EARLIER DIPLOMATIC HISTORY
1492–1713

Uniform with this volume

DIPLOMATIC HISTORY, 1713–1933

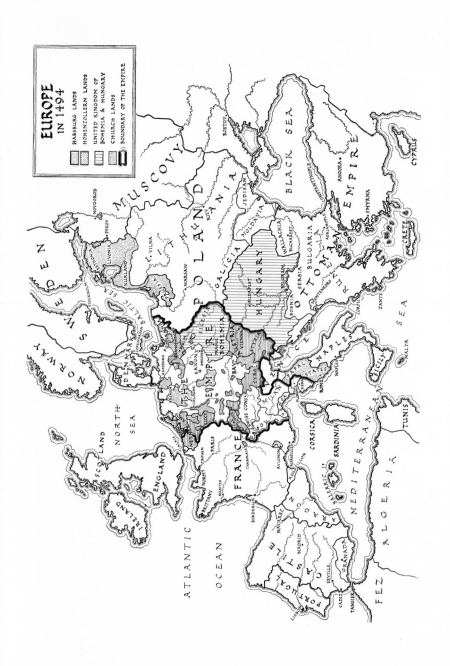

EUROPE
IN 1494

HABSBURG LANDS
HOHENZOLLERN LANDS
UNITED KINGDOM OF
BOHEMIA & HUNGARY
CHURCH LANDS
BOUNDARY OF THE EMPIRE

EARLIER
DIPLOMATIC HISTORY
1492—1713

By

SIR CHARLES PETRIE, Bt.

M.A. (OXON), F.R.HIST.S.

Corresponding Member of the Royal Spanish Academy of History.

LONDON

HOLLIS AND CARTER LTD.

1949

PRINTED IN GREAT BRITAIN FOR
HOLLIS AND CARTER LTD.
25 ASHLEY PLACE,
LONDON, S.W.I

First published 1949

PREFACE

THIS book is a companion volume to my *Diplomatic History*, *1713–1933*, and so far as possible it has been written along the same lines. For reasons of space, accounts of campaigns, as well as of the domestic affairs of the various Powers, have been cut down to the minimum necessary to understand international relationships.

My aim has been to deal with events either on a chronological basis or by episodes, and I have tried to avoid over-lapping: this has never been easy, and has not always proved possible, and chapters VI, VII, and VIII should be read together. In every case where there are variations of spelling the most familiar form has been employed.

CHARLES PETRIE

LONDON, *November 1948.*

CONTENTS

Power. Failure of Henry VIII. Mary I and Spain. Difficulties of Elizabeth. Position of Mary Queen of Scots. The Triumph of Elizabeth, and the "Auld Alliance". Policy of James IV. Battle of Flodden. Reigns of James V and Mary. Relations between James VI and Elizabeth.

Hamilton. Bolingbroke's Ultimatum to France. The Treaty
Signed. Its Provisions. Failure to Negotiate an Anglo-French
Commercial Treaty. Significance of the Settlement.

LIST OF MAPS

CHAPTER I

EUROPE AT THE END OF THE FIFTEENTH CENTURY

THE division of history into periods is doubtless, for scholastic reasons, a necessity, though a regrettable one, as it tends to obscure the progress (the word is used purely in an etymological sense) of the human race. One age can no more be isolated from another than one generation from the next, and, as has been well said, "the old generation melts into the new, as the night melts into day". All the same, there can be recognized in the story of mankind certain broad lines of division between different epochs, and it is not wholly without reason that the closing years of the fifteenth century have come to be regarded as a definite turning-point. Behind, stretching back to the fall of the Roman Empire in the West, lay the Middle Ages, ahead were the Reformation and the French Revolution, with all the changes they were to bring.

The mediæval conception of a universal Church under Pope and Emperor still existed in theory, but it had little foundation in fact. The Papacy had been on the decline for a number of years, and a variety of reasons. The first blows had been struck at the beginning of the previous century by Philip IV of France, while further causes of weakness were the so-called Babylonish Captivity, when the Popes were resident at Avignon, and the Great Schism, when, to quote Gibbon, "from the banks of the Tiber and the Rhone the hostile pontiffs encountered each other with the pen and the sword", and "the civil and ecclesiastical order of society was disturbed". These internal difficulties were reflected in the international sphere, and the decline of Papal power was very evident in the diplomacy of successive Popes during the Hundred Years' War between England and France. On the other hand, the spiritual supremacy of the Holy See was still unquestioned, and throughout the Middle Ages all challenges to it had sooner or later failed, the most recent being the Hussite Movement in Bohemia. Furthermore, if the Popes had lost ground as the arbiters of Christendom, they had consolidated their position as temporal sovereigns in Italy itself, and the States of the Church formed one of the more important principalities in that peninsula.

What was true of the Papacy was also applicable to the Empire: internal weakness had deprived the Emperor of the force necessary to maintain his old pretensions. These pretensions still existed, but little notice was taken of them beyond the frontiers of the Empire, and they were by no means always respected within those frontiers. The later Hohenstaufen, and particularly Frederick II, had been more interested in Italy than in Germany, and so their hold upon the Reich itself had been steadily weakened. Then had occurred the Great Interregnum, when the Empire was without a head and the centrifugal forces had full play. More recently the House of Habsburg had won the crown of Charlemagne, but it derived its strength rather from its hereditary dominions than from its Imperial position, and in Germany it was always liable to be thwarted by any or all of the seven Electors created by the Golden Bull of 1356, that is to say the Archbishops of Mayence, Cologne, and Trèves, and the four lay princes—namely, the King of Bohemia, the Count Palatine of the Rhine, the Duke of Saxony, and the Margrave of Brandenburg.

In spite, however, of the fundamental weakness of both Pope and Emperor, it cannot be too strongly stressed that the conception of a Christendom presided over by Papacy and Empire was still uppermost in men's minds, and in the closing decade of the fifteenth century the mediæval *façade* still stood. New forces, however, were coming into existence, and in due course they were to act as a dissolvent on the old order: they were the rise of the national kingdoms of Spain and France, and to a lesser extent England; and the threat from the East in the form of the Ottoman Turks.

During the Middle Ages the Iberian Peninsula had been divided into a number of Christian and Moslem states of varying sizes, but these had gradually been reduced to four—namely, the Christian kingdoms of Castille, Aragon, and Portugal, and the Moorish kingdom of Granada. In 1479 Aragon and Castille became united in the persons of Ferdinand V and Isabella I. The union of the two kingdoms, however, was purely personal; the two states did not become one, but remained distinct units, each with its own laws and institutions. There was no King of Spain as such, just as there was no common Cortes, and the monarch ruled his dominions under a variety of titles. This fact contributed largely to the weakness of Spain in her long struggle with France, which was much more centralized.

The first task of Ferdinand and Isabella, after the union of the Spanish kingdoms in themselves, was the conquest of the Moorish realm of Granada, and this was finally accomplished in 1492. There can be no doubt that a strong appeal was made, in order to obtain recruits for the enterprise, to the crusading spirit and to the religious enthusiasm which was so strong in the Spain of that day, but the policy that inspired the attack on Granada was dictated by necessity. The Crescent, as represented by the Ottoman Sultan, was supreme in the Eastern Mediterranean, and although there was a lull in Turkish operations after the death of Mohammed II in 1481, the next generation was to see the Osmanli supreme in North Africa as well as hammering at the gates of Vienna. The kingdom of Granada was the last foothold of Islam in the Peninsula, and the Catholic Sovereigns, as Ferdinand and Isabella were termed, feared that if they delayed too long the Moors would call the Turks to their aid. This was a very real danger, for the port of Malaga was in Moslem hands, and the threat was only averted by the conquest of Granada, which finally drove Islam out of Spain.

In the same year, 1492, there also took place the expulsion of the Jews. In this case, too, an appeal was made to religious prejudices to achieve what was primarily a political purpose. Rightly or wrongly, the Jews had long been regarded as extremely partial to the Moorish cause, and it was very largely to combat their activities that the Inquisition had been introduced into Castille in 1478. The Inquisition in Spain was always more of a secular than of an ecclesiastical organization, and it was rather an instrument of policy on the part of the State than of the Church. At the same time the two were so interwoven that it was impossible to say where the one began and the other finished, and the expulsion of the Jews is a case in point. Indeed, it would probably have taxed the ingenuity of Isabella herself to state whether she attacked the Jews because she considered them to be the enemies of Christianity or of Spain. What their expulsion did prove was Spanish inability to absorb the alien elements in the population, and with the passage of time this became an increasing source of weakness.

If the conquest of Granada and the expulsion of the Jews were in no small degree a legacy from the past, the discovery of America in the same year was an investment for the future. The wealth from the New World enabled Spain to play for upwards of a century a predominant part in Europe that would otherwise have been denied to her. With these resources she was enabled to support the celebrated *tercios* which for a hundred and fifty years were the masters of the European battle-fields. The very high proportion of foreigners in the Spanish service is also worthy of note. On the death of Philip III in 1621, of the thirty-nine *tercios* then in existence only seven were Spanish, and of the others thirteen were Italian, eleven Walloon, two Burgundian, and two Irish, while there were also nine German regiments. It was in no small measure her success in persuading so many foreigners to serve her in various capacities that enabled Spain to retain the position of a Great Power for so long, and when, in a later age, the growth of nationalism threw her back upon her own resources she could no longer maintain that rank.

There were also serious weaknesses in the Spanish administrative system which in due course were not without their influence upon international affairs. By the end of the fifteenth century the Cortes, like similar institutions in all parts of Europe, had lost much of its power, though it continued to be stronger in Aragon than in Castille. The Catholic Sovereigns took advantage of this to increase the power of the Crown, and they governed through councils, of which there were eleven in all, just as their Tudor contemporaries were doing in England. The Council of State dealt with questions of foreign policy; the Council of Castille acted as a judicial body, drafted laws, and possessed appellate jurisdiction; the Council of the Indies had charge of the administration of America; and the Council of the Inquisition was concerned with matters of religion. This system of administration had, in theory, much to recommend it, and so long as the monarchs of Spain were served by men of the ability of Cardinals Mendoza and Cisneros it did work quite well. The weakness of the Spanish governmental machine was seen when Philip II came to the throne, for he tried to do everything himself. The Spanish Empire was by this time too vast and too complicated for personal rule in matters of detail, and paralysis was the result. By the time that Philip II died in 1598 he was several years in arrears with his official correspondence. Yet he was an extremely conscientious man of no mean intelligence, and under his successors, who were not of his calibre, Spain alternated between periods of administrative chaos and of rule by not very competent favourites.

The financial system proved no more capable than the political of standing the test of time, and the incidence of taxation was calculated to inflict the maximum amount of damage upon commerce, while producing the minimum revenue. In these circumstances it is not surprising that the boom of the first half of the sixteenth century was to be followed by a slump from which there was no recovery. There was a tax upon all sales, while goods in transit from one part of Spain to another were subject to many duties of different sorts. The export of cattle and corn was forbidden, but foreigners were allowed, in return for loans, to compete in the home market in a way detrimental to the native producer. Indeed, it was oftener cheaper to buy goods from abroad than from another province. In normal conditions this system would have been difficult enough to work, but the steady influx of precious metals from the Americas was reducing the purchasing power of money. The statesmen of the day were bewildered by currency problems, and, faced with a rapid rise in prices, they merely applied the old methods with increased rigour. Spain was not a rich country, and with her resources crippled by a myriad economic restrictions she was in the end unable to maintain her position in the comity of nations. What is remarkable is not that she lost her supremacy so soon, but that she retained it for so long.

In France, too, the monarchy was getting an increasing amount of power into its own hands, and was in process of creating a French nation. At the beginning of the fourteenth century France had been the leading Power in Europe, and was pre-eminent both in arts and in arms, while her Court was the mirror of civilization. Then had come the disasters of the Hundred Years' War, the presence of foreign troops and the Free Companies on French soil, and the material and moral ruin to which these evils had given rise. France sank low in the eyes of Europe, and it was to London rather than to Paris that Christendom directed its gaze. England, however, had undertaken a task beyond her resources, and she proved too weak to hold a continental empire. After the death of Henry V in 1422 she became a prey to faction, and this facilitated the reconquest by the French of their own country. The expulsion of the English also necessitated the formation of a standing army, and this, in its turn, greatly strengthened both France and her monarch in negotiations with neighbouring Powers. It was no mere chance that both North and South of the Pyrenees the reconquest of the national territory was the prelude to a forward foreign policy.

B

Nevertheless, the France from which, with the exception of Calais, the English were finally driven in 1453 was a very different country from that which Edward III had invaded a hundred and fourteen years earlier. Then the monarchy had been supreme, thanks to the work of the later Capets and the first Valois; now it was little more than *primus inter pares*, for the great feudatories, nearly all cadets of the Royal House, behaved to all intents and purposes as if they were independent princes. Above all, there was the Duchy of Burgundy, whose rulers had done so much to support English rule in France earlier in the century and whose frontiers came to the Somme. When Charles the Bold succeeded his father, Philip the Good, as Duke of Burgundy in 1467 the danger became acute, for it was his avowed intention to unite his dominions to the North and East of France into one continuous whole, and to form them into an independent kingdom. Charles, however, was killed in 1477 fighting against the Swiss, and his heir was a daughter, Mary, who married the future Emperor Maximilian I shortly after her father's death. Nearly three hundred years later, standing by her tomb, Louis XV very justly observed, *"Voilà l'origine de toutes nos guerres"*.

Thus was initiated that Habsburg policy of expansion by marriage which has been so admirably summarized in the hexameter:

> Bella gerant alii, tu, felix Austria, nube.

The marriage of Mary of Burgundy and Maximilian of Austria, however, did not at once rouse French suspicions, for the Empire itself was so weak and divided that the union of its heir with the daughter of Charles the Bold was far from appearing to constitute that threat to the interests of France which subsequently developed, and which so influenced the policy of the later Valois and the earlier Bourbons. In the meantime it was the death of Charles, rather than the marriage of his daughter, that made the greater impression on Louis XI, and his feeling was one of relief, not of apprehension. No longer would his turbulent relatives be able to look across the Somme for support, and when he died in 1483 he had restored the power of the Crown to what it had been before the Hundred Years' War. Louis XI, it may be added, was never unmindful of the close connection between domestic and foreign policy: it was French internal differences which had so often played into the hands of the English, as they were later to play into those of the Spaniards, and peace at home meant peace abroad.

Louis XI was succeeded by his son Charles VIII, and as the new King was in his fourteenth year, no regency was necessary according to an ordinance of Charles V in 1374. All the same, for several years a controlling influence was exercised by the boy's sister, Anne of Beaujeu, whose husband in 1488 became Duke of Bourbon. She defeated repeated attempts by the nobility headed by Louis of Orleans, the heir-presumptive, to oust her from power, and to give the centrifugal influences full scope once more; she succeeded in this in spite of the fact that her opponents had such foreign supporters as Maximilian, Francis II of Brittany, and Richard III and Henry VII of England. Nor was this all, for on the death of the Duke of Brittany in 1488 she had interfered in the affairs of the duchy, and won by force of arms for her young brother the hand of Anne, the Breton heiress. By the marriage-contract the autonomy of Brittany was indeed acknowledged, but it was agreed that the duchy should fall to the surviving partner, and the Duchess Anne bound herself, in the event of her husband dying before her without children, to marry the next occupant of the French throne. By this means the way was prepared for the final incorporation into the monarchy of the last great semi-independent feudatory state, which had so often proved a thorn in the side of France.

Widely different as were the conditions obtaining in France and Spain, there was thus a certain amount in common between the policy of Louis XI and his daughter on the one hand, and that of Ferdinand and Isabella on the other: in both cases the doors, Granada and Brittany, had to be closed to the foreigner before it was possible to play a leading part on the stage of European politics.

Somewhat similar forces were at work in contemporary England, but she was considerably weaker than France or Spain for a variety of reasons. In the first place, she was far inferior to them in population and material resources; then, she had made her bid for European predominance, had failed, and was licking her wounds; while, lastly, the British Isles were politically disunited, and the "auld alliance" between France and Scotland was a standing threat to the English rear. On the other hand, the discovery of America had considerably increased the potential importance of England: prior to that event she had lain on the outskirts of the known world, henceforth she was to be in the centre of it; and this change in her geographical position was to prove of inestimable importance in future ages. At the end of the fifteenth century, however, England was a small and vulnerable state, not even controlling the whole of the island in which she was situated, and her only hope of influencing the course of events on the Continent was by throwing her somewhat inconsiderable strength first into the scale of one of the Great Powers and then into that of another. She had not herself been a Great Power for more than a generation, and many years were to elapse before she became one again.

The final victory of Lancaster over York in 1485 made very little difference in English foreign policy, for the reason that this was influenced by other considerations than dynastic. It is true that Edward IV was the brother-in-law of Charles the Bold, though they were by no means consistently on good terms with one another, but in any event the need for raw wool made Flanders economically dependent upon England. When Henry VII succeeded Richard III he definitely renounced any idea of Continental adventures on a big scale, and his policy was directed rather to the strengthening of the position of his dynasty on its shaky throne, as well as to promote English trade. It is true that he sent aid to the Bretons in their resistance to France, but this was as much to prove that he could be a nuisance as for any other reason: the hint was not lost upon Charles VIII, and by the Treaty of Etaples in 1492 the French monarch withdrew his support from Perkin Warbeck. Four years later the Magnus Intercursus, concluded with Maximilian, secured the expulsion of Warbeck from his dominions, as well as an increase in Anglo-Flemish trade. In 1502 Henry further secured his position by the marriage of his daughter, Margaret, with James IV of Scotland. The first Tudor was a realist who was under no illusion concerning his resources.

Finally, on the Eastern flank of Christendom was the growing power of the Ottoman Turks. Mohammed II had finally put an end to the Eastern Empire by the capture of Constantinople in 1453, and with Asia Minor and the Balkans firmly in his hands he seemed about to launch a general offensive against the West. In 1480 he had secured a bridgehead into Italy by the seizure of Otranto, and at the moment of his death in the following year he had collected a large force with which he may well have intended to invade the Italian peninsula, but his secret died with him. Mohammed II was succeeded by his eldest son, Bayezid II, and almost alone among the earlier Ottoman Sultans the new monarch was of a peaceful disposition. He reigned from 1481 to 1512, and during these years Central and Western Europe were spared any further Turkish invasions. One incident took place during the reign of Bayezid II which was ominous of the future, and that was the arrival at Constantinople of the first Russian ambassador, sent by the Tsar Ivan III. For the rest, the peace which marked this Sultan's reign was only the lull which precedes a storm.

In Spain, France, and England national consolidation was thus in process of accomplishment, and in each of these countries it was accompanied by the triumph of the monarchical principle after its long struggle with aristocracy. It was felt that the Crown represented the interests of the nation as a whole in opposition to those of any particular section of the community, and this was the secret of its strength. The monarchs thus came to typify the passions and aspirations of their subjects, who, realizing the identity of their interests, became aggressive where their neighbours were concerned. Nationalism was still several centuries in the future, but a consciousness of nationality was already in existence, though the Reformation was to cut across national loyalties to no inconsiderable extent, and to introduce ideological lines of division for several generations. In the struggle which ensued the Latin and Teutonic nations came into close if hostile contact; the theory of the Balance of Power became a dominant principle of international politics; and diplomacy in its modern form was born.

CHAPTER II

THE ITALIAN WARS, 1494–1518

To France and her young monarch, both avid of military glory, divided Italy seemed an easy prey. After the fall of the Western Empire that peninsula had lost all national cohesion, and in spite of fruitless attempts to establish a united kingdom the principle of disintegration had finally triumphed. The Holy Roman Emperors had, indeed, put forward very definite claims to supremacy, but since the death of Frederick II in 1250 these had possessed little reality, and the country had become divided into a number of states, of which five were of special importance.

First of all, in the Lombard plain, was Milan, whose territory had been considerably extended by the Visconti. The male line of this family became extinct in 1450, when Milan was seized by Francesco Sforza. In 1494 the state was ruled by Ludovico Sforza, *Il Moro*, as regent for his young nephew, Gian Galeazzo. The Sforza dynasty, however, was far from secure, for the House of Orleans, in virtue of its descent from Valentina, the heiress of the Visconti, looked upon itself as the rightful occupant of the ducal throne, and considered the Sforzas to be mere usurpers. The Orleans claim was represented by Louis, Duke of Orleans, cousin of Charles VIII, and himself heir to the crown of France. To the East of the duchy of Milan lay Venice, known as the Republic of Saint Mark. In earlier days she had concerned herself very little with the politics of Italy, and, securely entrenched behind her lagoons, she had concentrated on the Mediterranean and the Near East, whence came the source of her wealth. More recently, however, a different policy had been pursued, and expansion on the mainland had been effected. The last decade of the fifteenth century thus saw Venice in possession of considerable territory North of the Po stretching West to the Adda and northwards to the foothills of the Alps. This development rendered her a great deal more vulnerable than in the past, and that at the moment when she was seriously threatened in the Near East by the ever-growing power of the Ottoman Turks. Furthermore, Venice was soon to be weakened economically by the consequences of the discovery of

America, which marked the change from the thalassic to the oceanic phase of civilization.

Farther South lay Florence, in control of the watershed of the Arno, though not far away were the rival cities of Lucca and Siena, both of which were still independent. Florence was nominally a republic based on the trade-guilds, but actually all effective control was in the hands of the Medici. Lorenzo the Magnificent died in April, 1492, and under the rule of his son, Piero, the authority of the family was rapidly undermined. As in many Greek cities in classical times, so in Florence there were two bitterly antagonistic parties, and at this time the Medici were merely the leaders of one faction. The weakness of their position was soon to be demonstrated.

Next came the States of the Church, which were more imposing in extent than in real power. The Popes had never exercised much effective control over this territory, and in former days the Vicar of Christ had on more than one occasion been the puppet of the great nobles such as the Colonna and the Orsini. Recent Pontiffs had made a resolute effort to enforce their authority, and they had met with some success, though a good many years were to elapse before the Pope could be said to be master in his own house. Not the least of his difficulties was the dual rôle which he was called upon to play. In his spiritual capacity he claimed supremacy over all nations and their rulers, but as a temporal sovereign he was not of great account, and no particular notice was taken of him either by his neighbours or by the Great Powers. In the virtual impossibility experienced by successive Popes of reconciling these two characters lies the key to much Italian history until the latter half of the nineteenth century. There had, it should be observed, recently been a change in the occupancy of the Papal throne, for in 1492 there had succeeded to it Alexander VI, formerly Cardinal Rodrigo Borgia, a capable statesman if an unsuitable Pope.

Lastly, in the extreme South of the peninsula was the kingdom of Naples, now in possession of an illegitimate branch of the Aragonese Royal House, though Sicily and Sardinia belonged to the reigning King of Aragon, that is to say Ferdinand V, who was married to Isabella of Castille. As in Rome, so at Naples, there had recently been a change of sovereigns, and the Neapolitan throne was occupied by Alfonso II.

Such were the five principal states into which Italy was divided, and for some years peace had been preserved by an uneasy alliance between Milan, Florence, and Naples. The death of Lorenzo the Magnificent proved fatal to this coalition, for he alone realized that its continued existence was essential if the foreigner was to be deprived of all excuse for interference in Italian affairs. Piero, less wise than his father, set on foot an intrigue with Naples against the ruler of Milan, and so Ludovico, *Il Moro*, was driven to look elsewhere for support. In these circumstances he sent an envoy, in the words of Philippe de Commines, to " tickle Charles, who was but twenty-one years of age, with the vanities and glories of Italy, and to urge the right he had to the fine kingdom of Naples".

The King of France was certainly by no means unwilling to listen to the arguments of the emissary of the Sforza. Both he and his subjects were in the mood for adventures, and were desirous of regaining for their country that predominant position in the counsels of Europe which she had enjoyed before the Hundred Years' War. Charles was also influenced by a desire, not unnatural in the heir of Saint Louis, to pose as the champion of Christendom against the Turks, and for such a war Naples would prove an admirable base. It is also by no means improbable that in his more sober moments the French monarch reflected that it would suit him better if the wilder spirits in his country fought in Italy rather than against himself or each other at home. As for justification, there were the French claims on Milan and Naples. The former have already been stated, but they were not immediately applicable, in view of the fact that Charles was entering Italy as the ally, not the enemy, of *Il Moro*. In the case of Naples the position was less complicated. The House of Anjou had long disputed the title of the Aragonese dynasty, and had taken the view that Joanna II, who died in 1435, had left her territories to René, the head of the Angevin line. In 1481, on the death of René, these rights had fallen, together with Anjou and Provence, to the French crown, and Charles now determined to enforce them. In this way was inaugurated that policy of interference in Italian affairs which France was to pursue intermittently until 1870.

However adventurous Charles may have been, he realized that it would be folly to invade Italy without first of all securing France herself from attack by her neighbours, and he accordingly came to terms with all who had claims upon him. Henry VII of England, who was besieging Boulogne, was bought off by the Treaty of Etaples in November, 1492, when the Tudor monarch received a considerable sum in cash in return for a promise not to assist Maximilian or any other enemy of Charles; equally, France undertook not to give any countenance to Yorkist intrigues against Henry. Next year it was the turn of Spain, and by the Treaty of Barcelona in January, 1493, Roussillon and Cerdagne were ceded to Ferdinand and Isabella on their engagement, neither to give aid to the enemies of France except the Pope, nor to consent to any intermarriage between their children and the Habsburgs, Tudors, or the Royal Family of Naples. Finally, the Treaty of Senlis in May, 1493, restored Artois and the Franche Comté, which had been occupied by Louis XI, to Maximilian as the heir of Charles the Bold. Whether these sacrifices of solid French interests in the pursuit of problematic Italian thrones were justifiable is at least arguable, but having made them Charles VIII was at last able to take advantage of the opportunity which the position in Italy seemed to offer, and in September, 1494, he invaded that country at the head of an army which was far from being exclusively French, since it contained a considerable number of German and Swiss mercenaries.

The invasion proved to be little more than a military promenade. The Medici régime in Florence was, temporarily, brought to an end, and Piero sought safety in flight; in January, 1495, the Pope admitted the French King inside the walls of Rome; and on February 22nd Charles VIII entered Naples, where Alfonso II had abdicated in favour of his son, Ferdinand II. The way into Italy had been opened, and Charles, like the barbarians a thousand years or so before, had shown the world how easily it could be travelled.

The very rapidity of the French success militated against its permanence, and Charles was not the man to consolidate his conquests. His ambition was equalled only by his frivolity, and the situation which his campaign had created was one which demanded statesmanship of the highest order. Frenchmen were placed in all important posts, and no attempt was made to rally the sympathies of the Neapolitans to the new order, while the licence and cruelty of the French army alienated Italians of all classes and opinions. Nor was this all, for both within Italy and outside there was immediate alarm at this sudden increase in the power of France, and Alexander VI in particular had no desire to see himself threatened on the South by a French-controlled Naples, on the North by a French-controlled Milan. Accordingly, the Pope refused to invest Charles with the Neapolitan kingdom, and such were his diplomatic activities that by the end of March, 1495, he had formed the League of Venice against France. This coalition included the Papacy; Ludovico, *Il Moro*, who was terrified at the storm which he had raised; Venice; Maximilian, who was now Emperor; and Ferdinand and Isabella, who were able to invoke the clause in the Treaty of Barcelona which excluded the Pope from the number of those enemies of France with whom they had pledged themselves not to enter into an alliance.

Before this threat Charles had no option but to yield. He left a garrison in Naples, and retreated to the North, but he had to fight his way home. At Fornovo, in July, the forces of the League attempted to cut him off, but after a long and indecisive battle the French forced their way through, and by October their King was back in his own country. Meanwhile, Ferdinand II, assisted by Spanish troops under the command of that great soldier, Gonzalo de Córdoba, defeated the French troops, and re-entered Naples, while the Venetians occupied the Adriatic ports of the kingdom. Thus the Aragonese dynasty recovered their throne as easily as they had lost it, though Ferdinand II, who died without direct heirs in 1496, was soon to be succeeded by his uncle, Frederick. Two years later Charles VIII, while staying at the castle of Amboise, struck his head against the lintel of a door so violently that he never recovered from the blow. By the time of his death he had nothing to show in Italy for the concessions which he had been compelled to make elsewhere.

The French invasion had come and gone like a storm in summer, but in its passing it had destroyed the old political system of Italy. At the first glance the actual changes which had been effected did not, it is true, seem very great; the sixty years' domination of the Medici in Florence was, indeed, at an end, but a Sforza still ruled in Milan, and a prince of the House of Aragon was on the throne of Naples. Yet Charles had blazed a trail which others were to follow, while the weakness of the Italian military system had been exposed at Fornovo, where the French, although disorganized by retreat, had managed to escape disaster. The invasion, too, had destroyed, once for all, the balance of power between the Italian states. Above all, it had proved necessary to call in the aid of foreigners to expel a foreigner, that is to say the Spaniards and Imperialists to get rid of the French, and it is one of the ironies of history that a consequence of the League of Venice, which was to re-establish the liberty of Italy, was the marriage of Juana, the daughter of the Catholic Sovereigns, with Philip, the son of Maximilian, for of this union was born Charles V, who was finally to extinguish the independence of the Italian states.

Charles VIII was succeeded by his cousin, Louis XII, and so popular was the new monarch that he earned the title of *Pater patriae*. All the same he was resolved to press what he considered to be French interests in Italy, and he never forgot his own claims to the duchy of Milan as heir of the Visconti. First of all, however, he had to dissolve the League of Venice, but this was to prove no insuperable task. The Pope was more than ordinarily susceptible where his children were concerned, and in return for a bull sanctioning the divorce of his first wife Jeanne, and a cardinal's hat for George of Amboise, his chief adviser, the King of France invested Alexander's son, Cesare Borgia, with the counties of Valentinois and Diois, and gave him the title of duke: he also married Cesare to Charlotte d'Albret, and promised to further his designs on the Romagna. Venice was secured in 1499 by the Treaty of Blois, for by its terms the Republic of Saint Mark promised to assist the French against Milan by force of arms in return for certain territorial concessions at her expense when the victory was won.

Il Moro was now completely isolated, and bitterly did he regret his introduction of the French into Italy. Nowhere was there hope of an effective ally. The Pope and Venice had been gained over by the enemy, who had in any event much more to offer; Ferdinand of Aragon had no interest to serve by interfering in Lombard affairs, and he had very definite ambitions of his own farther South; Maximilian was too much occupied with a Swiss war and a quarrel with the Diet to render any assistance; and Frederick of Naples was solely concerned with his own threatened throne. In his despair Ludovico turned to the Sultan, and Bayezid II sent a force to ravage the Venetian territories in Friuli, an act which in no way helped *Il Moro* but which further exasperated his opponents. The results of his isolation were seen in the late summer of 1499: the French troops crossed the Alps in August, and by the middle of September the whole of the Milanese was in the hands of themselves and their Venetian allies, while Ludovico was in exile at Innsbruck.

It was not, however, long before Louis XII, like Charles VIII before him, found that it was easier to acquire Italian provinces than to consolidate his gains afterwards. This was in no small measure due to the fact that the French were neither popular nor competent, while the mercenary troops proved most unreliable. Evidence of this latter fact is afforded by the fate of the unhappy Ludovico, who in a last effort to regain his throne in 1500 was captured by the French owing to the refusal of the Swiss in his service to fight against their fellow-countrymen in the employ of France. This was, it may be added, the last appearance of *Il Moro* upon the international stage, and in 1508 he died in the dungeons of Loches in Touraine. With the failure of this last attempt the whole of the Milanese passed into the possession of France with the exception of the strip of country to the East of the Adda which fell to the Venetians, and the district round Bellinzona, which was seized by the Swiss in the pay of Ludovico and which belongs to Switzerland to this day.

Now that Louis was master of the Milanese he was able to turn his attention to Naples, but it was extremely doubtful whether he would be allowed to repeat the exploit of Charles VIII, owing to the opposition of Ferdinand V. That cautious sovereign, however, preferred partition to armed conflict, and Frederick of Naples played into his hand by appealing for help to Bayezid II. On this, Ferdinand suggested to Louis that they should divide the Neapolitan realm between them; mindful of his predecessor's experiences, the French King was by no means averse to the proposal, and in November, 1500, the secret Treaty of Granada was concluded. After deploring the discords of Christian princes, which weakened them in the face of the Ottoman power, the preamble asserted that "no other princes, save the Kings of France and Aragon, have any title to the crown of Naples, and as King Frederick has excited the Turk to the peril of Christendom, the two Powers, in order to rescue it from this danger and to maintain the peace, agree to compromise their respective claims, and divide the kingdom of Naples itself". The northern provinces, consisting of the Abruzzi and the land of Lavoro, with the royal title, were to go to Louis, while the duchy of Calabria and Apulia were given as a dukedom to Ferdinand. Until the preparations for putting this treaty into effect had been completed its conclusion was kept secret, but in June, 1501, it was publicly ratified by the Pope, who declared the deposition of Frederick as a traitor to Christendom, and invested Louis and Ferdinand with his dominions. By the following March all resistance was at an end, and thus in less than two years the two families, whose quarrels had first invited the foreigner into Italy, had lost their thrones.

The comment of Machiavelli on the Treaty of Granada was extremely apposite: "The French have little skill in matters of State, for whereas before, Louis was sole umpire in Italy, he now entertained a partner, and whereas Louis might have made the King of Naples his pensioner, he turned him out and put the Spaniard in his place, who turned out Louis himself". The truth is that, unlike the earlier Bourbons, the Valois never saw where the real interests of France lay, and it was to take many years of astute diplomacy and hard fighting in the seventeenth century to restore the position on the frontiers of France herself which had so lightly been thrown away in pursuit of Italian thrones.

A quarrel between Louis and Ferdinand over the spoils was not long in breaking out. In the original treaty of partition no definite mention had been made of the Basilicata, the Capitanata, and the two districts of the Principati. These territories furnished an easy cause of dispute, and the position was further complicated by the claim to the tolls paid on the flocks of sheep as they were driven between their summer pasture in the Abruzzi and their winter quarters in the Capitanata. The quarrel might possibly have been compromised had it not been inflamed by the internal factions of the country, for the old supporters of Anjou were strongest in Apulia, while the Spaniards found many adherents in the districts held by the French.

War broke out in July, 1502, and in its earlier stages the Spaniards fared none too well, for they were inferior in numbers to their opponents, who also possessed the command of the sea. While the issue was still in doubt the Archduke Philip, son-in-law of the Catholic Sovereigns, endeavoured to effect an accommodation, but Ferdinand would have none of it, and fortune gradually inclined to his side. The French were defeated at Seminara and Cerignola in 1503, and the first weeks of the following year witnessed their final expulsion from Neapolitan territory in spite of the efforts of Louis to cause a diversion by a direct attack on Spain. The victory of the Spaniards was due to their possession of Sicily, whence they could draw support, and to the French failure to retain command of the sea; to the exceptionally bad weather, which seems to have been felt more by the troops of Louis than by those of Ferdinand; to the widespread unpopularity of the French among the Italians; to the quarrels of the French generals;

and, above all, to the consummate ability of Gonzalo de Córdoba.

The years 1503–4 were marked by two other events of considerable importance: the one was a change in the Papacy, and the other was the death of Isabella of Castille.

Alexander VI died suddenly in August, 1503, in consequence, so the story went, of drinking from a poisoned cup which he had intended for one of the cardinals. He was succeeded by Pius III, who, however, lived only for a few weeks, and the choice of the Sacred College then fell upon Cardinal Julian della Rovere, who took the title of Julius II. It was of him that Ranke wrote, "Other Popes had laboured to procure principalities for their sons or their nephews: it was the ambition of Julius to extend the dominions of the Church. He must, therefore, be regarded as the founder of the Papal States." With these views he had little sympathy with the determination of Cesare Borgia to carve out for himself an Italian kingdom largely at the expense of the Papacy, and in due course he brought Ferdinand round to his way of thinking. Cesare was accordingly arrested while on a visit to Naples in 1504, and taken to Spain, after which he disappears from Italian history.

The death of Isabella in the same year meant that Ferdinand lost control of Castille, which passed to his daughter, Juana, and her husband, the Archduke Philip, henceforth known as Philip I of Castille. The resulting uncertainty as to his position in the Peninsula rendered Ferdinand more than usually circumspect in his foreign policy, and this in its turn caused an improvement in Franco-Spanish relations. It was not until Philip himself died in 1506, and the insanity of Juana became apparent, that Ferdinand once again enjoyed a free hand in Spain.

Julius II was not slow in turning to his own account this lull in the struggle between Ferdinand and Louis, and he determined to enlist the support of both in an attack on Venice. The Republic of Saint Mark had at that moment an unusually large number of enemies, and it must be admitted that this state of affairs was to some extent her own fault. In particular she had blundered badly by her alliance with Louis XII against Milan, for this established France on her Western frontier, while the occupation of the Apulian ports in 1495 had proved a bad investment now that Ferdinand was in possession of the rest of the kingdom of Naples. As for Louis, now that he had the Milanese in his pocket the friendship of Venice mattered nothing to him, while the temptation to extend at her expense the frontiers of his newly-acquired duchy was considerable. Then there was Maximilian, who had his eyes on Friuli. Lastly, the Pope had two causes of complaint against the Republic. The first was the independent attitude she adopted in religious matters, which at the moment had led her to refuse to allow the Pope to nominate to the vacant bishopric of Vicenza. "They wish to treat me as their chaplain," Julius complained. "Let them beware lest I make them humble fishermen as they once were." A second ground for hostility was the Venetian threat to the Romagna: Julius had no intention of saving it from Cesare Borgia for the benefit of Venice.

The outcome of these various grievances was the formation of the League of Cambrai in December, 1508, for the purpose of humbling the proud Republic. At first fortune favoured the allies, and the French won a notable victory at Agnadello in the following May. They captured Peschiera, Verona, and Padua, while Ravenna and Rimini fell to the Papal forces. Ferdinand confined his activities to the conquest of the Apulian ports, while the Emperor ravaged Friuli with a savagery which rallied the inhabitants to Venetian rule. The very success of the enemies of Venice, however, was fatal to their cause, for the Italians among them became alarmed at the progress of the French, and dissension soon made itself felt: moreover, the old subjects of Venice, not only in Friuli but elsewhere, gave obvious proof of their preference for her over those who claimed to be liberating them from her tyranny. The Pope was the first to take alarm at the trend of events, and in February, 1510, he came to terms with the Republic. In doing so he was influenced not only by a desire to further the Papal cause, but also of expelling the foreigner from Italy, that will-o'-the-wisp which so many Italian statesmen were to pursue for the next three and a half centuries.

The Papal conditions were hard, for in addition to the retention of the territory which he had conquered Julius insisted that the navigation of the Adriatic should be declared free to the citizens of the States of the Church. In addition, Venice had to acknowledge the justice of an excommunication which had been pronounced against her, to renounce the claim to tax the clergy or to nominate to bishoprics within the territory; and to promise that clerics should be tried only by ecclesiastical courts. So onerous were these terms that the Council of Ten recorded a secret protest against them as having been extorted by force, and subsequently repudiated them, but for the moment the Papacy had triumphed.

Having achieved his objective where Venice was concerned, Julius now turned his attention to the expulsion of the French from Italy, but neither for the first nor the last time it was proved that such an operation was beyond the power of any Italian state or group of Italian states. It is true that Julius himself, in January, 1511, took Mirandola by storm, but in May the French captured Bologna, and Louis adroitly turned the tables on his adversary by summoning a General Council. The Pope had taken on a task beyond his powers, and, like Alexander VI before him, Julius II was compelled to cast out one foreigner by means of another.

In this way there came into being in October, 1511, the Holy League, which was so designated because the Pope was at its head. It was joined by a number of Powers for a variety of reasons. Venice was burning for revenge. Ferdinand could hardly be suspected of sympathy for a policy of Italy for the Italians, but he was apprehensive of the growing might of France, and he hoped to acquire Navarre as his share of the spoils. The new King of England, Henry VIII, joined, partly to please his father-in-law, Ferdinand, and partly on the chance of being able to regain some of the lost French provinces. The Emperor came in later, and the bait which tempted him was the Milanese. These various aspirations were latent rather than patent at the formation of the Holy League, for its ostensible object was stated to be the protection of the Church, the recovery of Bologna, and the restoration to Venice of the territory which she had lost to France, but the stipulation that the Pope should confirm the Spaniards in any conquest made outside Italy pointed clearly to Navarre.

At first victory inclined to the French, as so often during these Italian wars, and the Spaniards were defeated at Ravenna on Easter Day, 1512. Soon, however, the tide turned, and this was in no small measure due to the Swiss. In previous campaigns they had been of great assistance to Louis, but lately the cantons had become alienated by his refusal to increase their subsidy, as well as by the obstacles which he placed in the way of their trade with the Milanese. The Swiss therefore changed sides, and with their help the French were driven not only out of Milan, but across the Alps, while the rule of the Medici was restored in Florence. The duchy of Milan went to Maximilian Sforza, the son of *Il Moro*, but he had to cede territory to the Swiss which made them masters of four of the most important passes over the Alps, namely the St. Gothard, the Splugen, the Maloja, and the Bernina. Nor was this all, for by the end of July, 1513, Ferdinand had conquered all the Navairese territory which lay on the Spanish side of the Pyrenees. The only member of the Holy League who had no cause for satisfaction was Henry VIII, for he soon realized that the troops which he had been so misguided as to send to Bayonne were intended by his father-in-law not to reconquer Guyenne, but to assist the Spanish occupation of Navarre.

While these events were taking place Julius II died, in February, 1513, and this implied the dissolution of the Holy League as such, for the new Pope, Leo X, a Medici, was nothing like so vigorous a personality as his predecessor. At the same time a new combination was called into existence by the Treaty of Mechlin in April of that year, and it was equally directed against France: it consisted of the Emperor, Henry, Ferdinand, and the new Pope. The months which followed were disastrous for France. In June an attempt to reconquer the Milanese with the help of the Venetians resulted in a resounding defeat of the forces of Louis at the hands of the Swiss, while in the North the English advanced from Calais, captured Tournai, and won the Battle of the Spurs. The French King endeavoured to restore the situation in this quarter by recourse to the alliance with Scotland, but in September his ally, James IV, lost his army and his life on the field of Flodden.

The darkest hour of France nevertheless marked the beginning of her recovery, for it was no part of the policy of Wolsey, the all-powerful minister of England, to reduce French power so low as to upset the balance of Europe. Accordingly, in August, 1514, Henry came to terms with Louis on the basis that his sister, Mary, should marry the French King. It is true there was a considerable discrepancy of age, for the bridegroom was a widower of fifty-two and the bride a girl of sixteen; Mary's scruples, however, were overcome by a promise that if she would on this occasion sacrifice herself to her brother's interests, the next time she should follow her own inclinations. She was not destined to have long to wait, for in January, 1515, Louis XII died.

He was succeeded by his cousin, Francis I, a young man of energy and ambition, who was determined to regain for his country all that she had lost in the previous reign. He at once confirmed the recent agreement with England, came to terms with Charles, the grandson and heir of the Emperor, and renewed the

C

alliance with Venice. With his rear thus secured, and with an ally on the other side of the Alps, Francis proceeded to invade Italy in August, 1515, and on September 13th his army, under four great generals—La Palice, Bayard, Trevulzio, and the Constable of Bourbon—utterly defeated the Swiss at Marignano. This victory not only dispelled the legend of Swiss military invincibility, but it restored the Milanese to France, and for a moment it looked as if Francis might become master of all Italy.

The French King, however, was not Napoleon, and the disasters which had overtaken his immediate predecessors in the South of the peninsula constituted a warning not to be lightly disregarded. The Pope showed himself only too eager to come to terms, and so an agreement was easily effected. Leo ceded Parma and Piacenza, while Francis promised to support the Medici in Florence, and to sanction a Papal attack on the duchy of Urbino, from which the ruler, Francesco della Rovere, was duly driven. After settling their political differences, Pope and King proceeded to share between them the liberties of the Gallican Church by the Concordat of Bologna in August, 1516. In January of the same year Ferdinand died, and Charles found himself at the age of sixteen ruler of Spain, the Two Sicilies (as the reunited kingdom of Naples and Sicily was usually termed), and the Americas, with the prospect of the early reversion of the Habsburg possessions in the Netherlands and Central Europe, if not of the Empire itself.

These responsibilities made Charles extremely reluctant to throw down the gauntlet to the King of France. His position, however imposing, was by no means secure; as a Fleming he was unpopular in Spain, and blood was to flow before he finally established himself there, while he wanted to have his hands free when his grandfather, Maximilian, died. He was thus in no condition to contest the possession of Milan with his French rival, and in August, 1516, the Peace of Noyon was concluded between France and Spain. The principal points of this settlement were that Francis retained Milan, but abandoned all claim to Naples; Charles promised to restore Spanish Navarre to the line of Albret; and Venice agreed to offer 200,000 ducats to Maximilian for Brescia and Verona. After a considerable amount of haggling, the Emperor accepted the terms of the Peace of Noyon, and sold the two towns to the Venetians. A few weeks earlier the Swiss, in return for a subsidy, made a "perpetual peace" with France at Friburg.

These events left England isolated, and Wolsey and his master had to make the best terms they could after their failure to uphold the Balance of Power. Therefore, by the Treaty of London in October, 1518, they sold Tournai to France, and the new-found friendship between Francis and Henry was confirmed by the usual marriage arrangements; according to these the English princess, Mary, a child of two, was betrothed to the Dauphin, who was not yet one. Wolsey then proceeded to claim credit for the general pacification which he had failed to prevent, but in this he was to be more successful with posterity than with his own contemporaries.

CHAPTER III

CHARLES V AND FRANCIS I, 1519–1547

IN January, 1519, the Emperor Maximilian died, and it at once became obvious that there would be three candidates for the succession, namely Henry, Francis, and Charles. The candidature of the first of these was never seriously considered, and it was only put forward by Wolsey to perpetuate the illusion that England was the equal of France and Spain. The Peace of Noyon had been a serious setback for English diplomacy, and so long as friendly relations existed between Francis and Charles the government in London carried little weight abroad; but as soon as there was the prospect of a breach between the Valois and the Habsburg, then the attitude of England became of importance, and she was courted by both sides. It is against this background that the candidature of Henry for the throne of the Holy Roman Empire must be viewed. With the passing of the years the geographical position of England, too, compelled Continental statesmen to take her increasingly into account, while there still lingered on the mainland of Europe the memory of those terrible archers who had proved the masters of so many battle-fields a century before, but this memory was fading as the use of gunpowder changed the character of warfare.

At first it looked as if Francis would be the successful candidate. The victory of Marignano, and his ambition for military renown, seemed to point him out as the most suitable leader of that crusade against the Turks which all Europe continually discussed, but never undertook; and the French monarch himself declared that, if elected, he would be in Constantinople within three years. He was not, however, content to appeal only to the better nature and Christian principles of the Electors, for he reinforced his arguments by dipping deep into the French treasury. How the voting would have gone had the Electors not been subject to external pressure it is impossible to say, but as the day of the election drew near German national feeling began to make itself felt. The Suabian League, headed by Duke William of Bavaria, declared for Charles, as did the Swiss, although traditional enemies of the House of Habsburg, and in the North the Duke of Brunswick-

Wolfenbüttel threatened to take up arms if he were not elected. Not less important was the attitude of the great banking family of Fugger, who showed where their sympathies lay by refusing to honour the bills of the French King. The Pope had originally supported Francis, for it was the traditional Papal policy to prevent Naples and the Empire from falling into the same hands; but when Leo realized in which direction opinion was moving he abandoned opposition to the Habsburg. Thus, in June, 1519, Charles was unanimously elected Emperor.

This decision was to have disastrous consequences for Spain. Her true interests lay in the Mediterranean and in the New World, but the circumstances of her monarch distracted her energies to the Netherlands and Central Europe. On all sides the possessions of Charles now surrounded France, and on repeated occasions she attempted to break out. This, in its turn, compelled Spain to strive to keep her enemy encircled, and so the struggle went on until the day came when Louis XIV was able to place his grandson upon the Spanish throne. As if this were not enough, the Reformation took place in the early years of Charles, and it was to Spain that he looked for the resources which might enable him to make headway against those who professed the new religion. The championship of the Roman Catholic Church meant war with England and the revolt of the Netherlands. Spain could not at one and the same time colonize America, hold the Turk at bay, keep France encircled, suppress heresy in the Netherlands, sustain the Austrian Habsburgs, and dispute the mastery of the seas with England. The secret of waging war on credit had not yet been discovered, and therefore actual gold was necessary for a war-chest. Yet the more the Spaniards distributed throughout Europe the gold which they obtained from the American mines the lower did the value of money fall, until the deficit in the revenue in Lombardy, which in due course fell into Spanish hands, had to be made good by Naples and Sicily, and sometimes from the Peninsula itself, which was poor enough. Yet Spanish pride would not admit that there was any discrepancy between the theory of omnipotence and the fact of debility, and the blood and treasure of Spain were wasted in quarrels in which she had nothing to gain and everything to lose.

On the other hand, the failure of Francis saved his country from a like fate. Had his candidature been successful, the hostility of Germany, and probably of the whole of Europe, would have been aroused, and the resources of France would have been exhausted in a struggle in which she was not really interested. The true French policy towards her German neighbour was not to control the whole Reich, as Francis I wished to do and as Napoleon I succeeded for a time in doing, but to keep it so divided that France could always find support there: this was the policy so successfully pursued by Richelieu and Louis XIV.

The election of Charles rendered inevitable the revival of hostilities in Western Europe, for the Habsburg power was now so great as to constitute a definite threat to France, while Francis personally was smarting under his failure. Nor was it difficult to find occasions for quarrel, since the terms of the Peace of Noyon had not been fulfilled. Francis complained with justification that Charles had not restored Spanish Navarre, but now that the Pyrenees had become the frontier of Spain in the West the new Emperor was determined that they should remain so. Charles, for his part, asserted that Milan was an Imperial fief, for which Francis should do homage, and he also claimed the restoration of the duchy of Burgundy as part of his inheritance from his grandmother. Yet neither side was ready to fight. Charles was not only short of money, as usual, but he was far from having consolidated his position either in the Empire or in Spain, while the first murmurings of the Reformation were beginning to make themselves heard. Francis was to a greater extent master in his own house, and strategically he held a central position, for so long as he retained the Milanese he cut the communications between the German and Italian possessions of his rival. On the other hand, French finances were seriously strained by the expense incurred in the previous war and by the canvass for the Empire, so it was impossible for Francis to take immediate advantage of the Emperor's difficulties, the course which sound strategy dictated.

In these circumstances, and with rivals so evenly matched, the attitude of England assumed considerable importance. The late A. H. Johnson summed up the situation admirably, "The opportunity was eagerly seized by Wolsey. To continue friends with both sides without offending either; to keep both asunder by fostering mutual suspicion; to prevent either from declaring war lest the aggressor might find England arrayed against him, and thereby to prevent if possible, if not to delay, the outbreak of hostilities; meanwhile, to gain for England the proud position of arbiter of Europe—this was the aim of Wolsey, a policy which for nigh two years met with such success that the two most powerful monarchs of Europe became the humble suitors of the Cardinal and his master." To what extent this was due to patriotism on the part of Wolsey, and to what to the hope of succeeding Leo X on the Papal throne, is another matter.

What a later age would have described as a series of conferences then took place. In May, 1520, Charles came from Spain to meet Henry at Sandwich, and in the following month there took place the interview between the English and French monarchs at the "Field of the Cloth of Gold" near Guisnes in the Pale of Calais. From there Henry passed to a second meeting with the Emperor at Gravelines in July. No diplomacy, however, could for long avert the appeal to force, and as the months passed both sides prepared for war. Even in the summer of 1521, when fighting had already begun in Spanish Navarre and in Luxembourg, Wolsey, whatever his motives may have been, strenuously endeavoured to preserve peace, and a conference under his chairmanship was held at Calais in August in an attempt to adjust the conflicting claims, but it was a failure, and England espoused the cause of the Emperor.

On this occasion it was the enemies of France who scored the first successes, and Milan, Parma, and Piacenza were occupied by Imperialist and Papal troops, for Leo had thrown in his lot with Charles. The English assistance was inconsiderable, for Henry's forces contented themselves with raiding the coasts of Normandy and Brittany, and with a foray into Picardy. In December, 1521, the general situation was modified by the death of the Pope, though at first Charles had great hopes of support from his successor, who was none other than his old tutor, Adrian of Utrecht, who had also once been regent of Spain. Nevertheless Adrian VI proved a different man from the Spanish regent, and he assumed a position of neutrality. This encouraged the Francophil elements in all parts of Italy, and after a good deal of indeterminate fighting, Francis in person regained Milan in October, 1524. By this time, indeed, Adrian VI was dead, and had been succeeded by another Medici, Clement VII, but the new Pope proved as unreliable as the old where Charles was concerned. One important success the Emperor did achieve, and that was the defection to his side of the Constable of France, the Duke of Bourbon.

The good fortune of Francis proved to be temporary, for at the end of February, 1525, his army was routed, and he himself was captured, at the battle of Pavia. It was the most disastrous day in French history until the surrender of Napoleon III at Sedan in

1870. The captive monarch was taken to Spain, and there, in January, 1526, he was compelled to sign the Treaty of Madrid. By this Francis promised to cede Tournai, to hand over Burgundy in full sovereignty, and to surrender all claims on Italy as well as the suzerainty over Flanders and Artois. He was to withdraw his protection from his allies, pay the debt incurred by Charles to England in the recent war, and to aid him against the Turk. The Duke of Bourbon was to regain all his possessions in France, and in addition he was to receive the duchy of Milan. In ratification of the treaty Francis promised to marry Eleanora, the widowed Queen of Portugal and a sister of Charles, and to leave his sons as hostages for the fulfilment of the settlement. The Treaty of Madrid, however, soon proved not to be worth the paper on which it was written, for before he signed it the French King announced to the representatives of France that he would not regard as binding promises extorted from him in this way, and he gave notice that he did not intend to keep them.

The battle of Pavia and the Treaty of Madrid alarmed all Europe, for they proved that the Balance of Power had been so completely upset as to render a Habsburg hegemony a distinct possibility. In these circumstances Francis, on his release, had no great difficulty in building up a coalition against Charles, and in May, 1526, there was formed the League of Cognac, consisting of the Pope, France, Sforza, Venice, and Florence under the protection of the King of England. It was agreed that Sforza should be confirmed in his possession of the Milanese; all Italian states were to be restored to the position they held before the war; Charles was to release the young French princes for a sum of money; and he was to pay his debt to England within three months. If the Emperor refused these conditions he was to be driven from Naples, which was then to be held by the Pope on payment of a yearly revenue to France. Henry VIII, it may be noted, politely declined the office of Protector of the League of Cognac, for the question of his divorce had already arisen, and he had no desire at the moment to push Charles too far.

The fighting which ensued was marked by a series of sudden reversals of fortune on both sides. Charles suffered from the initial disadvantage that his troops were in a mutinous condition owing to lack of pay, but they were veterans, and in July, 1526, they captured Milan. In the following month, far away in Hungary, the Sultan won the great battle of Mohacs, and another serious threat to the Empire developed. While Francis was still a prisoner in Spain he had approved of overtures to the Porte, and had thus initiated that policy of seeking allies to the East of Germany which was to be so prominent a feature of French diplomacy for the next four hundred years. Meanwhile the capture of Milan had set free considerable Imperialist forces in Italy, and in the early months of 1527 they began to descend on Rome. Charles, it is true, had little cause for satisfaction with the Pope, for not only had Clement joined the League of Cognac against him, but he had broken a four months' truce which he had subsequently signed; yet the Emperor would hardly have consented in advance to what was soon to follow. The Imperialist troops, thoroughly out of hand though nominally under the command of the Duke of Bourbon, and containing many Lutherans in their ranks, stormed Rome in May, and then put the city to a sack which has few parallels in history. Europe was thus within a few months treated to the spectacle of the Most Christian King in alliance with the common enemy of Christendom, and of the armies of His Catholic Majesty sacking the capital of the Vicar of Christ.

When news of what had happened in Rome reached the enemies of Charles they were stirred into action. Henry in particular abandoned his earlier reserve, for he saw his opportunity of earning the Pope's gratitude, and so of furthering his own divorce: accordingly, Wolsey had a meeting with Francis at Amiens in August, 1527, when the details of the Anglo-French alliance were worked out. French troops once more invaded Italy, though their King did not take the field again after his unfortunate experience at Pavia, and penetrated as far as Naples, having won Genoa to their side on the march South. Then, as on so many previous occasions, just when final victory seemed within their grasp, they experienced a crushing reverse which snatched from them all they had gained. The truth was that French diplomacy, however able, had not the requisite armed force behind it.

The Imperialist armies, whether composed of Germans or Spaniards, were ill-paid and badly fed, it is true, and they often broke out into mutiny, but they were no sooner called upon to meet the enemy than they proved themselves his superior, whether they were acting on the offensive or the defensive. They were, too, usually better led. In the present instance they were assisted by the fact that the French were not long in alienating their new Genoese ally, and so command of the sea passed to the enemies of

France. Naples could thus be supplied from Sicily, and in August, 1528, the Prince of Orange, who was in the service of Charles, routed the French at Aversa. This proved to be the first of a series of disasters, and before long the only places of importance in Italy which still held out for Francis were Asti and Alessandria, though Venice and Florence had not yet broken with him.

The position of France and her allies was further complicated by a reconciliation between the Pope and the Emperor. As the fortune of war turned against the French King, no course was left open to Clement but to come to terms with Charles; at the same time the sack of Rome had so shocked Christendom that it was not in the interest of the Emperor to drive the Pope too hard. These considerations were reflected in the Treaty of Barcelona, which was concluded in June, 1529. By this the Pope promised to invest Charles with the kingdom of Naples, and to crown him Emperor. For his part Charles undertook that the places seized from the States of the Church by the Duke of Ferrara and by Venice should be restored, while he also promised to re-establish the Medici in Florence. The Emperor, too, showed himself not unmindful of the fact that the King of England had been numbered among his enemies, for within three weeks of the conclusion of the Treaty of Barcelona he persuaded Clement to revoke the powers which he had given to Wolsey and Campeggio to try the question of Henry's divorce in England, and to cite the case to Rome.

The Treaty of Barcelona proved to be the prelude of a general pacification, and this was largely the work of Margaret, the Emperor's aunt, and Louise, the mother of the French King. The Peace of Cambrai, not unjustly termed the Women's Peace, was signed in August, 1529, and in more than one respect it modified the terms of the Treaty of Madrid. Francis was freed from the necessity of ceding Burgundy, and he regained his sons by a cash payment. On the other hand, he had to surrender all claims to Italy, as well as to the over-lordship of Artois and Flanders, and he undertook to force his allies, the Venetians, to give up some recent conquests on the Neapolitan coast. Lastly, his marriage with Eleanora was ratified. This settlement, as will have been seen, left Charles master of Italy, and he displayed statesmanship of a high order in the conciliatory policy which he pursued. The Republic of Saint Mark was, indeed, forced to surrender her acquisitions in the kingdom of Naples, and to restore Ravenna and Cervia to the

Pope, but she was not further punished. Francesco Sforza was left with the Milanese, though Charles was careful to place Imperialist garrisons in the citadels of Milan and Como. Savoy was strengthened as an outpost against France by the addition of the county of Asti. Only upon Florence did the Emperor's hand fall heavily, but it required an eight months' siege before the city consented to accept as its ruler, Alessandro Medici, a cousin of the Pope, who had married an illegitimate daughter of Charles.

For the six ensuing years Western and South-Western Europe enjoyed an uneasy peace, though it was clear from the beginning that Francis had never regarded the Peace of Cambrai as anything more than a truce. Charles had so many conflicting interests that he was peculiarly vulnerable, and at every turn he found the King of France intriguing against him: the German Protestants, the English, and the Sultan were all subjected to the wiles of French diplomacy. Nevertheless, it was not until 1535 that Francis found an opportunity to attempt to reverse the verdict of the previous war.

In that year the Duke of Milan died, and with him the Sforza dynasty came to an end, for the other branches had perished during the earlier vicissitudes of the family. At once a difference of opinion between Charles and Francis manifested itself. The Emperor claimed that as the Milanese was an Imperial fief it fell to him, while Francis demanded it for his second son, Henry. The King of France had, of course, no legal basis for his claim, but on other grounds there was some justification for his attitude, since if Milan went to Charles the chain of Habsburg possessions which encircled France would be complete. He was also fortunate in the time of Francesco Sforza's death, for Charles was fully occupied with the Turks and the malcontents in his own territories. In these circumstances the Emperor was forced to temporize throughout the winter of 1535–6, and it was not until the spring of 1536 that military operations on an extended scale commenced.

Fighting continued in Northern Italy and on the Northern and Southern frontiers of France for two years without any marked advantage being gained by either side. Such being the case, a truce for ten years was made at Nice in June, 1538. The Peace of Cambrai was confirmed: the rivals abandoned their respective allies; and each retained the conquests he had made. In practice this meant that the Duke of Savoy was made the scapegoat. Savoy and two-thirds of Piedmont were kept by Francis; the Swiss took the district of Vaud; and the rest went to the Emperor: all that was left to the unfortunate Duke being Nice itself.

For some time efforts were made by Charles to convert the Truce of Nice into a permanent peace. The Dauphin had died, and the third son of Francis was now Duke of Orleans: the Emperor offered to cede to him the Franche Comté and the Netherlands, if the French King, for his part, would give the young man the remainder of the duchy of Burgundy, abandon all claim to the Milanese and the suzerainty of Flanders, and restore his conquests in Savoy and Piedmont to the Duke of Savoy. A long negotiation then ensued, and it centred round the point whether the Duke of Orleans was to have immediate possession, and whether the territories should revert to the Emperor in the event of the Duke's death without issue. Finally, Charles lost patience with what appeared to be the insincerity of the French, and in October, 1540, he invested his son Philip with the duchy of Milan. A renewal of the war thus became inevitable.

The murder of a French diplomat in the Milanese on his way to Constantinople gave Francis an excuse for breaking the Truce of Nice in the summer of 1541, though war was not actually declared until the following year. Henry VIII turned a deaf ear to the blandishments of Francis, which was in no way surprising in view of the fact that he was at war with the French monarch's ally, James V of Scotland; and in other quarters, too, Francis was unfortunate in his search for allies. The Pope, Paul III, remained neutral, as did the German Protestants, who were satisfied with recent concessions from the Emperor. The Sultan, the Kings of Denmark and Sweden, and the Duke of Cleves alone joined France. Of these, Christian III of Denmark was irritated by the support which Charles had given to the claims of the Palatinate branch of the Wittelsbach family on his throne; Gustavus I of Sweden resented the favour shown in Imperialist circles to a revolt of his peasants; while the Duke of Cleves disputed the claim of the Emperor to the reversion of Guelderland.

The early fighting, which was inconclusive, mostly took place in the Netherlands and Roussillon, but it sufficed to show the fundamental weakness of Charles. Not only was he dealing with an enemy operating on interior lines, but he had so many distractions that he was never strong enough in any one place at any one time. In the beginning of 1543, for example, the Sultan was master of the greater part of Hungary, and was preparing for a further campaign in Central Europe; his admiral Barbarossa was on the point of joining the French in an attack on Piedmont; the Pope was none too pleased with the Emperor's concessions to the Protestants and with the talk of a General Council, so he began to lean towards France; Denmark had closed the Sound to Dutch ships; and it was very doubtful whether the powerful Elector of Saxony would consent to strong action against the Duke of Cleves, who was not only his brother-in-law, but also a man of convinced Protestant sympathies.

To improve his position Charles turned to Henry, who was far from unwilling to receive his advances, for the recent death of James V had done nothing to weaken the Franco-Scottish alliance, and England was thus still threatened on two sides. Accordingly, an agreement was reached in February, 1543, by which Charles and Henry pledged themselves to demand that Francis should give up his alliance with the Sultan; indemnify the Empire for what it had spent in the Turkish war; and, as security for the debts he owed the King of England, hand over Boulogne and other towns. If the French King refused these terms, the allies undertook to continue the war until Burgundy was restored to Charles, and Henry had made good his claim to Normandy and Guyenne, as well as to the crown of France.

Charles took the field himself, and it was in no small measure due to his own exertions that fortune began to favour him. He forced the Duke of Cleves to resign his claims to Guelderland, while a Franco-Turkish attack on Nice was foiled by Spanish naval and military armaments. The horror felt at this co-operation between France and the Sultan cost Francis dear, for at the Diet of Spires in February, 1544, the Empire as a whole came to the support of Charles, and largely in consequence of this Denmark abandoned the French alliance. It was now the turn of Francis to take alarm, for, although his army won a victory in April in Piedmont, the following month saw the Imperialists reach the Marne, while the English landed on the coast. Indeed, had Henry co-operated vigorously with his ally Paris might well have fallen: the English, however, contented themselves with besieging Boulogne, and although it eventually fell into their hands its capture had no effect upon the progress of the war.

The Emperor, annoyed at what he regarded as a breach of faith on the part of the English King, let it be known that he was ready to come to terms with Francis, and in September, 1544, the

Treaty of Crespi ended the last war between the two rivals. All conquests made since the Truce of Nice were to be abandoned. Charles renounced his claims on Burgundy, and Francis gave up his own on Naples, as well as the suzerainty of Flanders and Artois. The Emperor further promised to the Duke of Orleans, either the hand of his daughter with the Netherlands and the Franche Comté, or that of his niece with the duchy of Milan. Charles reserved to himself the right of deciding which of these two marriages should be carried out, and on the completion of the compact Savoy and Piedmont were to be restored to their rightful owner. This part of the settlement was nullified in the following year by the death of the Duke of Orleans, and his father was thus able to retain the two provinces. As for Henry VIII, he continued the struggle against France until June, 1546, when his depleted treasury compelled him to conclude the Treaty of Ardres, by which he undertook to restore Boulogne to Francis within eight years in return for a money payment.

In 1547 the Emperor lost both his rivals, for Henry VIII died in January, and Francis I at the end of March.

CHAPTER IV

THE REFORMATION, 1521–1559

THE Reformation, on its material side, may be said to have influenced Europe in two ways: it finally put an end to the theory of a universal Church of which the Emperor represented the spiritual arm, and it introduced fresh causes of discord based on ideological grounds.

As it was in Germany that Luther raised the standard of revolt, it was the Empire that experienced the first impact of the centrifugal forces which were now unloosed. To quote Bryce: "The Holy Empire is but another name for the Visible Church. . . . Mediæval theory constructed the civil on the model of the ecclesiastical society. . . . The Roman Empire was the shadow of the Popedom —designed to rule men's bodies as the Pontiff ruled their souls. Both alike claimed obedience on the ground that Truth is One, and that where there is One faith there must be One government. And, therefore, since it was this very principle of Formal Unity that the Reformation overthrew, it became a revolt against the principle of authority in all its forms." A few pages earlier the same author had written: "Hitherto it had seemed not impossible to strengthen the German state into a monarchy, compact if not despotic; the very Diet of Worms, where the monk of Wittenberg proclaimed to an astonished Church and Emperor that the day of spiritual autocracy was past, had framed and presented a fresh scheme for the construction of a central council of government. The great religious schism put an end to all such hopes, for it became a source of political disunion far more serious and permanent than any that had existed before, and it taught the two sections into which Germany was henceforth divided to regard each other with feelings more bitter than those of hostile nations."

The result of this was soon felt in international relations. The Protestant princes in the Empire found themselves from a military point of view inferior to their rivals, and at first they attempted to provide for their safety by the old device of forming leagues among themselves. "Soon they began to look beyond the Vosges, and found that France, burning heretics at home, was only too happy to smile on free opinions elsewhere." By 1552 things had gone so far that Henry II assumed the title of "Protector of the Germanic Liberties", and in future a pretext for French interference in Germany was never wanting. The example proved infectious, and there were few countries in Europe which were not, at any rate for a time, split into two camps. A French Catholic would feel that he had more in common with the Spain of Philip II than with his Huguenot fellow-countrymen, and would for that reason be willing to aid those whom in different circumstances he would have regarded as the bitterest foes of France; similarly, the Huguenots were quite willing to call their English co-religionists to their aid in spite of the terrible example of the Burgundians in the Hundred Years' War.

Much of this was still to come when Charles succeeded Maximilian as Emperor. One of his earlier acts was to settle his hereditary possessions. He kept only the Netherlands and the Franche Comté in his own hands, and he granted to his brother, Ferdinand, the whole of his Austrian territories together with claims on Hungary and Bohemia.

The disintegrating effects of the Reformation may be said first to have made themselves felt at the Diet of Worms in 1521, but for some years they were limited to the domestic affairs of the Empire. Civil war took place more than once, and it was the commitments of Charles elsewhere, more particularly in respect of France, which prevented him from taking any strong action. Indeed, it was not until after the Treaty of Crespi in 1544 that he was free to deal with the German Protestants. By agreement with Paul III the Council of Trent was summoned in March of the following year, though it did not open its sessions until December. Charles appreciated the strength of the Protestant position, and he realized that he must proceed with caution. The Germans had often petitioned for a General Council, and if one could get to work, it might institute certain reforms which would conciliate the more moderate, and so strengthen the Emperor's position. Unfortunately for this scheme the Council was badly attended; only some forty bishops came, and among them Spaniards and Italians were in a decided majority. In these circumstances the Protestants refused to acknowledge it as a free and general council, more especially as it was decided that the members should vote as individuals, not by nations, since this procedure would be greatly to the advantage of the Papal party.

Charles had more success at first in the military sphere, and he was able to deal individually with the members of the League of Schmalkalde, as the Protestant association of German princes was termed. At the battle of Mühlberg in April, 1547, he defeated and captured his chief opponent, the Elector of Saxony, John Frederick, who was compelled to resign the electoral dignity and most of his territories, though his life was spared. These events were soon followed by the Diet of Augsburg, where Charles found himself in a dominating position, and, in February, 1550, by the succession of Julius III to the Papal throne. His predecessor, as a Farnese as well as Pope, did not desire to see either Spain or France too powerful, and he was therefore apt to prove an unreliable ally, but Julius III, somewhat unexpectedly, ranged himself on the Imperialist side. In the words of Ranke, when his election "became known at the Imperial court, every face was lighted up with joy. For to the high pre-eminence of power and fortune, to which the Emperor had attained, was now to be added the ascent of the Papal throne by a man whom he might firmly calculate on finding devoted to his interests."

What strengthened the position of the Emperor not unnaturally alarmed his opponents, and the Protestants decided to invoke the aid of the King of France. In January, 1552, therefore, they signed the Treaty of Friedwald with Henry II. No actual mention of religious questions was made, although the French King had tried to get inserted a clause which recognized his right to interfere in Germany where they were concerned: in return for his promise to assist in the preservation of the liberties of the Reich he was empowered to occupy, as Vicar of the Empire, Cambrai, Metz, Toul, and Verdun, and thus began that extension of the frontiers of France to the North and East which was to form so important a part of the policy of the Bourbons. The Protestant princes also promised at the next vacancy of the Empire to support the candidature of Henry, or of someone agreeable to him. The moving spirit in the conclusion of the Treaty of Friedwald was Maurice of Saxony, who had long worked with Charles, but who had lately become distrustful of him both on public and private grounds.

In March the French invaded Lorraine, and Maurice swept down on Innsbruck, where the Emperor then was, too ill with gout to ride. With difficulty he fled across the Bremer in a litter, but when Maurice was urged to capture him, he replied, "I have no cage big enough to hold such a bird". It was, indeed, another of those sudden reversals of fortune which were so prominent a

D

feature of the wars of the first part of the sixteenth century, but it did not suit either side to push the quarrel to extremes. This could only benefit the French and the Turks. The Emperor's brother, Ferdinand, was quite ready to come forward as a mediator, for the Turkish pressure was such that he had no hope of making head against it with a divided Reich at his back. The result was the Treaty of Passau in August, 1552, which gave temporary peace to Germany, three years later to be consolidated by the Peace of Augsburg, but which did not include the French. The war against Henry, therefore, continued, but without any definite advantage for either combatant, and in February, 1556, a truce concluded at Vaucelles led to a brief cessation of hostilities, though by that date Charles had ceased to be King of Spain.

The vicissitudes of his reign and his many commitments had aged the Emperor before his time, and in 1555 he took the first step in relieving himself of the responsibilities that were proving too much for him. "Fortune is a strumpet," he declared, "and reserves her favours for the young", so he handed over the Netherlands to his son Philip, who was already King of the Two Sicilies and Duke of Milan, and, since his marriage with Mary Tudor, King of England. In the following year the crowns of Spain and the Indies were also transferred to Philip, while in 1558 Charles secured the election of his brother, Ferdinand, as his successor in the Empire. When all this had been done, the greatest monarch in the world betook himself to the seclusion of the monastery of Yuste, in Estremadura, where he died in the same year at the age of fifty-seven.

The immediate results of this division of the Habsburg territories were to constitute the major problem of European politics for a hundred and fifty years, and the ultimate consequences were to make themselves felt to a still later date. Spain under Philip II had to meet the liabilities which Charles had incurred on her behalf. In particular, there was the *damnosa hereditas* of the Low Countries, which were a perpetual source of weakness, and whose inclusion in the Spanish dominions it is extremely difficult to defend. Their possession entailed the control of the sea-route through the English Channel, and with the defeat of the Armada in 1588 this became highly insecure. There was, it is true, access to them by land from Lombardy through the Franche Comté, but that depended upon the inability of France to break through her bonds. Philip thus found himself compelled to interfere in French internal politics in order to keep France weak, and in the latter part of his reign this actually necessitated the presence of a Spanish garrison in Paris. The possession of the Netherlands also roused the hostility of England, always alarmed at the domination of the Low Countries by a Great Power, and this meant the harrying of Spanish America by English adventurers, and English assistance to the enemies of Spain in all parts of Europe. In the face of these difficulties, it may be added, Philip did none too badly, though signs were not wanting that Spain could not continue the fight much longer. At his death France was still surrounded by Habsburg possessions on all sides, but she was now united under Henry IV. The *tercios* still held Brussels, but the United Netherlands were independent in all save name. The English attack on Lisbon had failed, but the English mastery of the sea was becoming an accomplished fact.

Meanwhile, on his accession Philip was called upon to deal with the hostility of France in spite of the truce which had been concluded at Vaucelles. That this was the case was largely due to the Pope, and the policy he pursued at this time affords an admirable example of the difficulties of his position as a spiritual and temporal Power. Julius III had died in 1555, and, after the brief reign of Marcellus II, had been succeeded in May of the same year by Paul IV. This Pope was predisposed against the Spaniards, for he was a member of the Neapolitan family of Caraffa, which had always supported the Angevin party in that kingdom; he had himself early incurred the displeasure of Charles, who had opposed his appointment to the archiepiscopal see of Naples. An old man in his eightieth year, he remembered the days when Italy was free, and he considered the Spaniards to be the most dangerous of its enemies. Nor was he discouraged by the example of those who in the past had invited the French into the peninsula, for he said, "The French may easily be dislodged hereafter; but the Spaniards are like dog-grass, sure to strike root wherever it is cast". So the paradoxical spectacle was seen of the Pope taking the part, lately played by the German Protestants, of ally of Henry II against the King of Spain.

In December, 1555, Paul made a secret treaty with France for the purpose of driving the Spaniards out of Italy, and, in July of the succeeding year, this was extended to include an arrangement by which the kingdom of Naples was to be conferred on one of Henry's sons, with the exception of a strip on the Northern frontier

that was to go to the Pope. A French army under the Duke of
Guise thereupon entered Italy, but that was the measure of allied
success in this theatre. The Duke of Alba invaded the Papal States,
and only his own and his master's scruples prevented him from
occupying Rome itself. As for Guise, he failed in his attempt on
Naples, and was shortly afterwards recalled to retrieve the
situation in France. There the French had in August, 1557,
suffered a severe defeat at St. Quentin at the hands of a Spanish
army commanded by Emmanuel Philibert, the dispossessed Duke
of Savoy, and, had Philip been so disposed, there was little to have
prevented his forces from reaching Paris, but he was content that
they should go into winter quarters. Guise used this opportunity
to capture, in the depth of winter, Calais from Philip's ally, Mary,
and so to close forever that door through which the English had so
often entered France during the previous two hundred years.
Guise followed up this success by the taking of Thionville in June,
1558, but shortly afterwards another French army was defeated
at Gravelines.

By this time the belligerents were desirous of peace. The
Queen of England was dying, and it was more than likely that her
successor, Elizabeth, would adopt a different foreign policy.
Charles, too, was approaching his end, and the situation in Spain
demanded the presence of Philip. Above all, the financial position
of the Spanish monarchy was giving cause for grave disquiet. On
the side of Henry, too, there were forces working in favour of a
settlement, and not the least of them was the fact that the Pope had
already made peace with Philip. He had, in fact, no alternative,
but the Spanish King, mindful of the unpopularity which his
father had incurred by the sack of Rome in the days of Clement
VII, was ready to let Paul off very lightly. Alba, indeed, remarked
of the terms that "they seem to have been dictated by the vanquished instead of the victor". The more important stipulations
were that the territories of the Church were to be restored intact,
and that such French troops as still remained in Italy were to be
allowed to return home without interference. So determined was
Philip to preserve appearances that Alba had to ask pardon, and
receive absolution, from the Pope, for having taken up arms
against him.

The settlement between France and Spain was effected by the
Treaty of Cateau Cambrésis in April, 1559. By this Henry was
allowed, with the consent of the Emperor, to retain Metz, Toul,

and Verdun, and he also kept Calais, but he had to surrender all his other conquests to Philip and his allies, with the exception of Turin, Saluzzo, Pignerol, and a few other places in Piedmont: these he was allowed to hold until his claim to the duchy of Savoy had been decided. On his part Philip surrendered some towns in Picardy which he had captured. The two Kings further pledged themselves to do their best to bring about the meeting of a General Council, which they deemed necessary both for the reformation of abuses, and for the restoration of union and concord to the Church. Lastly, the treaty was to be ratified by a double marriage: Philip was to marry Elizabeth, the eldest daughter of Henry, then a girl of thirteen, who had at first been suggested as the bride of his son, Don Carlos; Margaret, the sister of the French monarch, was to wed the Duke of Savoy. In the tournament which was held to celebrate the marriage of Philip with the French princess, Henry received a wound from which he died. He was succeeded by his son, Francis II, who was married to Mary, Queen of Scots.

The Treaty of Cateau Cambrésis may be said to have marked the end of the period in European history which began with the French invasion of Italy in 1494, and in which France had been continually the aggressor. All she had to show for a vast expenditure of men and money were Calais, Metz, Toul, and Verdun: she was surrounded by Habsburg territory on all sides, and Philip was undisputed master of Italy. The effort to secure the first place had also proved too much for her, and for a generation she was to be a prey to internal dissension to an extent which recalled her experiences in the Hundred Years' War. Spain, it is true, emerged the victor, but the price which she had to pay was, as we have seen, the sacrifice of her true interests. In these circumstances it is difficult to resist the conclusion that the residuary legatees of the long struggle were the Protestants and the Sublime Porte.

While these events were taking place in Central, Western, and Southern Europe, far away in the North other changes were being effected which were destined to exercise considerable influence upon the Balance of Power.

Ever since 1397 the three kingdoms of Denmark, Norway, and Sweden had been united by the Union of Kalmar. By this agreement the three states were to be irrevocably joined under the same monarch. Each was to retain its own laws and institutions, but treaties with foreign Powers were to be binding upon all. At first this scheme did not work too badly, but before long jealousy be-

tween Denmark and Sweden began to make itself felt. Denmark
was the centre of the federation, and her monarch was the King of
the Union, a fact which the Swedes increasingly resented with the
passing of the years. The result was that although the federal King
nominally ruled over the three kingdoms, in two-thirds of his
dominions he soon came to have very little power indeed. When
Christian II ascended the throne in 1513 he determined to revive
the royal supremacy, and he lost no time in attempting to give expression to his views. Sweden had for long been governed by two
distinguished nobles, the Stures, who called themselves Stadt-
holders, but who were in reality more powerful than the King, and
in Norway the influence of Christian was no greater than it was
in Sweden; in addition, all three kingdoms were commercially dependent upon the Hanseatic League in general and upon Lübeck
in particular, which still ruled the sea. Christian determined to
put an end to this state of affairs, and to restore the royal authority:
in 1520 he marched into Sweden with an army largely consisting
of mercenaries, suppressed all opposition, and entered Stockholm.

His success would appear to have convinced Christian that he
had only to deal with a handful of recalcitrant nobles, and he
determined to eliminate them. Accordingly, he organized the
massacre of some eighty of his leading opponents in the capital,
and an unspecified number of people were put to death in other
parts of Sweden. Christian then returned to Denmark apparently
master of the situation, but in actual fact his severity had caused
a revulsion of Swedish opinion against the Union of Kalmar, and
this feeling soon found a leader in Gustavus Vasa, whose father had
been one of Christian's victims. In 1523 he was elected King, and
in due course he carried his country into the Protestant camp,
though not without considerable opposition from the Swedish
people.

The accession of Gustavus I marked the beginning of an epoch
which was to see Sweden take her place among the Great Powers,
and which lasted until the death of Charles XII in 1718. Yet at the
beginning of his reign Gustavus was far from being in a strong
position, for to establish himself on the throne he had been compelled to have recourse to the aid of Lübeck, which was only too
willing to assist the dissolution of the Union of Kalmar, and she
used this fact to exploit Sweden to the uttermost, while the Swedish
King bided his time. His opportunity came in 1534, for in that
year the burghers of Lübeck over-reached themselves by attempt-

ing to force a monarch on Denmark. Christian II had finally been deposed by his own people, and his successor, Frederick I, had died eight months later, so that the Danish throne was vacant. Lübeck supported the claim of Count Christopher of Oldenburg against Christian, the son of Frederick I, and sent an expedition to aid her candidate to assert his rights. Gustavus saw his chance, broke with Lübeck, and openly espoused the cause of Christian.

The hostilities which ensued were known as the Count's War, and their result fully vindicated the policy of the Swedish King. By the spring of 1535 his ally, now Christian III, was in possession of the greater part of Denmark, and in the following summer one Lübeck fleet was driven under the guns of Copenhagen, which still held out for Christopher, while another was annihilated in Svendburg Sound. The Danish capital fell in July, 1536, and this marked the end of a contest which was much more than a mere contest for the throne of Denmark. The hegemony of Lübeck in Scandinavia was gone for ever, and in future Danes, Norwegians, and Swedes were masters in their own houses. Another consequence was the consolidation of the Reformation in Denmark and Norway, for Christian III was a devoted Protestant. To Sweden the Count's War was an unmixed benefit, for it led at once to an armistice with Lübeck, arranged by Christian III, and ultimately in 1537 to a five years' truce by which the city abandoned all her old exclusive privileges in return for exemption from tolls in Stockholm, Kalmar, Söderköping, and Åbo. Thus was abolished that external control which had for centuries handicapped the free development of Swedish trade.

The Union of Kalmar might have come to an end, but one of the immediate consequences of the Count's War was to strengthen the friendly relations between Sweden and Denmark which had resulted from the assistance given by Gustavus to Christian III, and an offensive and defensive alliance was concluded by the Peace of Brömsebro in September, 1541. As has been shown in a previous chapter, both Scandinavian monarchs had at this time causes of complaint against Charles V, and their close friendship was by no means uninfluenced by apprehension regarding the Emperor's intentions. It was at this date, too, that there was signed— at Sceaux in 1542—the first of the many treaties of alliance between Sweden and France. As the danger from Charles receded there was a revival of jealousy between Denmark and Sweden, but so long as Gustavus I and Christian III lived their relations continued peaceful. It was, however, otherwise where Russia was concerned, and in 1556 there was a short, and inconclusive, Russo-Swedish war in Finland over frontier questions. Gustavus entertained very real fears of his Eastern neighbour's intentions, and he attributed to Ivan IV the design of turning the Baltic into a Russian lake. Ivan, it must be confessed, adopted an extremely offensive tone in his dealings with Gustavus, and it was only with difficulty that a settlement was reached in 1557. During this struggle an attempt was made by the Swedish King to persuade Mary Tudor to break off the recently formed commercial relations with Russia by way of Archangel, but as Sweden had nothing sufficiently lucrative to offer in return he was unsuccessful.

Owing to her geographical position Denmark was more closely affected than Sweden by the progress of events in the Empire, and both on political and religious grounds Christian III inclined towards the German Protestants and their French ally: in 1541 he concluded with Henry II the Treaty of Fontainebleau, which was the counterpart of the agreement made by Sweden with France at Sceaux. In the ensuing campaign against Charles V the Danes played their part, but they were ignored, both by the King of France and the German princes when they had served their purpose. Christian then decided to enter into direct negotiations with the Emperor, and these were brought to a successful conclusion in May, 1544. The Danish monarch promised to renounce the French alliance, and to open the Sound which he had closed to shipping from the Low Countries. Charles on his part undertook to withdraw his support from the Wittelsbach claim to the Danish throne. This settlement represented a definite diplomatic victory for Denmark.

The foreign policy of Christian's later years was dictated by this arrangement. He carefully avoided all external complications, and cultivated the friendship both of Charles V and of his successor, Ferdinand I. He steadily refused to assist the Protestant princes in the Schmalkaldic War, ostensibly because it was of a purely political nature, but really because he still resented what he considered to be their desertion of him on an earlier occasion. Christian died in the same year as Henry II of France, namely 1559, and in 1560 he was followed to the grave by Gustavus I.

The Reformation in Scandinavia was not the result of a popular religious movement, but rather of the domestic political situation; it was a lever of a secular revolution which brought a change in the religious sentiments of the people in its train; but in both Denmark and Sweden there followed a realization of national consciousness on the part of the population which was wholly wanting in the Reich. Elsewhere the consequences of the Reformation were also having their effect upon national and international politics. In France the death of Henry II ushered in a period of religious strife, the repercussions of which will receive attention in a subsequent chapter. In the British Isles many an old political landmark temporarily disappeared; England had less to fear from foreign intrigue in Scotland, but a great deal more where Ireland was concerned. Yet, as was to be the case after the French Revolution, once the waters began to subside the old landscape reappeared, changed in some respects, but still easily recognizable. Values had been transformed, and new catch-words took the place of the old in the mouths of statesmen, but the attitude of the various Powers towards one another was not for long vitally affected.

CHAPTER V

HEIGHT OF OTTOMAN POWER, 1512–1566

I N 1512 Bayezid II was dethroned by his son Selim I, not in-
appropriately termed "The Grim", and the immunity from
Turkish attack which Christendom had enjoyed for nearly a
generation came to an end. Before, however, discussing the relations between the Porte and Europe it is necessary to look a little
more closely at the bases of Ottoman power, for these exercised
considerable influence over the foreign policy of the Sultans.

The Turks conquered Asia and Africa from Europe, not, as is
often supposed, Europe from Asia and Africa. The Crescent flew
over the greater part of the Balkans long before it was seen in
Damascus, Baghdad, or Cairo, let alone in Tunis or Algiers. Indeed, it was to no small extent the Ottoman hold on the Balkan
peninsula that enabled Mohammed I (1413–1421) to restore the
situation after the disasters which had been inflicted upon the
Osmanli by Tamerlane. Nor is this surprising in view of the fact
that it was from the European provinces of the Empire that were
recruited the Janissaries, who proved the deciding factor in many
a battle. In effect, the capture of Constantinople in 1453 rounded
off the Turkish conquests in the Balkans; it did not originate them.

On the other hand, as a modern authority has put it, "The
Sultan had but one arm, it was a long arm and a strong one, yet
it could reach only a fixed distance, and it could strike but one
blow". There was only one army, so there could be only one
serious war. If, while war was in progress on one frontier, conditions became critical on the other, it was necessary to make peace
on what terms could be had, and carry the army to the extremity
of the empire. Thus, Suleyman I concluded peace with Charles V
in 1533, and with Ferdinand in 1547, in order to be free to act
against Persia: had either Habsburg wished to go back on his
word he could have marched to Constantinople with very little
opposition. Had the Ottoman standing army been divisible, or
separable from the person of the monarch, the Sultan could have
kept up a steady pressure on both frontiers, and considerably
extended his dominions both to East and West.

In this connection it is interesting to note that the Empire

46

possessed two great advantages over Persia in the wars with Turkey. The Osmanli did not wish to pass the winter in the cold
North, but they did not seriously object to staying in Aleppo or
Baghdad. This attitude may well have saved Vienna for Austria
and lost Baghdad for Persia. Then, again, since the journey from
Vienna to Constantinople was much easier than that from Tabriz
to Constantinople, the Imperialists could have reached the Turkish
capital while the Ottoman army was in the East, whereas the Persians could not have got there while the Osmanli were in Austria.
In the sixteenth century, however, this advantage remained
theoretical, since neither the Emperor nor the Shah was ever in a
position to attempt such a stroke.

The earlier Sultans, too, unlike their successors in the eighteenth and nineteenth centuries, had no cause to fear co-operation
between their enemies abroad and their Christian subjects at
home. The non-Moslem population of the Ottoman Empire was
predominantly Orthodox in religion, and at that time the chief
antagonists of the Turks, such as Spain, Austria, and Venice, were
Roman Catholic Powers, with whom the Christian peoples of the
Balkans had no sympathy. Indeed, there were many occasions
when the *rayahs* gave clear proof of the fact that they preferred the
Sultan to those who acknowledged the Pope. It was not until
the rise of Russia that the situation changed, and the Christian
subjects of the Porte began to give active assistance to its
enemies.

The first two years of the reign of Selim I were spent in the
elimination of potential and actual rivals, and it was not until 1514
that he was able to return to that expansion of the Ottoman Empire which had been suspended under his more pacific father. He
turned first of all against Persia, and the prize of a successful campaign was the incorporation of Diarbekir and Kurdistan in his
dominions. Having secured himself against attack from the East,
the Sultan then proceeded against the Mamelukes who ruled Syria
and Egypt; once more success rewarded his efforts, the Mameluke
dynasty was overthrown, and their dominions became Ottoman
pashalics. These victories, it may be noted, were to no inconsiderable extent made possible by the skilful way in which the Osmanli
handled their artillery, as well as to the training of the Janissaries.
As so often in the course of history, the rise of a new Power was
due to the development of a new weapon or a new strategy.

The conquest of Egypt by Selim I had not only a material

significance, for it entailed the incorporation in the Ottoman Empire of the Holy Cities of Mecca and Medina. Nor was this all, for in Cairo there lived, under Mameluke protection, Al-Mutawahkil, the titular Caliph of Islam and the descendant of the great Abbasid line. Selim took him to Constantinople, where in due course the Caliph was persuaded to hand over to the Ottoman Sultans his shadowy office, together with its symbols, the standard and cloak of Mohammed. Henceforth the heirs of Selim assumed the title of Caliph and Protector of the Holy Places, and on occasion they used their position to stir up the Moslem subjects of the British and Russian monarchs when it suited their purpose, though such attempts were never particularly successful, for the Caliphate did not prove to be a very effective weapon in the Turkish diplomatic armoury.

In less than eight years Selim nearly doubled the extent of his dominions, but it is significant that during all this warfare he never crossed swords with a Christian Power: he realized the limitations imposed upon him by the Ottoman military system, and he wished to be assured of a secure position in Asia and Africa before he tried conclusions with Europe. By 1518 such a state of affairs had been established, and the Sultan spent the last two years of his reign in organizing a navy. He died in 1520.

Selim I was succeeded by his son, Suleyman I, known to Europe as "the Magnificent", and to his own people as "the Lawgiver". He was a worthy contemporary of Charles V, Francis I, and Henry VIII, and under his rule the Ottoman Empire may be said to have attained the zenith of its power. When Suleyman ascended the throne he saw that there were two points of conspicuous weakness. In the North the gate into the Balkans, namely the fortress of Belgrade, was in the hands of the Hungarians, and so long as this remained the case the road from Vienna to Constantinople was open. In the South there was another complication. The Knights Hospitallers still held Rhodes, in spite of the efforts of earlier Sultans to dislodge them, and so long as they remained there they constituted a perpetual menace to the maritime communications between Constantinople and the newly acquired conquests of Syria and Egypt.

Suleyman decided to reduce Belgrade first, as he did not wish to be exposed to attack from Hungary while he was engaged in the siege of Rhodes. He accomplished this immediate purpose in 1521, and it is an illuminating sidelight on contemporary conditions that when the Hungarian defenders of Belgrade had decided to blow up the citadel, their project was betrayed to the Turks by the Orthodox clergy. The way was now clear for the attack on Rhodes, and this was at once undertaken. It was, however, only after a gallant defence lasting nine months, during which the Osmanli losses were in the neighbourhood of fifty thousand, that the fortress capitulated. By the terms of surrender, which Suleyman faithfully observed, the survivors of the garrison with all their personal property were to be conveyed to Crete in their own galleys. In 1530 the Knights moved from Crete to Malta, where in those early years of Suleyman's reign they seemed to be too far away to constitute any threat to the Sultan's dominions.

This consolidation of his position enabled Suleyman to play his part on the stage of European politics, and to extract the maximum advantage out of the struggle between Charles V and Francis I; in other words, he began to pursue in the East much the same policy as Henry VIII was attempting in the West. The progress of events soon provided him with an opportunity of intervention, for the defeat of the French at Pavia was a great day not only for the Habsburgs but also for the Turks. In his despair Francis invoked the aid of Suleyman to take the pressure off his country by an attack upon the Empire from the East.

This was not the first official contact between Paris and Constantinople. As long ago as 1483 an envoy had been sent by Bayezid II to regulate some matters concerning the Knights Hospitallers, and to offer certain holy relics to the French King, but Charles VIII had refused to receive him. Again in 1500 the Sultan had asked for the intervention of Louis XII in his differences with the Republic of Saint Mark, and after the conquest of Egypt all the privileges which the French had enjoyed under the Mameluke regime were confirmed to them by Selim I. Nevertheless, until disaster overtook him Francis was not to be tempted, and he adopted the traditional rôle of the French monarchy as the champion of Christendom against the infidel. A crusade was one of the main planks in his platform in the contest for the Empire, and he promised the Electors that within three years he would be in Constantinople or his coffin. Adversity, however, proverbially makes strange bedfellows, and before long Europe was horrified by *"l'union sacrilège des lys et du croissant"*. All the same, the ensuing agreement between France and Turkey was destined to supply one of the most important and one of the most continuous threads in the fabric of European diplomacy for more than three hundred years.

The preliminary approach was not actually made by Francis himself, for he was a captive in Madrid, but by the French regent, Louise of Savoy, though the new policy was at once confirmed by the King as soon as he heard of it. The first envoy sent from Paris was murdered on his way through Bosnia, but in December, 1525, there arrived in Constantinople one Count John Frangipani with a letter for Suleyman from Francis. At the end of the following April the French King wrote to the Sultan, "*Nous n'avons pu que ressentir un vif plaisir en voyant l'insigne générosité de votre coeur qui vous porte à nous promettre des secours dans cette triste situation de nos affaires, en nous offrant de grands trésors et toutes vos forces*". From the beginning Francis would appear to have been under no illusions about the unpopularity of his policy in Christendom and of the possible repercussions of this among his own subjects; he was therefore careful to lay great stress upon the exertions which he was making to secure from the Sultan an amelioration of the lot of the Catholics in his dominions, while he did all in his power to obtain for the French every kind of commercial advantage in the Ottoman Empire.

No formal engagements between the two Powers were entered into at this time, and Suleyman's subsequent invasion of Hungary was certainly not pre-arranged with the King of France. The opportunity was tempting enough in itself. Hungary and Bohemia were linked in an uneasy personal union under the young King Louis II, the last of the Jagellon dynasty, and in the event of attack the international situation was clearly such that he could not rely upon foreign support. In the spring of 1526 the Sultan fell upon Hungary like a thunderbolt, and in August he routed its army at Mohacs, largely owing to the skilful employment of his artillery; Louis was drowned in his flight from the field, and the two kingdoms which he had ruled at once fell apart. Buda itself capitulated in the following month, and had it not been that the Sultan was called away by troubles in Asia Minor, there seemed to be nothing to prevent an Ottoman advance into the heart of the Empire. In 1529 Suleyman was repulsed before the walls of Vienna, and a definite limit had been put to Turkish aggrandizement in Central Europe, though another century and a half was to elapse before this was definitely proved. The wave once again dashed as far; but only to be again broken, and then to recede for ever. For the rest of his reign the Sultan was engaged in intermittent warfare against Ferdinand, who claimed to be the heir of the Jagellons, on the Austro-Hungarian frontier, but although there were repeated truces no final settlement was reached.

As we have seen, the Turks were unable to fight simultaneously on two fronts, but Suleyman's campaigns against Persia were also remarkably successful, and during the course of them large portions of Armenia and Mesopotamia, including the city of Baghdad, were added to his dominions. All the same, he was no more able finally to subdue the Safavids than the Habsburgs.

Meanwhile the relations between France and the Porte were becoming closer. In 1528 Francis sent a representative to Constantinople to ask for the return to Christian use of a church in Jerusalem which had been converted into a mosque. The Sultan refused, but in the most courteous manner, and he made a number of more material concessions. Freedom of movement and trade in Egypt was granted to the subjects of the French King; the jurisdiction of French consuls over their fellow-countrymen in that country was recognized except in the case of prisoners arrested on a capital charge; the right to certain churches in Alexandria was admitted; and all French consuls, factories, and merchants were placed under the protection of the Sublime Porte. In 1534 Francis decided to take the matter a stage farther, and Jean de La Forest arrived in the Turkish capital with full powers to conclude a definite alliance against Charles V on the basis of the acquisition by France of the Milanese, Flanders, and Artois, and the recognition of Suleyman's nominee, John Zapolya, as King of Hungary.

These proposals resulted in the following year in a definite treaty between France and the Porte. The Sultan extended throughout the Ottoman Empire the privileges which he had already accorded to the French in Egypt. Frenchmen were to enjoy complete freedom of trade and navigation in all Turkish ports, subject to a uniform duty of five per cent; no foreign vessel might sail in Turkish waters except under the French flag; French traders were to be under the exclusive jurisdiction, both civil and criminal, of their own consuls, and the Turkish officials guaranteed the execution of all judgments in the consular courts; French settlers in the Ottoman Empire were to enjoy peculiar privileges in respect of the transmission of property by will, and even of intestate estates; they were to have not only complete religious liberty for themselves, but also the custody of the Holy Places, and thus to exercise a kind of protectorate over the Christian subjects of the Porte. The King of France, alone among the European sovereigns, was to be regarded and treated as an equal by the Sultan, and in future he was to be described in official documents as Padishah instead of Bey.

In addition, a secret offensive and defensive alliance was concluded between Francis and Suleyman, by which the Sultan undertook to invade Hungary and the Two Sicilies, and the French King promised to commence hostilities by an attack on the Milanese. The treaty made by La Forest was confirmed by Henry II in 1553, and it was further stipulated that any towns in Italy captured by the Ottoman fleet should be handed over to the French, but not until they had been sacked by the Turks and the inhabitants had been carried off as slaves.

France thus ensured that whenever she was at war with the Habsburgs, they should fight on two fronts: she might herself be surrounded by the territory of the House of Austria, but her enemy was now exposed to attack from Sweden, Denmark, and the Turks. Twenty years later a Valois prince ascended the throne of Poland, and that country was included in the French system of alliances. The assistance of the Sultan was particularly valuable to France in the sixteenth century. With very brief intervals, as we have seen, she was at war with the Habsburgs from 1535 to 1559, and there was no real settlement until the Treaty of Vervins in 1598, in spite of the attempt to reach one at Cateau Cambrésis. Throughout the whole of this period, and indeed much beyond it, France could count upon the loyal co-operation of the Turks. In this connection it must be confessed that the loyalty of the Porte to its engagements was a good deal more constant and continuous than that of the French. Francis I and his successors were only too glad to take advantage of the alliance whenever, and for as long as, it suited their purpose, but they never hesitated to come to terms with the Sultan's adversaries when their own interests appeared to dictate such a course. On the other hand, they always had to weigh carefully the material advantages to be derived from Turkish aid against the moral reprobation which such aid inevitably roused in the rest of Christendom.

During the earlier years of his reign Suleyman had come into conflict with Charles V in the Habsburg's capacity as Emperor, but a series of events on the coast of North Africa produced a clash between the Sultan and Charles as King of Spain.

FRANCHE COMTÉ

SWISS CONFEDERATION

TYROL

CARINTHIA

KINGDOM of HUNGARY

GENEVA

SAVOY

TRENT

VENETIA

CARNIOLA

CROATIA

OTTOMAN EMPIRE

AOSTA

MILAN

VERONA

MANTUA

VENICE

POLA

DALMATIA

FRANCE

TURIN

PINEROLO

SALUZZO

PARMA

MODENA

FERRARA

BOLOGNA

ADRIATIC REPUBLIC

NICE

GENOA

PISA

LEGHORN

FLORENCE

URBINO

ANCONA

CORSICA
(TO GENOA)

BASTIA

ELBA

SIENA

PERUGIA

PAPAL STATES

PESCARA

SEA

AJACCIO

ROME

CAPUA

BENEVENTO

BARI

NAPLES

SALERNO

TARANTO

TERRANOVA

SARDINIA
(TO ARAGON)

TYRRHENIAN

SEA

COTRONE

CATANZARO

MEDITERRANEAN

PALERMO

MESSINA

REGGIO

SICILY
(TO ARAGON)

CATANIA

SEA

ITALY
1494 — 1559

BOUNDARY IN 1494

BOUNDARY OF THE HOLY ROMAN EMPIRE

Ⓐ TO FRANCE 1559, TO SAVOY 1601 Ⓑ TO FRANCE 1601 Ⓒ LOST TO SAVOY UP TO 1536

BECAME SPANISH DEPENDENCIES UNDER CHARLES V

4

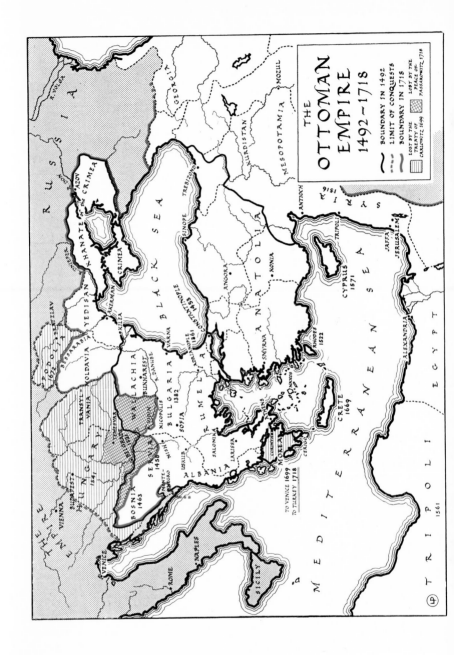

THE
OTTOMAN
EMPIRE
1492~1718

BOUNDARY IN 1492
LIMIT OF CONQUESTS
BOUNDARY IN 1718
LOST BY THE TREATY OF CARLOWITZ 1699
LOST BY THE PEACE OF PASSAROWITZ 1718

RUSSIA

R. VOLGA
R. DON
AZOV
GEORGIA
KURDISTAN
MESOPOTAMIA
MOZUL
ANTIOCH
SYRIA 1516
TRIPOLI
CYPRUS 1571
JAFFA
JERUSALEM
ALEXANDRIA
EGYPT
TRIPOLI 1561

KHANATE OF THE CRIMEA
YEDISAN
CRIMEA
AKERMAN
KILIA
BLACK SEA
TREBIZOND
SINOPE
ANATOLIA
ANGORA
KONIA
SMYRNA
RHODES 1522
MEDITERRANEAN SEA
CRETE 1669

PODOLIA 1672
BESSARABIA
MOLDAVIA
WALLACHIA
BUCHAREST
R. DANUBE
NICOPOLIS
BULGARIA
SOFIA 1382
VARNA
ADRIANOPLE 1361
CONSTANTINOPLE 1453
RUMELIA
SALONIKA
LARISSA
CORINTH
MOREA
CERIGO

TRANSYLVANIA
HUNGARY
BUDAPEST 1541
THE EMPIRE
VIENNA
TEMESVAR
SERVIA
SEMENDRIA 1458
BOSNIA 1463
NISH
USKUB
ALBANIA
MONTENEGRO

TO VENICE 1699
TO TURKEY 1718

VENICE
ROME
NAPLES
SICILY

④

This littoral was divided between a number of Moslem dynasties which had grown up on the collapse of the Almohad empire in the middle of the thirteenth century, but their principal occupation was piracy, and they were a perpetual menace to those engaged in commerce in the Mediterranean. The conquest of Granada had brought Spain face to face with the problems of North Africa, and for reasons of security she had occupied a number of strong points there, such as Peñon de Alger, Oran, and Tripoli. At this stage there appeared various corsairs, who sometimes operated on their own and sometimes on behalf of the Sultan; the most important were Barbarossa and his brother Kheyr-ed-din, Dragut, and Piale. Under their pressure both the local dynasties and the Spaniards were forced to give ground. Barbarossa had taken Algiers as early as 1516, and three years later his brother was recognized by Selim I as Governor-General of the province of Algiers, though the Spaniards held Peñon de Alger until 1530 and Oran until 1706. Tunis had belonged to the Hafsids for some three centuries, but in 1534 it was occupied by Kheyr-ed-din in the name of Suleyman. The threat to the Two Sicilies which was thus constituted was too great to be ignored, and in the following year Charles V recaptured the city; he restored the dethroned Hafsid, and left a Spanish garrison to support him, but by 1574 both Tunis and the surrounding country were wholly in Turkish hands. Farther along the coast the Sultan became master of Tripoli in 1552, it having been conquered by Dragut, who had already established a base to the West in Morocco.

These successes changed the whole Balance of Power in the Mediterranean. Ferdinand and Isabella had hoped by the conquest of Granada to close the door by which Islam had so often invaded the Peninsula, and yet here were the Osmanli apparently sweeping along the coast of North Africa like the Ommeyad Caliphs in the seventh century. Nor was this all, for that command of the sea which had so greatly contributed to the defeat of the French in Naples had passed out of Spanish hands. The conquest of Egypt and the support of the corsairs had contrived to produce one of those rare occasions when the Crescent was superior to the Cross at sea, and in 1538 the Turks defeated the combined Papal, Venetian, and Spanish fleets off Prevesa. To the statesmen of Madrid the Ottoman power appeared in the not inappropriate guise of a crescent, one horn of which pointed at Vienna and the other at the Straits of Gibraltar. Nor was this all, for there was no

E

telling how far the descendants of the conquered Moors in Spain itself might not be preparing to display active sympathy with their Ottoman co-religionists, while the Sultan had an ally on the Pyrenees in the person of the King of France. So long as the mastery of the Mediterranean was in dispute, the strength of the Habsburg ring round France was likely to prove more apparent than real.

With Ottoman power thus extended to the West, the fate of Malta, which seemed of little importance to Suleyman at the beginning of his reign, assumed very different proportions at the end of it. Malta became, as has been emphasized on more than one subsequent occasion, the key to the Western Mediterranean. If the Turks could drive the Knights Hospitallers from the island, then it would form an admirable advanced base from which, in conjunction with French squadrons based on the ports in the South of France, to harry the Balearic Islands and the coast of Spain itself. So it came about that the last warlike operation of Suleyman the Magnificent was against the same enemy as his first, namely the Knights Hospitallers. The attack was launched in May, 1565, and the siege lasted until September, when the Turks broke it off on the news of the impending arrival of a Spanish force. The Ottoman advance in the Mediterranean had been halted as it had been halted in Central Europe, but he would have been a bold prophet who would have foretold, when Suleyman died in the following year, that this advance was destined to go no farther.

It is impossible to understand the workings of European diplomacy in the sixteenth century unless allowance is made for the Ottoman threat from the East, first by land and then both by land and sea. It was continually present to European statesmen, and those responsible for the destinies of Spain and the Empire had always to take into account the probability that a war with France would mean one with the Turks, though the contrary was not always the case. On the other hand, the Sultan had to be assured of the inactivity of the Persians before he could embark on a campaign in Central Europe.

CHAPTER VI

REIGN OF PHILIP II, 1556–1598

PHILIP II landed in Spain in 1559 on his return from the Netherlands at the close of the war with France, and he never afterwards left the Peninsula. He was laborious and conscientious, and he regarded, in all sincerity, his position as a trust for which he must one day render an account to God. He conceived it to be his duty to defend the faith and to maintain the Spanish Empire, but he was by inclination opposed to the warlike methods by which his father had sought to achieve these ends. Philip was essentially a man of the study, and he had a firm belief in time as an ally. On official occasions no one could be more haughty; he took the greatest pains to cultivate a manner equal to his pretensions; and he inspired with awe those who obtained an audience of him: the icy coldness, the fixed stare, and a paucity of words all contributed to the result he desired. As a monarch he was often both cruel and treacherous, but when his great palace of the Escorial was being built he would mingle freely with the workmen, and on Sunday would wait his turn with them to receive Communion from the village priest. He was a fanatic, and did not hesitate to include murder among the weapons in his diplomatic armoury.

Yet, if Philip ill-used others, he certainly did not spare himself. Sometimes his conscientiousness had ludicrous results, as, for example, when he came to England to marry Mary Tudor, and drank English beer until he was sick in a vain attempt to make himself popular. He was also a generous patron of the arts, devoted to children, and a lover of flowers. In effect, Philip was a naturally good man, cursed with mental obliquity and a lack of due sense of proportion.

His reign was to be marked by more than one of those paradoxes which are so prominent in Spanish history. It was to the interest of Spain that he should continue the old struggle against the Moslem, but the logical result of that struggle, namely the persecution of the Moriscoes—that is to say, the descendants of the Moors—in the Peninsula was to her economic detriment. A friendly England was essential if the sea-route to the Netherlands was to be secure, and Elizabeth's refusal to continue her sister's pro-Spanish policy really left no alternative but the subjugation of the kingdom by force. Yet if Elizabeth was dethroned her heir was Mary, Queen of Scots, who had been Queen of France and who would clearly further French, rather than Spanish, interests. It was not until shortly before Mary's death that Philip dared to strike directly at Elizabeth, and by then it was too late. In France itself Spanish armed intervention became essential during the Wars of Religion, but it had the effect of accelerating the revival of the country under Henry of Navarre.

One of the first problems which Philip was called upon to face was the insecurity of the Spanish communications with Naples and Sicily owing to the Turkish successes of recent years. The relief of Malta in 1565 certainly alleviated the situation, but the danger remained, and it was aggravated by the presence in the Peninsula of the Moriscoes, who could only sympathize with their co-religionists. After the conquest of Granada they had been allowed many privileges, such as permission to wear their national costume, and although, on the morrow of the Sultan's invasion of Hungary, these were curtailed in 1526, the regulations of that year were not generally enforced. Philip, fearful of the negotiations which he knew were going on between the Moriscoes on the one hand and the Turks and Barbary Corsairs on the other, applied such harsh measures that in 1568 the Moriscoes rose in revolt. They chose a King, and proof that Philip's fears were by no means groundless is afforded by the fact that the insurgents' choice was confirmed by the Pasha of Algiers in the name of the new Sultan, Selim II.

For two years Andalusia and Murcia were the scene of a war in which quarter was neither asked nor given, and at the end of that time Philip's troops were victorious. The Moorish settlements were broken up, and their inhabitants scattered in La Mancha, Castille, Estremadura, and Galicia; all Moriscoes were forbidden under penalty of death to approach within thirty miles of Granada; and all Arabic books were ordered to be destroyed, while the possession of one rendered the unfortunate owner liable to punishment in the galleys. In 1609 Philip III, having discovered that the Moriscoes were intriguing with the French, completed his father's work by expelling them from the country altogether. Domestic and foreign policy were closely connected in all states in the sixteenth century, but nowhere more than in Spain. The Moriscoes were the best husbandmen, artisans, and metal-workers in the Peninsula, but in the interest of national security they had to go, whatever might be the consequences in the economic field.

The rising of the Moriscoes had not yet been crushed when, in May, 1570, Philip's aid against the Turks was invoked by Pope Pius V. The death of Suleyman the Magnificent had not resulted in the cessation of Ottoman aggression, although Selim II possessed none of his father's abilities, for the men trained by the old Sultan were still in charge of the civil and military administration. Nor had the reverse at Malta damped Turkish hopes, and at the close of 1569 an expedition was sent from Constantinople to reduce the island of Cyprus, then a Venetian possession. It was in consequence of this action on the part of the Porte that the Pope had asked Philip for help. In due course an agreement was reached between Spain, the Papacy, and the Republic of Saint Mark to form a perpetual alliance not only against the Sultan but also against the corsairs of Tunis, Tripoli, and Algiers. The signatories promised to defend each other's territory, and not to make any separate peace. The supreme command of their joint forces was to be given to Don John of Austria, an illegitimate son of Charles V, and consequently half-brother to Philip II.

The formation of this league throws much light on the position of the Spanish King, which was a great deal more formidable on paper than in practice. Twelve months elapsed between the Pope's appeal reaching Madrid and the conclusion of the agreement between the three Powers, so that it is hardly surprising that Cyprus should have been subdued by the Turks before the allies could come to its effective assistance. On July 30th, 1571, the last Venetian stronghold, Famagusta, fell; its defender was flayed alive; and his skin was stuffed and sent as a trophy to Constantinople. The explanation of this delay was that Philip was perpetually short of money, and that his commitments were so extensive that he always experienced the greatest difficulty in assembling a sufficient force at the right time and at the right place. Towards the end of his reign he was to find this difficulty for all practical purposes insurmountable.

The loss of Cyprus galvanized the allies into action, and on October 7th, 1571, Don John of Austria won the great naval battle of Lepanto. On the morrow of this victory voices were raised in favour of an immediate attack on the Turkish capital, but it was considered by those in authority that the season was too far advanced to encourage hopes of success. Moreover, once the immediate danger was removed differences revealed themselves between the allies, for Philip wished to turn his arms against the coast of North Africa, whence came the main threat to Spanish shores, while the Venetians were chiefly concerned for their commercial position in the Levant. To complicate the situation still further, in May, 1572, Pius V, to whose inspiration the formation of the league had been so largely due, died. In these circumstances the Venetians decided that the time had come to shift for themselves, and in March, 1573, they came to terms with the Porte: Cyprus was formally renounced, and the Republic of Saint Mark subsidized the Sultan's recent efforts against her and her allies.

The subsequent Spanish operations against the Turks in the Mediterranean were of merely local importance. Don John captured Tunis in 1573, but it was retaken in the following year. It is true that the Sultans never again seriously threatened the South-West of Europe; but whether this was due to the battle of Lepanto, or to the internal decay of the Ottoman Empire, is at least arguable.

In the Italian peninsula, too, Philip never forgot that he was the heir of Aragon, and the settlement of Cateau Cambrésis, which had left him master of Italy, was not seriously called in question during his reign. Two important factors combined to render it more lasting than the treaties earlier in the century. In the first place, France, who had the most cause for dissatisfaction, was for many years unable to make an effort to reverse the decision owing to the internal troubles which distracted her from Italian affairs. Secondly, and because of French inability to interfere, Spain had no reason to upset the settlement, for it gave her such a control over Italy that she was almost as powerful in the nominally independent states as in the Milanese and the Two Sicilies. Furthermore, Philip had no desire to extend his dominions; the mere lust of possession made little appeal to him; and the aim of his policy was rather to support a *status quo* which was very much in the interest of Spain.

After two generations of strife this policy made a strong appeal to the Italians themselves, and typical of their attitude was the opinion expressed by a contemporary Venetian of Philip II: "May he live long, because he always loves peace and quiet and the princes who love these, placing his own interests behind this object. . . . . It is indeed wonderful how, with such fortune and greatness, so many states and such great armies, he is of so moderate and

composed a mind, and so far removed from passions and ambitions."

Spanish control over Italy protected the East coast of Spain itself, and Philip was under no illusions on this score. At the beginning of his reign he had extracted from Cosimo I of Tuscany five
ports on the Tuscan coast, known as the *presidi*, which would provide Spain with a door into Italy should Genoa ever be closed
against her. Then, again, the ships of the Italian states were dis-
tinctly useful in the wars against the Turks and the corsairs.
Crippled by lack of money, as well as by his growing commitments
in the Atlantic and the English Channel, the Spanish King was
never able to build a really efficient fleet for service in the Mediterranean, and so he was dependent on the fleets of the Italian
Powers. Above all, his hold on Italy, particularly on the Northern
part of the country, enabled Philip to move troops to Flanders by
land through the Franche Comté, and as the sea-route became
increasingly unsafe this proved to be an increasingly valuable
asset.

To ensure the continuance of these advantages perpetual vigilance was necessary. Little was to be feared from Vienna, for
although no great love was lost between the Habsburg cousins, the
Austrian branch of the family was too dependent on the Spanish to
assert the ancient Imperial rights in Italy, and not much was heard
of them until the very end of the seventeenth century. Savoy, on
the other hand, required careful watching, for its geographical
position rendered it strategically important in the event of a revival of French interest in Italian affairs. For this reason Philip
was careful to foster Savoyard resentment against France in consequence of the duchy's recent sufferings from French aggression;
nor did he entirely object to the retention by France of Saluzzo,
since it was a thorn in the side of Savoy, and helped to keep alive
the ill-feeling between her and her neighbour. The Republic of
Saint Mark constituted an even more difficult problem. She resented her encirclement by the Habsburg possessions, more particularly while France was too weak to be used as a counterweight;
she feared that Philip might revive old Milanese claims to her
territory: she knew that at Rome the Spanish representatives were
continually casting doubts on her orthodoxy; and her commercial
interests suffered in the perpetual war between Spain and the
Turks.

On the other hand, the connection between Venice and France,

in spite of His Christian Majesty's political and commercial dealings with the Sultan, had been close since the abandonment of the
French claim to the Milanese, and during the reign of Philip II it
became even more intimate. The Republic lent money to Henry
III during his short-lived royalty in Poland, and he was lavishly
entertained in Venice on his way back to France. When he was
murdered in 1589 the Republic immediately recognized Henry of
Navarre as his successor, to the scandal of the orthodox, and it was
Venice which was mainly instrumental in obtaining Papal absolution for him. In short, the Republic desired to see the Balance of
Power restored by the revival of France, and for that reason she
favoured the French retention of Saluzzo as an open door into
Italy. None of this agreed with the views of Philip, but he did not
wish to push matters to an open quarrel, partly because of her
geographical situation, and partly because both Spain and Venice
had a common interest in the preservation of peace in Italy. In
these circumstances it is not altogether surprising that when the
moderating influence of Philip II was removed, the wilder spirits
among the high officials who served his son should have been implicated in the mysterious Bedmar conspiracy against the Republic
of Saint Mark.

If Philip, in Italy and the Mediterranean, may be said to have
pursued an Aragonese policy, in the Peninsula itself he never forgot
that he was King of Castille, and never was this more clearly
proved than in the affairs of Portugal. In August, 1578, the Portuguese monarch, Sebastian, was killed in battle in Morocco, and his
successor was his great-uncle, Henry, who was sixty-six years of age
and a Cardinal. Henry himself died in 1580, and Philip determined to complete the work of Ferdinand and Isabella by uniting
the whole of the Peninsula under one ruler. He had a very good
claim to the Portuguese throne through his wife, and the only
serious rival was Antonio, prior of Crato, who was the illegitimate
son, by a converted Jewess, of a brother of Henry, but he had been
secretly legitimized by his father. Philip sent an army into Portugal under the Duke of Alba to enforce his claim, and he was soon
accepted by the country as its monarch. Antonio, on the other
hand, was forced to wander round Europe begging assistance
against the Spaniards. Both Elizabeth and Henry III encouraged
him from time to time, but neither of them did much for him, and
he eventually died in exile.

The fact that owing to the maladministration of Philip's successors Portugal recovered her independence in 1640 cannot obscure the soundness of the policy which dictated her incorporation in the Spanish monarchy. Had Antonio been allowed to establish himself on the throne, Portugal would have become another Granada, that is to say an open door through which the foreigner could always enter Spain. As it was, Philip secured in Lisbon a most valuable harbour both for the American trade and for ships on their way to the Low Countries, while his enemies were deprived of what would otherwise have been a most useful base for operations against him. Nor was this all, for the wealth of Brazil was now at the service of Spain.

Further North, that is to say where France and England were concerned, Philip was primarily affected as heir of the Duke of Burgundy, for no real Spanish interest was at stake. As in the case of Louis XIV, Napoleon I, Wilhelm II, and Adolf Hitler, his commitments became so many and various that no crisis could arise anywhere in which he and his subjects were not almost certain to be embroiled. Nor was this all, for, as so often in history, Philip passed without noticing it the point where defence of his own interests became defiance of those of others. Napoleon went to Moscow in quest of security for France; the Armada disappeared into the fogs of the North Sea in quest of security for Spain. In both cases the outcome was the very reverse of what had been intended.

In succeeding chapters will be found an account of the international repercussions of the Wars of Religion in France and of the Revolt of the Netherlands, but even at the risk of repetition some allusion must be made to them in any analysis of the foreign policy of Philip II.

In June, 1583, there died the Duke of Anjou, heir-presumptive to the French throne on the death of his brother, the reigning King Henry III. The next in the line of succession was the Protestant Henry of Bourbon, King of Navarre. Until this event Philip had not interfered very actively in the French civil war, for as long as France was divided, and there appeared no chance of any party hostile to Spain gaining the ascendancy, the existing chaos suited Spanish interests very well indeed. The death of Anjou, however, meant that the next King of France would not only be a Protestant, and as such opposed to Philip on religious grounds, but also a Navarrese, who had a long account to settle with Spain in temporal matters. The time had clearly come when Philip would either have to appear as a principal in French politics or run the risk of seeing a united France ranged on the side of his enemies.

The danger, from the Spanish point of view, was very real. The Netherlands were in full revolt, and their sovereignty was on offer to Henry III; it seemed by no means impossible that he might accept it, and effect a reconciliation with his Protestant heir. Fortunately for Philip the prospect was on ideological grounds equally repellent to many French Catholics, and above all to the powerful House of Guise. For many years the Guises had been anti-Spanish in their views, and the family had made its reputation in the wars of Henry II. For this reason, as has been shown, Philip had been most unwilling to see their kinswoman Mary, Queen of Scots, on the English throne, and this reluctance had handicapped him in his dealings with Elizabeth. Now the situation was changed, and the imperative necessity of preventing the French from assisting the Dutch, or the incorporation of any part of the Netherlands into France, caused Philip to modify his views. Accordingly, in January, 1585, there was concluded the Treaty of Joinville between Spain, the Guises, and the Holy League, by which the signatories bound themselves to eradicate heresy, and to recognize the Cardinal of Bourbon, the Catholic uncle of Henry of Navarre, as King of France on the death of Henry III; as the price of his support Philip was to receive Navarre and the viscounty of Béarn.

For the ensuing four years it looked as if the Spanish King was to be justified by events in the course he had adopted, for it seemed as if the Guises and the League would prove strong enough to resist Henry of Navarre, without too serious a drain upon the resources of Spain. The King of France submitted to what appeared to be superior force, and the Pope, Sixtus V, excommunicated the Navarrese heir. Appearances, however, were deceptive, and in particular no reliance could be placed by either party on the last of the Valois. In an effort towards the end of 1588 to assert his independence Henry had the Duke of Guise murdered in his palace at Blois, but the dead man's brother roused the French Catholics against the King, who then threw himself into the arms of Henry of Navarre. In July, 1589, Henry III was himself assassinated, and the lists were set for the first round of the contest between Bourbon and Habsburg.

In the situation which had now arisen Philip found himself increasingly called upon to come to the aid of the Duke of Mayenne, the surviving brother of Guise, and the League, and this at a time when his forces were urgently required in the Netherlands, and when the defeat of the Armada had rendered his communications by sea hazardous in the extreme. Slowly, too, national spirit revived in France, and began to centre in Henry IV, who before long proved his superiority in the field. In 1590 he won an important victory at Ivry, and proceeded to lay siege to Paris, which was only saved by the arrival of Parma with a Spanish army from the Netherlands. Two years later Parma had to intervene once more to prevent the fall of Rouen. Philip had become implicated in French politics to a greater extent than his resources would stand.

Events now began to move more rapidly, and much to Spain's disadvantage. The year which witnessed Henry's triumph at Ivry was also marked by the death of the Cardinal of Bourbon, or Charles X as he was termed by the enthusiasts of the Holy League. Philip then proposed that the French throne should go to a member of the Habsburg family, but this suggestion was too much for all save the more extreme Leaguers, and its only effect was to strengthen the position of Henry. Then, in July, 1593, the Bourbon became a member of the Roman Catholic Church, and in the following March the French capital opened its gates to him, as the Spanish garrison marched out of the city. Once more in history a civil war in which the foreigner had intervened had become a national war in the course of which the foreigner was to be expelled. Ever since the death of the Duke of Anjou in 1583 the course of events had tended in this direction, and in January, 1595, war was officially declared by France against Spain.

In the fighting which ensued the Leaguers did not prove of much assistance to the Spaniards, but on more than one occasion Philip's veterans were too much for the French. Cambrai and Calais fell into Spanish hands, and all Henry's efforts to retake them were unavailing. Nevertheless, open war against the foreigner had the effect of uniting France: one by one the chief adversaries of the new dynasty became reconciled to it, though the price paid to secure their submission was often very high, and in April, 1598, the Edict of Nantes secured religious peace. Meanwhile, Philip was dying, and he wished to leave his son at peace with France: Henry, too, had no desire to continue the struggle, for his country was exhausted after so many years of foreign and civil war. Accordingly, in May, 1598, the Treaty of Vervins was signed between the two Powers, and its provisions well reflect the exhaustion of the combatants, for it scarcely involved any territorial changes. The Spaniards surrendered all their conquests in France except Cambrai, while Henry restored the county of Charolais. The Duke of Savoy gave up Berre, the only place which he held in Provence, while the future of Saluzzo, which he had acquired during the struggle, was referred to the arbitration of the Pope. (In 1601 Henry relinquished his claim to it in exchange for Bresse, Bugey, and Gex.) Neither the Dutch nor the English were included in the settlement.

The Treaty of Vervins registered the fact that Spain, as a Great Power, was past her prime, though many years were to elapse before this was realized by the statesmen of Europe, for the conditions in which warfare was carried on in the sixteenth and seventeenth centuries made it possible for her to conceal her weakness in a way that would have been out of the question in a later age. Armies were small in size; they lived to a large extent on the country in which they were operating; they retired into winter quarters for several months of each year; and most campaigns were little more than a succession of sieges. All this enabled Spain to maintain the appearance of her ancient power long after this had ceased to be a reality. She was, moreover, in possession of all the strategic points on the French frontiers, and in the later wars, while generally remaining on the defensive, she was able to fight for years with the minimum of loss. Even in the days of her decline, during the latter part of the reign of Philip IV, her armies threatened Paris.

In this way Spain was able on land to keep up for many years an illusion of strength which was far from corresponding with the facts, but at sea this was not possible, and by the date of Philip's death Spain no longer possessed command of this element save to a very limited extent. That this should have been the case was due to the rising power of England.

Her importance during the latter part of the sixteenth century was mainly owing, as we have seen, to her geographical position, and the value of this had been enhanced by the Spanish possession of the Low Countries. In earlier days English intentions had hardly called for notice on the part of Spanish statesmen save during the relatively brief period when John of Gaunt had designs upon the throne of Castille, but with the expansion of Spanish power had come an extension of Spanish liabilities, and the *damnosa hereditas* of the Low Countries had brought Spain into close contact with the island state on the English Channel. Moreover, if there was one guiding principle of English foreign policy even in these early days it was opposition to the possession of the Low Countries by one of the Great Powers, and it was at least arguable that Edward III had embarked upon the Hundred Years' War for this reason. Thus the Spanish lines of communication with the Netherlands passed along the coasts of a Power which by tradition was disinclined to regard them with a favourable eye.

Then, again, there were the sea-routes with the Americas to be taken into account. Spanish power in the Old World very largely depended upon the wealth which she drew from the New, and if there was any serious interruption of this, the results in Europe would certainly be serious, and might easily become disastrous. It was true that Ferdinand and Isabella had in 1493 obtained a Papal Bull conferring on them and their successors all lands discovered in the Americas not belonging to any other Christian Power, and that in the following year a territorial settlement with Portugal had been reached by the Treaty of Tordesillas, but there was not the slightest likelihood that the English would recognize these arrangements. Indeed, Philip had not been long on the throne before his sovereignty in the New World was seriously challenged, and his source of wealth proportionately threatened, by the activities of a swarm of adventurers who set out from the ports of South-West England to harry Spanish commerce and to plunder Spanish towns. There might be official peace between Philip and Elizabeth in Europe, but there was perpetual war between their respective subjects in the Americas.

In spite of the fact that Spain was the first Power in the world, while England was, by comparison, of no great account, Philip was in no position to force a settlement with her such as his interests dictated, quite apart from the fact that his commitments were always so extensive, and his financial resources so restricted, that he was rarely able to concentrate sufficient force upon any one object at any one time. As has been shown, the alternative to Elizabeth was Mary, Queen of Scots, and as she was a relative of the Guises, her accession to the English throne would merely mean that London would pass under the control of Paris: furthermore, a direct attack on England might be followed by some form of agreement between Huguenots and Catholics in France which would range that kingdom on the side of Elizabeth, in which case the retention of the Low Countries might prove impossible. Such being the case, the Spanish King was compelled to employ diplomacy rather than force. At first he attempted, by an offer of marriage, to renew the personal union between Spain and England which had existed while he was the husband of Mary Tudor, and when this failed he had perforce to put up with the exceedingly dubious neutrality of England in his relations with the rest of the world.

Elizabeth was thoroughly aware of the advantages to be derived from this situation, and she took full advantage of them. Henry VIII had left England a good deal weaker than he found her, and the reigns of Edward VI and Mary I had reduced her still further: their successor was under no illusions on this score, and she realized that a period of peace was essential if the national strength was to revive. Fortunately for her, Philip's difficulties provided her with just the opportunity she wanted, so she gave underhand aid to his enemies, and let her seamen interrupt his commerce, but she was careful never to goad him too far. Thus England obtained the much-needed respite, and when Philip could at last strike, both she and her Queen were ready.

Even before the death of the Duke of Anjou the Guises had been wondering whether it might not be better policy to abandon their hostility to Spain, and as early as 1580 Philip had received a message from the imprisoned Mary, Queen of Scots, to the effect that she would in future follow his wishes. The Treaty of Joinville completed the understanding between Spain and the Guises, and resulted in an immediate stiffening of the Spanish King's attitude towards Elizabeth. Thereafter, events moved rapidly, and in June, 1586, Mary wrote to the Spanish ambassador in London to the effect that she had by her will disinherited her son, James VI, and made Philip her heir. Elizabeth's reply on the morrow of the discovery of the Babington conspiracy was the execution of Mary in 1587. After nearly thirty years the latent crisis in Anglo-Spanish relations had come to a head.

What followed was to mark the beginning of the decline of Spain as a Great Power. Philip launched the Armada against England in 1588, and when it failed he had lost command of the sea, as was made plain to all eight years later when the English sacked Cadiz. A country that could not protect its principal port from capture by the enemy could certainly not ensure its line of communications through that enemy's home waters. In consequence, the long land-route to the Low Countries, from Milan through the Franche Comté, became increasingly important, and the struggle to retain it against a resurgent France was one of the guiding principles of Spanish policy during the earlier years of the seventeenth century. It is true that once Philip was embarked upon war with England he neglected none of the weapons in his armoury, least of all the ideological: if Elizabeth could intrigue with his Protestant rebels in the Low Countries he could fan Irish Catholic hatred into flame. His weakness, however, lay in the fact that it was much easier for geographical reasons for the English to aid the Dutch than for him to send troops to Ireland: also, like the assistance which Louis XIV a century later gave to James II in the same country, it was on too small a scale to affect the issue, and its main result was to convince the English Government of the advisability of extinguishing the last remnants of Irish independence.

Philip died in September, 1598, and not long before his death he is said to have observed, "God, who has given me so many kingdoms, has denied me a son capable of ruling them. I fear that they will govern him." It was, indeed, a splendid, if difficult heritage, which was left to Philip III, for in spite of the reverses which had marked the last years of his father's reign, Spain still held the hegemony of Europe, and her prestige was very high indeed. Apart from the United Provinces, which had detached themselves from the Spanish monarchy, but to which Madrid had not yet by any means abandoned its rights, Philip II passed on to his son the same wide dominions which he had himself inherited from Charles V. The King of Spain was still master of Naples and Sicily, the Milanese, the Franche Comté, Artois, and Flanders, while all of the New World that was yet inhabited by white men was subject to his rule. The dead monarch had even added to this vast heritage by the annexation of Portugal, which also meant the incorporation in the Spanish Empire of Brazil, as well as of the various Portuguese colonies in the East. The preoccupation of Philip's immediate successors was to be the maintenance of this *status quo*. To preserve this closest connection with Austria, and to let nothing be decided in Europe without the consent of Madrid and Vienna; to preserve free communication with Germany and Flanders through the Tuscan ports and the Milanese (this was specially important in view of the growth of English and Dutch naval power); and to hold France in check by the menace of the Flemish garrisons. These were to be the objects of the diplomacy of Spain during the reigns of her last three Habsburg monarchs.

CHAPTER VII

WARS OF RELIGION IN FRANCE, 1559–1589

T HE civil war which divided France during the reigns of the last three Valois monarchs has been not inaptly compared with the Thirty Years' War in Germany. There was the same religious and political fanaticism; the same interference from abroad; and the same fearful hatred which usually marks such an internal conflict. The difference, of course, is to be found in the consequences: for whereas Germany remained divided for two centuries, the monarchical and centripetal influences in France were sufficiently strong to restore to that country its lost unity within the space of a few years. Possibly, also, this contrasted outcome was due to the fact that although foreign armies fought on French soil during the Wars of Religion intervention from abroad was on nothing like so extensive a scale as in the Thirty Years' War in Germany. At the same time, the temporary eclipse of France as a Great Power undoubtedly prolonged the Spanish hegemony in Europe, for had it been otherwise, the many weaknesses of Philip's empire would have been discovered much sooner.

The details of the struggle belong to the domestic history of France, but from the beginning foreign influences were strong, and this could hardly fail to be the case in view of the origin of some of the protagonists. The Queen Mother, who exercised so great a hold over her three sons, who successively occupied the throne, was an Italian, Catherine de Medici; the Guises were cadets of the House of Lorraine, and were only half Frenchmen; while even Henry of Bourbon, who was eventually to unite the country, was a Navarrese. Nor were these external affinities confined to those in high places, for many a humble Huguenot felt that he had more in common with his English or Dutch co-religionists than with his Catholic fellow-countrymen. As always, ideology knew no frontiers, and it was responsible for many an unnatural alliance until a reaction set in, and Frenchmen once more began to concentrate on what they had in common rather than upon what was keeping them apart. In the interval foreign Powers fished in the troubled waters of French politics, and on more than one occasion the clue

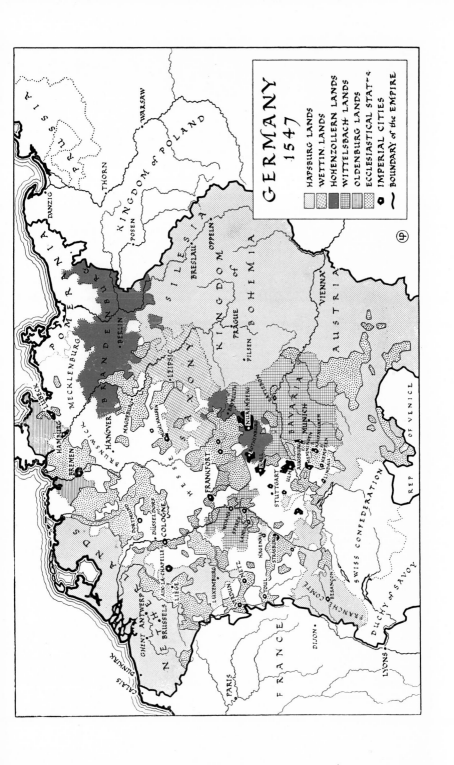

GERMANY
1547

HAPSBURG LANDS
WETTIN LANDS
HOHENZOLLERN LANDS
WITTELSBACH LANDS
OLDENBURG LANDS
ECCLESIASTICAL STATES
IMPERIAL CITIES
BOUNDARY of the EMPIRE

THE
NETHERLANDS
IN
1702

GRONINGEN

FRIESLAND

DRENTHE

ZUYDER
ZEE

AMSTERDAM

LEYDEN

THE HAGUE
RYSWICK

UTRECHT

GELDERLAND

ROTTERDAM

R. RHINE

NIMEGUEN

GERTRUYDENBURG

UNITED NETHERLANDS

GENERALITY

THE EMPIRE

FLUSHING
CADSAND

ZEELAND

KAISERSWERTH

OSTEND

BRUGES

ANTWERP

ROERMONDE

GHENT

R. SCHELDE
DENDERMONDE

BRABANT

R. DYLE

FLANDERS

SPANISH

YPRES

OUDENARDE

COURTRAI

BRUSSELS

LOUVAIN

COLOGNE

R. MEUSE

Bishopric of LIEGE

MAESTRICHT

AACHEN

LIMBURG

BONN

WATERLOO
RAMILLIES

LANDEN

LIEGE

LILLE

ATH

HAINAULT

NETHERLANDS

HUY

NAMUR

FONTENOY

MONS

VALENCIENNES

BOUCHAIN

DENAIN

R. SAMBRE

CAMBRAI

BISHOP

LUXEMBURG

TREVES

ROCROI

FRANCE

LUXEMBURG

THIONVILLE

LP

to the action of the belligerents is to be found far beyond the frontiers of France.

When, in 1559, Henry II was succeeded by his son, Francis II, all power passed into the hands of the Guises, who were the uncles of the Queen, Mary of Scots. Their policy was to place their niece and her husband upon the English throne, and then to constitute a close alliance between France, England, and Scotland. This scheme, though for different reasons, was equally objectionable to Elizabeth and Philip, and it might have produced an Anglo-Spanish understanding but for the fact that it was not destined to proceed very far. The Tumult of Amboise in March, 1560, proved to the Guises how strong was the opposition to them in France, while four months later the death of their sister, the Scottish Regent, led to the Treaty of Leith between Mary, Queen of France, and Scotland on one hand, and Elizabeth on the other: it resulted in the withdrawal of French troops from Scotland, but it was never actually ratified by Mary, on the ground that one clause in it implied her abandonment of her claims to the English succession. In December of the same year Francis II died suddenly, and the control of French policy was soon seized by the Queen-Mother, Catherine.

The new King, Charles IX, was a boy of ten, and a regency was in consequence necessary. This should have been exercised by the young monarch's senior relative, Anthony of Navarre, but he was persuaded to renounce his right in favour of Catherine. Years later, Anthony's son, then Henry IV of France, said of the Queen-Mother, "What could a poor woman have done, with her husband dead, five small children upon her hands, and two families who were scheming to seize the throne—our own and the Guises? I am astonished that she did not do even worse." The judgment is not inapposite. Catherine's object was to preserve the throne for her sons, and she considered that the best way to do this was to preserve a balance between the various rival factions at home while resisting the influence of Philip abroad. Her difficulty lay in the fact that the Crown was too weak, and the parties were too strong, for her purpose. Her sons, though not devoid of intelligence, were lacking in character, and were regarded as puppets by the contending factions. In effect, Catherine had adopted a policy beyond her power. She was, too, a foreigner, and consequently regarded with considerable suspicion. The consequence was that she fell back on intrigue to an extent reminiscent of her relative, Clement

F

VII; this in its turn introduced further complications into French politics, until the monarchy, which it had been her object to sustain, fell into a disrepute unparalleled since the early years of Charles VII.

It was not long before the inherent weakness of Catherine's position was made clear by the outbreak of the First Civil War in 1562. The geographical distribution of the two parties, it may be noted, did nothing to support the belief that there is any natural affinity between Protestantism and the Teutonic races, or between the Celtic and Romance nations and Catholicism. It is true that the lower classes in Celtic Brittany were strongly Catholic, but then so was the North-East of France, in which the Teutonic element was strong, while the Huguenots found their chief support in the South-West, which was Romance. The main stronghold of the Huguenots may be described as a square enclosed by the Loire, the Saône, and the Rhone on the North and East; the Mediterranean, the Pyrenees, and the Bay of Biscay on the South and West; while Dauphiné and Normandy were their outposts. In view of the fact that from the beginning both sides looked for foreign support, these geographical details acquire added importance.

It was only in Eastern Languedoc and in Dauphiné, and later at La Rochelle, that the Huguenots really held their own, or that they were supported by the majority of the population irrespective of class. Elsewhere, in those provinces where the nobles inclined to Protestantism, the peasants generally remained Catholic. With the exception of the House of Condé, the Huguenots had few supporters among the high aristocracy, and they found their chief support among the smaller nobility and the commercial classes in the towns. On the Catholic side were to be found the majority of the greater nobles, the official classes, the peasants except in the Cevennes and Dauphiné, and the urban masses, especially in Paris. The Catholics also possessed the great asset of the King's person and of the financial resources of the central government.

War had hardly begun before the Huguenots turned to Elizabeth for help, which she was not unwilling to give, for she feared that a victory of the Guises might be followed by an attempt to place the Queen of Scots upon her throne. The temptation to intervene was considerable, for the old conditions, under which the disruption of France between the Burgundians and the Armagnacs had induced Henry V to invade the Continent, seemed to have reappeared in another form. Accordingly, Elizabeth in 1562 concluded the Treaty of Hampton Court with the Huguenots, and by this she promised to assist them with men and money, while as security she was to receive Havre at once, and was ultimately to be given Calais. From the beginning the treaty proved unsatisfactory from the English standpoint, for even the Huguenots proved most unwilling to hand French forts over to English garrisons. The First Civil War was brought to an end in March, 1563, by the Pacification of Amboise, which was in no small measure the work of Catherine. One result of this settlement was a united French attack on Havre, from which the English were duly expelled, while Elizabeth was forced to abandon her claim to the restitution of Calais.

Between 1563 and 1570 there were two more civil wars, neither of which seriously affected the balance of parties, but the second of these conflicts was followed by a change in the foreign policy of the court. For the previous ten years Catherine had alternated between two lines of conduct: at one time she had tried to act as mediator between the two religious parties, and at another she had endeavoured to preserve the equilibrium by throwing her weight into the scale of the weaker. Neither policy had succeeded, and she began to incline to a foreign war against Spain with the object of dividing the Netherlands with William of Orange, who was the moving spirit in the Dutch revolt. In this Catherine was supported by Admiral Coligny, the Huguenot leader, and the King himself was seriously alarmed at the possible increase of Spanish power which it was felt might result from the victory of Lepanto in October, 1571.

William of Orange welcomed the advances which were now made to him, for he had long been of the opinion that if the Low Countries were successfully to make head against Spain they must have foreign support. Elizabeth, in spite of her continued quarrels with Philip, was less enthusiastic: she had already burnt her fingers once by interfering in French politics, and in any event she had no desire to see Antwerp and the mouth of the Scheldt in the hands of the King of France. To meet this objection it was suggested that she should marry one of the younger brothers of Charles IX, that is to say either the Duke of Anjou or the Duke of Alençon, and that a separate kingdom should be created for him in the Netherlands. Meanwhile, events began to move apace: in April, 1572, the Comte de le Marck, a Flemish refugee, seized Brille and Flushing, and the provinces of Holland and Zealand rose against Philip; in May, with the connivance of Charles IX, a French force, largely Huguenot in composition, took Mons; and even the cautious Elizabeth allowed English volunteers to cross to Flushing. It seemed as if the unity of France had been restored and Charles was about to emulate the example of his father and grandfather.

It was this moment that Catherine chose to accentuate the internal divisions of France by the perpetration of the Massacre of Saint Bartholomew, and her motives must always remain a source of dispute, particularly because her action ran counter to the policy to which she had of late appeared wedded. As one authority has said, "She had at once a constitutional liking for diplomatic intrigue, and a nervous horror of war. Consequently more than once she shrank back from the conflict which her aggressive policy had done much to kindle." It may, too, be that she began to doubt the result of an appeal to arms as reports came in of the superiority of the Spanish troops over anything that could be brought against them. Then the Venetians sent a special envoy to Charles beseeching him not to break with Spain, as this would only play into the hands of the Sultan, and Catherine was always susceptible to the arguments of her fellow-countrymen. Furthermore, although a great deal depended upon the co-operation of England, the attitude of Elizabeth was far from reassuring, and it was widely believed in France that she was preparing to betray Flushing to the Spaniards.

These, however, are conjectures: what is certain is that Catherine had become profoundly jealous of the influence of Coligny over Charles. She saw that power which she coveted above all things slipping from her, and she feared a return to the obscurity which had been her lot while her husband, Henry II, was upon the throne. Had the attempt upon Coligny on August 22nd proved fatal, it is possible that his death would have sufficed, but he stooped to adjust his stirrup, and the wound he received was unlikely to prove mortal. The outspoken threats of the Huguenots, the indignation of the King, his determination to run the perpetrators of the crime to earth, and the fear of her complicity being discovered, may well have driven Catherine into a panic which caused her to drown her guilt in the blood of the whole Huguenot party. Whether the Massacre was premeditated or not, it is quite clear that the Queen-Mother did not intend that it should be taken to imply any change in French foreign policy; all she aimed at was to recover the reins, and though she might moderate the pace, she had no intention of altering the direction.

The repercussions abroad were not in the long run unfavourable. It is true that the immediate effect upon the Pope and Philip was to cause them to believe that the French court had finally broken with the Huguenots, and upon Elizabeth to reject the idea of an alliance with France against Spain. The Emperor, Maximilian II, converted his genuine horror to diplomatic uses, and pointed out to the Poles the part played in the Massacre by the Duke of Anjou, who was a candidate for their vacant throne. This mood, however, soon passed. In a few months Henry of Anjou was elected King of Poland, where he was received with honour, having been escorted on his way by the most uncompromising of German Calvinists. The Prince of Orange renewed his negotiations with France, and was soon taking subsidies from the hand which he had declared could never be cleansed from the blood of Saint Bartholomew. As for Elizabeth, within three months of the Massacre she had consented to act as godmother to the French King's daughter, and was listening not unfavourably to proposals of marriage from the Duke of Alençon.

Where Catherine failed was at home, for the success of her foreign policy was nullified by the loss of French unity. Once more Catholics and Huguenots were at each other's throats, and France ceased to be an object either of hope or of fear. Twenty years were to elapse before the promise of the summer of 1572 was fulfilled. The truth is that Catherine saw where the true interests of France lay, but she was temperamentally incapable of concentrating upon their realization. She was far from being a Richelieu, and she was not even a Mazarin. Yet she never showed any inclination, Italian as she was, to interfere in the affairs of Italy as the Valois had done between 1494 and 1559, and she realized the importance of pushing back the Northern frontier, from which the enemy was continually able to threaten Paris. Farther afield, Catherine saw the value of Poland as a check on the German Reich, and the election of her son as King presaged the policy of Louis XIV. In short, what she lacked was not the will or the ability requisite for statesmanship, but the temperament and the means.

In 1574 Catherine's power was somewhat weakened by the death of Charles IX and the succession of Henry III, the former Duke of Anjou, who thereupon returned to France from Poland. Armstrong describes him as "at once pathetic and contemptible.

By nature gifted with taste and talent, he was cursed by hereditary disease and a predisposition to premature vice. Zealously Catholic, even to his disadvantage, naturally chivalrous and honest, all his good qualities were nullified by lack of will. He was everything by turns and nothing long. It is hard to believe that the abnormal effeminacy, the hanging ear-rings, the frizzed head, the puppy dogs, the girl-like admiration for his favourites, were not the result of constitutional ill-health. Yet he had fought at Jarnac and Moncontour, and he never faltered when Guise had to be struck down. When Clément stabbed him he tore the dagger from the wound and plunged it in the assassin's jaw. No one realized more clearly that he was unfit to be a King. Retirement and pleasant society were his ideal. Yet, when forced to business, he showed intelligence. Twice he thwarted the Estates General of France, twice he out-manœuvred Guise." Unlike Charles IX, the new King took advice from others beside his mother, but Catherine's was the dominant influence during the greater part of the reign.

When Henry came to the throne the Fifth Civil War was dragging its weary course, and the country was being ravaged by half-a-dozen independent armies, including one under the son of the Elector Palatine which was financed by Elizabeth. English diplomacy at this time was particularly tortuous in its methods, for at the very moment that the Palatine troops were invading France the Queen of England signed a defensive alliance with Henry III. If, however, the means employed by the English Government were obscure, its ends were perfectly clear, and they were to preserve a balance in North-West Europe: to this end everything else was subordinated. Elizabeth had no more desire to see France dominant in the Low Countries than she had to see Philip all-powerful there, and whenever there appeared to be a chance of either of these situations occurring she threw her weight into the opposite scale; the result was that neither Madrid nor Paris trusted her, but equally they could not ignore her. In these circumstances it is hardly surprising that throughout the reign of Henry III the Wars of Religion in France, the Revolt of the Netherlands, and the political situation in England should have been inextricably interwoven.

The centre of intrigue was Francis, the new Duke of Anjou and former Duke of Alençon, though at no time was he himself anything more than the puppet of others. William of Orange still despaired of shaking off Spanish domination without foreign aid, and he knew that ultimately he must have some Catholic support or the Belgian provinces would go back to Philip. Equally, Elizabeth could not be ignored. To what extent religion entered into these royal and princely calculations it is difficult to say. Upon William of Orange religious convictions sat but lightly, for he had in turn been a Catholic, a Lutheran, and a Calvinist; while as for Elizabeth, she was at this time writing to Philip with regard to his Dutch subjects, "What does it matter to Your Majesty if they go to the Devil their own way?" However this may be, William still held the view which had prevailed during Coligny's short-lived ascendancy in French politics, namely that the best solution would be for a Valois to rule the Netherlands and to marry Elizabeth. With this end in view, Francis of Anjou was in August, 1578, proclaimed Defender of the Liberties of the Netherlands, and in the following October he reopened matrimonial negotiations with the English Queen.

How far either party was serious must be a matter for conjecture, but the project was not without its influence upon French internal politics, for when the Seventh Civil War broke out in 1580 Elizabeth restrained the German Calvinists from joining in the fray, while Anjou persuaded his brother not to press the Huguenots too hard. Meanwhile events in the Low Countries were affecting the situation to an increasing extent. Religious conviction destroyed any hope of united opposition to Spain, and while the Catholic provinces came to terms with Philip, the Protestant enos abjured his sovereignty; five of them offered it to Anjou, but two, Holland and Zealand, preferred William of Orange. Francis accepted the offer by the Treaty of Plessis les Tours in September, 1580, and this acceptance was ratified at Bordeaux in the following January. Elizabeth made no pretence of approval of these proceedings, and an interesting light is thrown upon what were probably her real views when she wrote to Anjou, "Pardon me if I tell you that for my part I see in me no right to take that which belongs to another; still less was there any reason to accept a gift from those who have no title to make it". Expediency might render necessary English support to those who were in rebellion against Philip, but this did not mean that Elizabeth had any real sympathy with them or their objects.

All the same an Anglo-French alliance seemed inevitable. Ten years had passed since Coligny had urged Charles IX to break with Spain, and the wheel had revolved its full cycle. The recent acquisition of Portugal by Philip had also alarmed both London and Paris, and had done a good deal to bring the two courts together. In August, 1581, Sir Francis Walsingham arrived in the French capital to arrange the details of the alliance, and some very hard bargaining thereupon ensued. Henry, who desired above all things to be rid of his brother from France, insisted on the marriage as the price of an alliance, while both he and Elizabeth fought hard to avoid any financial liability for Anjou's commitments in the Netherlands. That same autumn Francis tried to force the Queen's hand by a visit to England, but this did not take him very much farther. Elizabeth told him that any promise of marriage was conditional upon her ability to overcome her repugnance to the matrimonial state, while Henry must declare war on Philip, abandon the old Franco-Scottish alliance, maintain the campaign in the Low Countries at his own expense, and surrender Calais and Havre to England as guarantees that he would keep his word. There was a good deal to be said for the contemporary French point of view that the real object of English diplomacy was to embroil France with Spain, and to cast upon Henry the onus of any breach between Elizabeth and Anjou.

Francis stayed in England until February, 1582, when he left for the Low Countries, accompanied by the Earl of Leicester and with a recommendation from the Queen to the Dutch that they would receive him as her other self. Leicester returned before long, remarking that he had left Anjou stranded like an old hulk on the sandbanks of the Netherlands; and Elizabeth was soon apologizing to William of Orange for having shot so much rubbish on his land. Nevertheless, the sovereignty of the Netherlands was conferred on Anjou as soon as he arrived from England, and the next twelve months were marked by a very definite anti-Spanish policy on the part of the French court. In June, 1582, an expedition was sent to the Azores in support of Philip's rival for the Portuguese throne, the Prior of Crato, but it was unsuccessful, as was another in the following year.

On the other hand, with the exception of William the Silent, the allies were not serious. Henry III had neither the will nor the means to embark on full-scale war with Spain, while the object of Elizabeth was merely to embroil Philip and the French King without allowing the Netherlands to become incorporated into France, and she had no real intention of marrying her Valois suitor. Anjou, too, soon became impatient of the restraint to which he found himself subject, and he attempted, in January, 1583, a *coup d'état* to give himself more freedom of action. This failed disastrously, and the so-called "French Fury" at Antwerp was long remembered against him and his fellow-countrymen. This event put an end to any hope which Anjou might have had of establishing himself in the Netherlands, and in June he left the country for ever, to the ill-concealed delight of Elizabeth. A year later he died, shortly afterwards (June, 1584) to be followed to the grave by William of Orange, murdered by Balthazar Gérard.

In view of the deep-seated belief of William that aid from abroad was essential if the Dutch struggle against Spain was to be carried to a successful conclusion, and of his further conviction that this aid could only come from France, it is in no way surprising that after his death the statesmen of the United Provinces, as that section of the Netherlands which had declared its independence had come to be called, should have turned to Henry III in spite of the fact that the memory of the "French Fury" was still fresh. At the beginning of 1585, therefore, their emissaries arrived in Paris, and offered the crown to the King of France; they were kept waiting some weeks for an audience, were then most courteously received, and their offer was politely declined. Thus terminated the connection between the House of Valois and the Low Countries.

The truth was that events had passed beyond Henry's control, even if he wished to control them. By the time that the Dutch envoys offered him the crown at the Louvre all effective power in France, as has been shown in the previous chapter, was divided between the Holy League, the Guises, and Philip on the one hand, and Henry of Navarre on the other. The death of Anjou had made it clear to all where their real interests lay. Henry III had himself only four more years to live, and there are two schools of thought as to his policy during this period. The older historians have little use for the last of the Valois, and hold that he was a mere cork bobbing on the troubled waters of French politics. Bainville, on the contrary, describes the murder of the Duke of Guise as *"cet inestimable service rendu à la France"*, and he goes on to say, *"Henri III était mort pour une idée: celle de l'Etat, de la monarchie, de l'unité nationale"*. It is certainly arguable that by playing for time until the defeat of the Armada revealed Philip's weaknesses, and then by throwing in his lot with his heir, Henry III rendered much easier the transference of the crown from the Valois to the Bourbons, and so frustrated those who would have seated a foreigner on the throne of France.

Another nine years were to elapse before the Treaty of Vervins brought about a general, though not a universal, pacification, and in the meantime the French Wars of Religion became merged in the Franco-Spanish contest. In the history of France they represent one of those periods of disorder—the Fronde in the following century is another example—into which that country from time to time has a habit of falling: from the international standpoint they undoubtedly enabled Philip to retain his hold on the Southern part of the Netherlands, which he would not have been able to do had France enjoyed internal peace, and taken in conjunction with the Revolt of the Netherlands, they allowed Elizabeth full scope for her policy of keeping the Spanish danger away from her own door until she was ready to face it.

CHAPTER VIII

REVOLT OF THE NETHERLANDS, 1559–1609

I T would be impossible to exaggerate the importance of the Revolt of the Netherlands in the history of European diplomacy during the second half of the sixteenth century, and it produced a general situation which might otherwise never have arisen. Had Charles not made the fatal mistake of burdening Philip with what remained of the duchy of Burgundy, the decline of Spain might well have been delayed: she would have been able to concentrate upon what were her real interests in Southern Europe, the Mediterranean, and the Americas, and this task would in all probability not have overtaxed her resources. Equally, the clash with England would have been postponed, if not altogether avoided, for during Elizabeth's reign the real cause of dispute between London and Madrid was neither religion nor rivalry in the New World, but English dislike of the control of the Low Countries by a Great Power, and to prevent this England had fought on many a previous occasion just as she was to fight many times in the future. The Netherlands were no concern of Spain, and in her effort to retain them she ruined herself, with consequences which were felt throughout Christendom.

At the same time it would, perhaps, be unfair to blame Charles V overmuch for developments which it would have been difficult for him to have foreseen. He had himself been born at Ghent, and as a Fleming he had never lost his personal popularity in the seventeen provinces which constituted his inheritance in the Low Countries. His strength and weakness lay in the differences which existed between his subjects. In Flanders, Brabant, and Hainault there was a powerful landed aristocracy; Ghent and Bruges enjoyed a civic independence comparable with that of the cities of Northern Italy in the earlier Middle Ages; and in Holland and Friesland there was a seafaring population with very decided views as to its own rights, and by no means amenable to any control by the central government. More recently, religious differences had added to the general lack of cohesion, for on the whole the North tended to be Calvinist, while the South remained true to Rome. The Netherlands, it may further be added, had traditional ties with France, England, and the Empire, but none at all with Spain. Charles knew his own fellow-countrymen, and although he had to crack the whip over them from time to time, his administration was tactful and moderate; furthermore, he was throughout his reign aided by the fact that England was no serious danger, and on many occasions was his ally.

Of the seventeen provinces which formed the Netherlands at the accession of Philip II, the greater number had been gradually collected together by the various Dukes of Burgundy in the previous century either by marriage, or cession, or conquest. The tie which bound these provinces together was purely personal, and they were held by different titles. Four were duchies, five were lordships, six were counties, and two were margravates. Each province had its own peculiar government; many had special privileges guaranteed to them by charter; while no native of one province could constitutionally hold office in another.

During the earlier years of the Revolt of the Netherlands the international repercussions were unimportant. The neighbouring Powers were largely occupied with their own problems, and in any case it was by no means clear how much was at stake. Hostility to Spain was at this stage on national grounds, and there were many Catholics who objected to any increase in the power of the Inquisition, while the whole population was practically united in its resentment at the presence of Spanish troops. Nor was there any general wish to sever the connection between the Low Countries and Philip; what the malcontents desired was that he should govern less autocratically and should respect their traditional privileges. In effect, the King of Spain was the innovator, and his opponents were the champions of the old order. Various governors were sent from Madrid to govern the Netherlands, and the most famous was the Duke of Alba, who was there from 1567 to 1573, but they all experienced the same difficulty. They never had enough money to pay their troops, whose discipline in consequence became extremely lax, and the *tercios* on more than one occasion lived on the country. This did nothing to endear them to the inhabitants, who displayed an increasing reluctance to vote the money out of which the soldiers might have been paid, and thus more easily controlled by their officers. In this way, the vicious circle was complete, and none of Philip's representatives succeeded in breaking it.

As has been described above, the years 1570–72 witnessed a definite threat of French intervention in the Netherlands, and that this did not materialize was due to the miscalculations of Catherine de Medici regarding the consequences of the Massacre of Saint Bartholomew in France itself. The protagonist of the resistance to Philip, namely William of Orange, was firmly convinced that foreign aid was essential, and to the day of his death he never faltered in this belief, whatever rebuffs he might receive from Paris and London. His career is an excellent illustration of the cosmopolitanism of the age in which he lived, for the man whose name was for all time to be associated with the cause of Dutch independence was a German by birth, had commanded the armies of Charles V, and took his title from a principality on the Rhône.

Assistance from France might become more remote as that country relapsed once more into civil war; but on November 4th, 1576, there took place an event which, temporarily at any rate, united the whole of the Low Countries: this was the so-called "Spanish Fury" at Antwerp, when a horde of Philip's unpaid soldiers sacked that city in their quest for loot. No distinction was made on the score of age, sex, or religion, and eight thousand people are said to have lost their lives. Four days later the Pacification of Ghent united the whole seventeen provinces. By this treaty it was agreed that the Spaniards should be expelled from the Netherlands, and that an Estates-General from all the provinces should be summoned to take measures for the common safety and future government. The Prince of Orange was to be lieutenant admiral, and general for Philip in Holland and Zealand. There was to be freedom of trade and communication between the provinces. All prisoners should be released, and all confiscated property restored. The placards and ordinances against heresy should be suspended until the Estates-General had come to a decision on the point. No attack, however, should be made on the Catholic religion outside the provinces of Holland and Zealand, and if the property of prelates and other ecclesiastics in the North were alienated, this should not be done without compensation. In January, 1577, the Pacification of Ghent was confirmed by the Union of Brussels.

Philip's next governor was Don John of Austria, whose ambitions were by no means limited to the Netherlands, for he had conceived the romantic project of crossing into England, marrying the imprisoned Mary, and sharing the English throne with her. This scheme came to nothing, although it alarmed Elizabeth, but the more moderate methods adopted by Don John had the effect of sowing dissension among the signatories of the Union of Brussels. An attempt by some of the Catholic malcontents to bring in against him the Archduke Matthias was not a success, and when Don John died in 1578 he had done much to prepare the way for the Duke of Parma, who succeeded him.

One of the foremost soldiers and statesmen of the sixteenth century, Parma had an easier task than his predecessor. The racial and religious differences between the Northern and Southern provinces were every day becoming more marked, and the Pacification of Ghent had been as much due to panic on the morrow of the "Spanish Fury" as to any feeling of national solidarity. Then, again, Elizabeth, unwilling to use her own troops for fear of precipitating an open breach with Philip, had subsidized German mercenaries to aid William, and their behaviour was driving the Catholics back into the arms of Spain. Lastly, if the choice was to be between a Spanish and a French ruler—and William's partiality for the Duke of Anjou seemed to pose this alternative—then many preferred the Spaniard, if only because he was more remote. In January, 1579, Parma secured his first triumph with the formation of the Union of Arras between the provinces of Artois and Hainault, and the towns of Lille, Douai, and Orchies; in the following May the signatories came to terms with him on condition that the foreign troops should be dismissed and provincial privileges respected.

The Northern reply to this was the Union of Utrecht between the seven provinces of Guelderland, Holland, Zealand, Utrecht, Friesland, Groningen, and Overyssel. Allegiance to Spain was not definitely repudiated, but the provinces bound themselves to protect each other against any attempt to coerce them, even by Philip. Each province, while renouncing its right to make separate treaties, was to retain its special privileges, and to decide on the religion it should adopt, although individual freedom of conscience was to be allowed; the Roman Catholic provinces were to be asked to join on the same terms. The confederacy was to be ruled by a General Assembly formed of deputies from each provincial assembly, and it was to have a common currency, a common system of taxation, and an executive council responsible to the General Assembly. In the Union of Utrecht lay the germ of the Dutch Republic, just as in the Union of Arras was to be found that of the reconstituted Spanish Netherlands.

This cleavage between North and South was cleverly exploited by Parma, and the year 1579 was marked by a number of Spanish military successes. Encouraged by these events, Philip in the following year published a ban against the Prince of Orange, whom he declared to be a traitor and a miscreant. William replied by falling back on French support, and what may be described as the second phase of the Revolt of the Netherlands began. As in the case of the Wars of Religion in France, what had been an internal struggle assumed an international significance.

William did not, it may be added, turn to the Duke of Anjou because he placed any special confidence in the House of Valois, but rather because there was no hope in any other quarter. The Germans were impossible, and the English were unreliable, so by the Treaty of Plessis-les-Tours in September, 1580, the Duke of Anjou was granted the hereditary sovereignty over the Netherlands, though with considerable limitations upon his power in many respects. He was always to reside in the country, never to appoint a foreigner to office, not to attempt any alteration in the government, and not to interfere with the privileges of the provinces; he was to procure the assistance of the King of France, but not to surrender any territory to him. In July of the following year, 1581, the Estates followed this up by finally renouncing their allegiance to Philip.

What then ensued has already been related in a previous chapter. The French proved distasteful as allies, and the "Spanish Fury" at Antwerp was matched by a "French Fury". Even had he been a man of different calibre, it is doubtful whether Anjou could have established himself in the Netherlands. From the beginning Holland and Zealand were extremely distrustful of him, and they only consented to acknowledge him on the definite understanding that, so far as they were concerned, no alteration should be made in the practical supremacy of the Prince of Orange, whom they had chosen as their Count in 1581. Furthermore, Elizabeth, in spite of her matrimonial intrigues, viewed Anjou by no means favourably, for she had no more desire to see the Low Countries a dependency of France than of Spain. In spite of this, William did not abandon hope of French help to the day of his assassination in July, 1584, and even after that event the sovereignty of the Netherlands was offered to Henry III, who, as has been shown, refused it, as he was by that time to all intents and purposes a prisoner of the Holy League. The United Provinces then turned to Elizabeth.

The succeeding negotiations were lengthy. The English Queen may have been flattered at the offer of sovereignty which was now made to her, but neither she nor her advisers were the sort of people to allow ambition to get the better of prudence. Nor did Elizabeth wish to be committed too far to an anti-Spanish policy, though this was, of course, exactly what the Dutch desired. Meanwhile, events were proving that the two parties had very considerable need of one another. Philip and the Guises had come to terms, and in August, 1585, the city of Antwerp surrendered on terms to Parma. The only effective opposition to the Spaniards came from Holland and Zealand, where Maurice, the seventeen-year-old son of William of Orange, had been elected Captain-General. This growing threat brought the English and Dutch together, and in November, 1585, an agreement was reached. Elizabeth declined the proffered sovereignty, but promised to maintain in the Netherlands a permanent force of five thousand foot and a thousand horse at her own expense; as a pledge for the repayment of the charges thus incurred, Brille and Flushing were to be handed over to England, and were to be garrisoned by a further contingent. Elizabeth was also to have the right of nominating two out of the eighteen members of the Council of State, to which the administration of affairs had been entrusted after the death of William the Silent.

The closing weeks of 1585, therefore, witnessed the beginning of the third, or English, phase of the Revolt of the Netherlands. The Earl of Leicester was appointed to command the troops; the governorship of Flushing was given to his nephew, Sir Philip Sidney; and that of Brille to Sir Thomas Cecil, a son of the statesman Lord Burghley. The Dutch experience of an alliance with England was, however, to prove as disappointing to them as that with France.

Probably with the purpose of still further implicating Elizabeth, in view of her refusal of the sovereignty, Leicester was on his arrival offered the post of Governor-General of the United Provinces, with supreme military command by land and sea, and with paramount authority in matters civil and political. He was to swear to maintain the ancient laws and privileges of the country and to govern with the assistance of the Council of State; he might, however, summon the States-General at his will, and was to enjoy the right of appointment to all offices, civil and legal, from a list presented to him by the States of the province where the vacancy should occur.

Leicester was dazzled by this brilliant offer, which he accepted, and he was reported to have observed that his family had been wrongly deprived of the English crown, in view of the fact that his brother had been the husband of Lady Jane Grey. At once the anger of Elizabeth was aroused. The Tudor suspicion of a possible rival was excited, as was a woman's jealousy that a favourite should accept honours from any other hands than her own; above all, she feared that Leicester's precipitate act would drive Philip to extremes. The illuminating spectacle was thus witnessed of the Queen of England publicly disowning her own commander-in-chief, and censuring those who had conferred these wide powers upon him. It was not until April, 1586, that she agreed that Leicester should, at any rate provisionally, retain the authority of "absolute governor".

The quarrel between the Queen and her representative might be at an end, but the damage it caused outlived it. The disgust of the Dutch was not diminished by the memory of their unfortunate experience with the Duke of Anjou, and now rumours, by no means unfounded, began to spread that Elizabeth was in negotiation with Parma in the hope of averting that direct attack upon England to which Philip had at last reconciled himself. It was true that the English Government always maintained that it would not make any separate peace with Spain, but its previous conduct afforded no security that if the necessity arose Dutch interests would not be sacrificed. Even at this late hour Elizabeth believed that she could by diplomatic means ward off the impending Spanish blow, while the Dutch had no confidence in anything save force. Between these two views there was no room for compromise, but plenty for suspicion.

In spite of this difference of outlook, Anglo-Dutch relations might have remained on a more satisfactory footing had Leicester been possessed of the most elementary attributes of statesmanship. He was not long in quarrelling with the governing class in the area under his control, and he soon broke his promise that no person should hold office in any province of which he was not a native. In commercial circles he and the English Government gave great offence by their refusal to remove the staple for English cloth from Embden in East Friesland to Amsterdam or Delft, and by the prohibition of all exports to Spanish territories, for this latter measure did far more harm to Dutch trade than it did to that of Spain. Furthermore, Leicester's religious policy was diametrically

G

opposed to the conciliatory methods adopted by William the Silent and laid down at the Union of Utrecht. Leicester declared that Roman Catholics must necessarily favour Philip, so he banished seventy of the leading members of that faith from Utrecht, and he allowed them to be maltreated elsewhere. In short, to quote Motley, "Leicester, in spite of his good qualities—such as they were—had not that most necessary gift for a man in his position, the art of making friends. No man made so many enemies. He was an excellent hater, and few men have been more cordially hated in return. He was imperious, insolent, hot-tempered. He could brook no equal. He had also the fatal defect of enjoying the flattery of his inferiors in station. Adroit intriguers burned incense to him as a god, and employed him as their tool."

The upshot of all this was that Leicester, instead of uniting all parties in common opposition to the Spaniard, became a partisan, made enemies of those who had been the most strenuous advocates of the English alliance, and did much to deepen those provincial, class, and religious differences which henceforth were to be the chief bane of the United Provinces. At the same time it would be unfair to place the whole of the blame upon Leicester, for the real culprit was Elizabeth. Her refusal to accept the sovereignty and to throw herself heartily into the cause of the Netherlands, the niggardliness of her supplies, the harshness of her terms, and the suspicions aroused by her negotiations with Parma: these had at least as much to do with the strain put upon Anglo-Dutch relations as had the imprudence of Leicester. In this attitude the Queen was at variance with all her leading advisers. Men like Burghley and Walsingham had no belief that open war with Spain could be postponed much longer, and they felt it to be sounder policy to meet Parma and his veterans on the soil of Flanders rather than to await his arrival in London. That events turned out contrary to their fears cannot conceal the risks which Elizabeth took during the two years preceding the defeat of the Armada.

In view of the Anglo-Dutch differences, it is hardly surprising that the allies should have done badly in the field, and 1586 was a year of almost unbroken disaster for them. Military failure was bad enough, but the tension between the English and Dutch was considerably increased when two of Leicester's officers turned traitor and surrendered to the Spaniards the places confided to their keeping. During the winter of 1586–7 Leicester was in England,

and the political situation was to some extent restored by the tact of Lord Buckhurst, who was the English representative in his absence. However, with the return of Leicester in July, 1587, the quarrels broke out again, and before long his designs were being compared with those of Anjou. By the end of the year the position had become impossible, and in December the Earl was finally recalled. It was not uncharacteristic of Elizabeth that she would not hear a word of criticism of her favourite, and in her letter of recall she put the blame entirely on the Dutch. She upbraided them for their ingratitude, their breach of faith, and their false and malicious slanders against the Earl. The Queen concluded, nevertheless, with a promise that she would continue her subsidies for the present, and that if she came to terms with Philip she would see that the Dutch were included in the settlement.

It is illustrative of the Spanish monarch's inability to be strong at the right place at the right time that he was unable to take advantage of these dissensions among his enemies completely to reestablish his power in the Low Countries. As it was, he was fully occupied at home with the preparations for the Armada, while the attention of Parma was continually being diverted from the Netherlands to the need for sustaining the Guises and the Holy League in France. Thus there was allowed to slip an opportunity which was never to recur.

Although English troops remained in the Low Countries after the departure of Leicester, and English subsidies continued to trickle in to the Dutch, the English phase in the Revolt of the Netherlands may be said to have ended in December, 1587. It had not reflected any particular credit upon the English Government, and it had not done much to revive the lustre of English arms, while not a little of the harm which Leicester inflicted upon his allies was destined to live after him.

The outstanding figure of this last, and most successful, phase of the Revolt of the Netherlands was Maurice of Nassau, but it is no disparagement of his achievements to point out that he enjoyed several advantages which had been denied to his predecessors. In the first place, hardly had he come to the front than the defeat of the Armada and the accession of Henry IV to the throne of France dealt Philip two severe blows from which Spain never recovered. The security of the sea-route to the Netherlands was gone for ever, while Parma's activities became principally concentrated on France, where only his troops enabled the League to make head against the new King. Then in 1592 Parma himself died, and in him Philip lost the most competent statesman and the ablest general who ever served him. Gone were the days when the Dutch cause depended upon the whims of the shifty Elizabeth or the Machiavellian Catherine, and when so much rested on foreign help. Maurice also possessed another invaluable asset in that he was himself one of the foremost soldiers of his age, and he turned the Dutch army into an extremely efficient military machine; indeed, to serve a campaign under Maurice became one of the ambitions of the adventurous in every Protestant country.

Gradually the Spaniards were driven from the places they still held in what had now become the United Provinces, and when in January, 1595, Henry IV officially declared war on Spain, the hands of Maurice became freer than ever, for all Philip's forces in the Low Countries were required for service against the French. The old differences with England, dating from the time of Leicester's campaign, were forgotten, for in October, 1596, the Dutch joined the alliance which Henry and Elizabeth had concluded against Philip; a few months earlier their forces had participated in a successful English expedition against Cadiz.

In spite, however, of these triumphs, there was no immediate prospect of the recognition by Spain of the independence of the United Provinces. For this reason the Dutch refused to be a party to the Treaty of Vervins which Henry made with Philip in 1598. All the same, the Low Countries were not entirely unaffected by this settlement, for there was a definite change, even though it proved to be but temporary, in the position of the Spanish Netherlands. Philip consented to renounce his claim to them, as well as to the Franche Comté, on the condition that the sovereignty should be conferred on the Archduke Albert, who was to marry his daughter, the Infanta Isabella. It was, however, stipulated that these provinces should revert to Spain if there were no issue of the marriage (as proved to be the case), while by a secret treaty the Archduke promised to allow Spanish garrisons to hold the cities of Antwerp, Ghent, and Cambrai. A desultory war, which did not materially affect the issue, continued between Spain and the United Provinces until 1609, when the Twelve Years' Truce was concluded. This virtually recognized Dutch independence, though the formal acknowledgment was delayed until the Treaty of Westphalia.

The seven United Provinces which thus broke away from Spain

were Guelderland, Utrecht, Friesland, Overyssel, Groningen, Zealand, and Holland. The geographical position of the new state was as important as the political. It occupied a stretch of country on the shores of the North Sea, running from the old duchy of East Friesland to the estuary of the Scheldt, both sides of which it held, thus cutting off Antwerp, the chief port in the Spanish Netherlands, from access to the open sea. On the East and South the frontiers were East Friesland, the territories of the bishopric of Münster, the duchy of Cleves, the bishopric of Liége, and South Brabant.

A new Great Power had, in effect, been born, and for a hundred years the United Provinces were to remain such; then, worn out by efforts which were too great for them, they sank, after the Treaty of Utrecht, into the second or third rank. Away in the North, the seventeenth century was to witness a similar rise and fall in the case of Sweden, and more than once during this period the fortunes of the two nations were closely linked. In the case of the Dutch, long before they had achieved their independence they were well on the way to becoming the carriers of Europe, and they were supplanting the Portuguese as the colonizers of the East. Yet the growing importance of the United Provinces was fraught with dangers which were one day to prove fatal. The closing of the Scheldt was a one-sided measure which was certain to be contested sooner or later by the possessor of Antwerp, while it was peculiarly unfortunate that the rise of the United Provinces should have coincided with the revival of English power. Their overseas commitments and their land frontiers were liabilities which in the long run made them no match for England, and when the clash came in the latter part of the seventeenth century it was the beginning of the end.

Internally, too, there were germs of weakness. The government was a loose federation of provinces of very unequal size and wealth, and each province was in its turn a federation of municipal councils. The authority of the States-General, which was the legislative body, and that of the States-Council, which formed the executive, was continually being called in question by the Provincial Councils; while the burgher aristocracy which governed the towns was disliked by the nobles of the countryside and regarded with jealousy by the unenfranchized. A nominal unity was, indeed, provided by the Stadtholder, when such existed, but he tended to be at variance with the burgher aristocracy, and to

look to the unprivileged classes to give him a more extended
sovereignty. Lastly, there were the religious differences which
Leicester had done so much to exacerbate. These weaknesses in
the new state were all in existence at the date of the Twelve Years'
Truce, but they did not become operative until later in the century.

CHAPTER IX

ENGLISH AND SCOTTISH FOREIGN POLICY,
1492–1603

FROM the accession of Henry VII in 1485 to the death of his grand-daughter Elizabeth in 1603 a certain unity is to be observed in the conduct of English foreign policy, and this was due to the circumstances of the internal situation. None of the Tudors was ever really safe on the throne, with the possible exception of Elizabeth during the last fifteen years of her life. Henry VII had to encounter the groundswell of the Wars of the Roses, and this force had by no means spent itself by the date of his death; Henry VIII had in addition to deal with the difficulties and disorders caused by his religious policy; the reigns of Edward VI and Mary I can only be described as chaotic; and Elizabeth was never for a moment free from the rivalry of Mary, Queen of Scots, until the latter's execution in 1587. In these circumstances it is not surprising that the keynote to Tudor foreign policy is to be found in the determination to deprive claimants to the throne of foreign support, and to ensure that no War of the English Succession was fought on English soil. That this policy was successful was in no small measure due to the fact that Britain was an island.

For several centuries there had been a close connection, based on common economic interests, between England as the producer of wool and the Low Countries as the consumer. It was therefore important for any government in London that this trade should proceed with as little interruption as possible, while it was undesirable, on the ground of national safety, that the Low Countries should come under the control of a Great Power. Indeed, economics played a more important part in the shaping of English foreign policy during the Tudor period than is always realized, and in the latter part of the sixteenth century their rôle definitely increased in scope. Englishmen saw no reason why the riches of the New World should be the preserve of the King of Spain, and they made little scruple about trading with the Americas whatever the Council of the Indies at Seville might say; nor did they fail to meet with a certain amount of encouragement from the Spanish colonists themselves. Spain and England, from about the middle of the century, were always at war in the New World, and this did not tend to improve relations between them in the Old, whatever might be the personal predilections of individual statesmen in London and Madrid.

As these factors remained constant throughout the period, they tended, as has already been suggested, to give a unity and a continuity to English foreign policy during the last years of the fifteenth, and the whole of the sixteenth, century by which it had not to the same extent been characterized before, and which it was to lack on more than one later occasion.

On an earlier page some mention has been made of the background against which Tudor foreign policy was necessarily set, and this must be constantly borne in mind. In the fourteenth and fifteenth centuries England had attempted to secure the hegemony of Europe, just as Spain, France, and Germany were to attempt to secure it in later ages. The effort had been too much for her in spite of brilliant initial successes; she had failed disastrously, and she had then relapsed into civil war. At the same time her neighbours, in particular France, had no guarantee that England would not resume her career of aggression when circumstances allowed, and they were justified in their suspicions by the fact that her sovereigns continued to style themselves Kings of France. To what extent the Tudors believed in the possibility of regaining the lost provinces of the Plantagenets is another matter, and the indications are that none of them ever took it very seriously. The return of Normandy and Guyenne does, it is true, figure in many of the negotiations with foreign rulers, but it is difficult to resist the conclusion that it was included partly to alarm the French, and partly as a sop to the more bellicose spirits at home.

The sixteenth century was not very far advanced before European fears of a revival of English aggression on the Continent were finally set at rest. Wolsey's attempt to hold the Balance of Power in the end deceived no one except the Cardinal himself; the religious issue then came to cause dissension at home; and, later, the Elizabethan expeditions to France and the Low Countries proved that whatever else Tudor England might be she was not the England of Crécy and Agincourt. Nevertheless, while she was sinking steadily as a military Power she was as steadily rising as a naval one, although this fact might be hidden from contemporaries. Her geographical position on the flank of what had since 1492 become the main trade-routes of the world enabled her to utilize her growing maritime resources to the full, and if her rise to naval greatness was not as spectacular as that of the Dutch, it was much more solidly based. In effect, when the sixteenth century began England was still under the shadow of her overthrow in the Hundred Years' War; when it ended she had set her house in order, and was ready for the maritime and colonial expansion which was to mark her history under the Stuarts. The Tudor period must thus be regarded as one of transition.

As the first of a new dynasty, Henry VII was particularly susceptible to the difficulties of his position, and his foreign policy was in the main pacific; like Walpole, in not wholly dissimilar circumstances, he realized that war would provide many opportunities for those who wished to dispute the succession to the throne. Not the least of Henry's embarrassments was Perkin Warbeck, who claimed to be the younger of the two sons of Edward IV who had been murdered in the Tower; at one time or another Warbeck was recognized as Richard IV by the Kings of France and Scotland, as well as by Margaret of Burgundy, the widow of Charles the Bold, herself a sister of Edward IV. A great deal of diplomatic energy had to be expended by Henry before this foreign support was withdrawn from his rival. The help he sent to Brittany in her struggle against Charles VIII was very largely to prove to the French monarch that he could be a nuisance if he were so disposed; the hint was taken, and by the Treaty of Etaples in 1492 Charles withdrew his support from the Pretender. James IV of Scotland was persuaded by Henry's ally, Ferdinand of Aragon, to marry the daughter of the English King, and this in turn was followed by his abandonment of his father-in-law's rival; Maximilian, too, eventually adopted the same course. Thus, Warbeck, deprived of his allies, was forced to put his fortune to the test by a direct bid for the crown which he claimed. He did this in 1498, but signally ailed; he was captured and was finally executed. The whole affair was a masterly piece of diplomacy on the part of Henry VII in circumstances that might well have defeated a lesser statesman.

Where Maximilian, the master of the Low Countries, was concerned, more than dynastic considerations were involved. The close understanding which had been effected by Edward IV with Charles the Bold had done much to keep London and the English commercial classes loyal to the House of York, and Henry dared not alienate this interest if he was to preserve his throne. In February, 1496, a general settlement was reached by the so-called

Intercursus Magnus, which provided for a complete renewal of the old commercial intercourse between the two countries. No duties, save such as had been paid during the previous fifty years, were to be imposed upon the merchants of either nation, and all restraints upon trade were to be removed, save that power was reserved to either government to lay duties upon its own subjects and to prohibit the export of food-stuffs in time of need. Finally, it was specially provided that neither party should give countenance to the other's rebels, and if Margaret of Burgundy defied this arrangement she was to be deprived of her dower lands. It was little wonder that two years later Perkin Warbeck was forced to set out on his ill-starred expedition.

Henry was indeed well-advised not to take any chances, for between the conclusion of the Intercursus Magnus and Warbeck's attempt the fundamental weakness of the Tudor monarch's position was revealed by the Cornish rising, when a body of obscure rebels, armed with no better weapons than bills and bows, without cavalry or artillery, proved able to cross the whole of Southern England unmolested save for a brief skirmish at Guildford.

The Tudor monarch's interest in commercial matters was not, it may be observed, by any means confined to Flanders, for he was desirous both of curtailing Hanseatic privileges and of opening up the Baltic to English trade. With this end in view a treaty was in 1490 concluded with King John of Denmark, by which were confirmed to Henry's subjects all the privileges which they had at any time enjoyed in the Scandinavian kingdoms, which were still united by the Union of Kalmar; admission to the Icelandic trade; most-favoured-nation treatment; the right of holding real property in Bergen, Schonen, the island of Seeland, in Finnish Lovisa, or anywhere in Denmark; and the special protection of the Danish King in all criminal cases. Henry was not quite so successful in his dealings with the Hanseatic League, and in 1504, in order to prevent them harbouring Yorkist exiles, he had to agree to the passing by Parliament of an Act to the effect that no step should in future be taken to abridge their privileges. All the same, he may be said to have indicated the road which the Kings of Denmark and Norway were soon to follow.

It may thus be claimed for Henry VII that when he died in 1509 his foreign policy had been remarkably successful. He was in no position to embark upon adventures, even had he been temperamentally inclined towards them, but what he set out to do he did.

When he wrested the crown from Richard III it seemed to contemporaries abroad that Bosworth was just another round in the Wars of the Roses, and that since the House of York might regain power, as it had done only fourteen years earlier, after Warwick's *coup d'état*, it would be just as well to show some favour to its temporarily exiled representatives; when Henry died he had proved that the odds against the rival dynasty were very long indeed, and that friendship with him was much the best policy for his neighbours. At home his trade negotiations with foreign Powers had rallied to him those very commercial classes which had for so long been the mainstay of the Yorkists. All this, too, had been effected without war on a scale which England could not afford.

From the beginning of his reign Henry VIII showed himself desirous of playing a more spectacular part than his father on the international stage, and for a short time events seemed to favour him. Valois and Habsburg were fairly evenly balanced, and so by throwing his weight first into one scale and then into the other, the English monarch was able to delude himself into a belief that he was preserving the Balance of Power in Europe. Furthermore, the money which Henry VII had saved for a time obscured the real poverty of England. In his ambitious schemes the new King was encouraged by Wolsey, who had a personal interest in the matter, as he hoped to get himself elected Pope.

The details of the struggle between France and Spain have been discussed in an earlier chapter, and they only concern us here in so far as they illustrate English foreign policy. At first Henry continued his father's alliance with Ferdinand, typified as it was in his own marriage with Catherine of Aragon, largely because of the traditional hostility to France. Ferdinand, however, did nothing to assist towards the reconquest of Guyenne, to which the English Government was committed, so Henry allied himself with France, and married his sister Mary to Louis XII. The early successes of Francis I alarmed Wolsey and his master, so in spite of the Field of the Cloth of Gold they swung back to the side of Charles, only to change again when the battle of Pavia seemed to threaten a Spanish hegemony in Europe. The end of this vacillating policy was, however, in sight, for in 1529 the Peace of Cambrai was concluded between Charles and Francis without the consent of Wolsey, whose failure either to impose his master's will upon Europe or to gain the Papacy for himself was now clear for all the world to see. Circumstances had enabled King and Cardinal for a short time to play a rôle which they could not sustain, but from the beginning their policy contained the seeds of its own failure.

Meanwhile, Henry and his minister had been encountering opposition at home. Their schemes for the Continent—not least Wolsey's repeated candidature for the Papacy—were proving extremely costly, and the first Tudor's reserves were soon exhausted. By 1523 it was necessary to have recourse to Parliament for supplies on a considerable scale, and opposition at once began to develop. Then came the question of Henry's divorce from Catherine, and it was necessary to conduct the country's foreign policy with an eye to the successful outcome of this negotiation. It is not without significance that the year in which the Peace of Cambrai was concluded also marked the fall of Wolsey, for it finally displayed the bankruptcy of his statesmanship in international matters.

The disgrace of the Cardinal and the divorce of Henry from Catherine of Aragon ushered in the Reformation in England, and this in its turn brought about further complications in foreign affairs. The English King had henceforth to be on his guard against the possibility of a Catholic alliance against him, and it was a matter of absolute necessity to keep alive the hostility which always marked the relations of Charles and Francis; at home the surviving Yorkists were hunted down with merciless severity in case they might become a rallying-point for a rising with foreign support. Thomas Cromwell in 1539-40 persuaded his master to seek allies among the German Protestant princes who were in opposition to the Emperor, and the outward sign of this policy was the marriage of Henry with Anne of Cleves. "The Flanders mare", as the bridegroom somewhat impolitely described her, did not, however, prove to the English monarch's liking, and the German princes were an unknown quantity, so the new policy was not continued. Anne of Cleves was divorced, and Thomas Cromwell was sent to the scaffold.

Henry's diplomacy during the last years of his life was as adroit as the employment of his armies was incompetent, and he succeeded in preventing the formation of a Franco-Spanish alliance against him. It was well that this should have been the case, for in 1545 it was only with considerable difficulty that a French attempt at invasion was defeated. By this time it was financially impossible for England to continue the war, and in June, 1546, there was concluded the Treaty of Ardres, by which Henry undertook to restore Boulogne to France within eight years in return for a money payment.

The reigns of Edward VI and Mary I constitute a period during which England was so weak that she counted for very little in the counsels of Continental Powers. Edward's ministers desired to have their hands free to deal with Scotland, and they therefore tended to incline towards France, for experience had shown that the way to Edinburgh not seldom lay through Paris. Boulogne was accordingly given up to Henry II, and the original money payment scaled down. Religious considerations, too, drew the English Government to France, for although the French King persecuted Protestants at home, he had not the slightest objection to their alliance abroad, and a policy which did not reject Suleyman the Magnificent was hardly likely to boggle at Somerset and Northumberland. With the accession of Mary there was another change, with which ideological factors had not a little to do, and England became the ally of Spain. This, in its turn, involved the country in war with France, and Calais was lost. In this connection it is not without interest to note that this Spanish alliance marks one of the earliest occasions on which foreign policy became an active issue in English domestic politics, for Wyatt's rebellion in 1554 was a definite protest against the Queen's attitude towards Spain and her prospective marriage with Philip. Had that marriage been blessed with children, the history of Europe must have been very different, though how long a dual monarchy of Spain and England would have endured is another matter, and this might well have depended upon the extent to which the Spaniards would have been willing to allow the English to participate in the trade with the Americas.

When Elizabeth came to the throne in 1558 she was in much the same predicament as that in which her grandfather, Henry VII, had found himself on the morrow of Bosworth. The country was rent by civil strife, and her own claim to the crown was fiercely disputed. In short, much of the work of the first Tudor had to be done again. On the other hand, the new Queen enjoyed two very considerable advantages. In the first place, Philip II was unable for many years to make any direct move against her, for this might easily result in her replacement by Mary, Queen of Scots, which would represent a triumph for France, and in the second, the success of the Reformation in Scotland rendered that country more amenable to English influence than had been the case in the past.

From the standpoint of foreign policy the reign of Elizabeth falls into three well-defined periods, of which the first lasted from the Queen's accession until Mary, Queen of Scots, took refuge in England in 1567. During these nine years the real threat came from a Franco-Scottish alliance, for France had not yet been wholly disrupted by the Wars of Religion. Elizabeth endeavoured to avert the danger by giving support to the Huguenots and to the Scottish Protestants, but she was more successful in Scotland than in France. Her real strength, however, lay in the fact that she enjoyed the support, albeit most unwillingly given, of Philip II, who had no desire to see the British Isles dependent upon the Court of France. In 1567 Mary was defeated by her rebellious subjects, and fled South of the Border. From that moment Elizabeth enjoyed all the advantages—and disadvantages—of having her rival safe under lock and key. Moreover, Mary's son, James VI, showed no disposition to allow his filial piety to push him so far as hostilities against his mother's gaoler.

The second phase of Elizabeth's reign may be said to have begun with the captivity of Mary in 1567 and to have ended with the defeat of the Armada in 1588. During this period relations between England and Spain became increasingly more strained, very largely owing to the activities of the English seamen on the Spanish Main; the danger from France diminished as that country passed into the grip of the Wars of Religion; and the situation in Scotland became a great deal more favourable from the point of view of the English Government, since the Protestant party there had to lean on its support. It was not until shortly before Mary's death that Philip threw the weight of Spain on her side, for until then he had suspected her as an instrument of French policy. At the same time Elizabeth had been unwilling to push matters to extremes, and she refused to listen to those who urged that it was better to meet Parma in the Low Countries than at the gates of London. Accordingly, her aid to the Dutch was tardy and insufficient, and her final success cannot blind us to the very great risks that she ran. In the end, Philip realized that he would never crush the Netherlands so long as a hostile England lay athwart his lines of communication, so he launched the Armada in the hope of re-establishing his position in North-West Europe.

The third period into which the reign of Elizabeth falls is that which covered the years between the defeat of the Armada and the Queen's death in 1603. One of the few really decisive battles of the world had been fought, and the danger from without was at an end. Elizabeth has been blamed for not following up her victory, but it may be argued on her behalf that her country's resources were extremely scanty, and that recent precedents for sending English forces overseas had been none too encouraging. It may even be that in the old woman's shrewd brain there existed a belief that Spain was beginning to decline, and that it was no part of England's business to pave the way for the ascendancy of Bourbon France. At home the reign of Elizabeth, like that of every member of her family, was marked by an unending series of plots and rumours of plots with varying objectives, and the last conspiracy of all, that of the ill-fated Essex, occurred only two years before the Queen's own death.

Scotland, of which James IV became King in 1488 at the age of sixteen, on the murder of his father, was an even poorer country than England when compared with the great monarchies of the Continent, and its recent history had been every bit as stormy. The basic weakness of the Northern Kingdom lay in the succession of minorities by which the House of Stuart had been characterized and by the opportunities which this had placed in the way of the centrifugal factors in a turbulent and self-seeking nobility. The resulting situation was well adapted to foreign intrigue, and throughout four reigns, until James VI came to the English throne in 1603, the policy of the Tudors was to buy Scottish traitors and to attempt to secure the person of the Scottish monarch.

Ever since Edward I had endeavoured to subjugate Scotland it had been the policy of the Northern kingdom to work in alliance with France, and for England a war with one Power nearly always led to hostilities with the other. From the French point of view this had everything to recommend it, and the rôle played by the Turks, the Poles, and the Swedes in relation to the Empire was enacted by the Scots where England was concerned, that is to say they were the allies of France, who could be relied upon to attack her enemies in the rear. In these circumstances it is hardly surprising that the English should have decided to put an end to this nuisance once for all, so as to have their hands free whenever they were engaged with a Continental Power. The Wars of the Roses paralysed the action of England for a generation, but once they were at an end both Edward IV and Richard III adopted a definitely aggressive policy in respect of their Northern neighbour.

Henry VII had too many domestic problems on hand to allow him to pursue the Scottish policy of his immediate predecessors, and this in spite of the fact that James IV was giving support to Perkin Warbeck, whom he went so far as to marry to his own cousin, Catherine Gordon. At this point Spanish diplomacy began to work upon the Scottish monarch, for Ferdinand did not wish to see his ally, Henry VII, distracted from the task of checking the designs of Charles VIII and Louis XII. In August, 1503, James was married to Henry's daughter, Margaret, and exactly a century later this wedding was to bring their great-grandson to the English throne. The immediate results of the marriage, however, were not so successful, for the repeated forays on the Border perpetuated uneasy relations between London and Edinburgh. In addition, there were soon to be bitter family quarrels between Henry and James over Margaret's dowry. All the same, Anglo-Scottish relations did not deteriorate into war so long as the English throne was occupied by Henry VII, and this represented a very marked improvement upon what had been the case for many years.

With the accession of Henry VIII the strain upon Anglo-Scottish relations increased, and a crisis was reached when Pope Julius II persuaded the English monarch to join the alliance which he had formed against France. Louis XII called upon James to create a diversion by attacking England, and the appeal was not made in vain. James believed that if France went down in the struggle, the turn of Scotland would soon come, so he marched South with the entire strength of his kingdom. At Flodden, in September, 1513, the Scots were heavily defeated, and their King was killed. Once again there was a minority, for his successor, James V, was only a year old.

The catastrophe of Flodden darkened the history of Scotland for two generations, and the country was a prey to the intrigues of the Tudors and their advisers, who wished to take advantage of its weakness to force its incorporation in the English monarchy. Murder and kidnapping became definite instruments of policy, and throughout the entire period England was the home, and her monarch the ally, of every domestic foe and traitor to the Scottish throne. Nor was there much help to be obtained abroad, for France was herself hard put to it to make head against Charles V. As James V grew to manhood he found the problem still further complicated by the progress of the Reformation, and when Henry VIII broke with Rome a not inconsiderable minority of Scots wished their King to follow his uncle's example. James, however, was too suspicious of Tudor policy to copy any aspect of it, and when he was able to take control he espoused the cause of Catholicism and France. In 1538 he married Mary of Guise, and in the following year he appointed Cardinal Beaton, the head of the Francophil party, to the see of St. Andrews. Henry regarded these moves as an insult to himself and a revived threat to his country, and there was renewed fighting on the Border; in the midst of it, in December, 1542, James V died, leaving as his heir a new-born baby, Mary, Queen of Scots.

The disorder of Scottish politics now degenerated into something approaching anarchy, and domestic and foreign problems became hopelessly involved. The Protestant party inclined towards England as the chief hope of securing the triumph of the Reformation, so the Catholics moved in the direction of France, while the nobility changed their allegiance as their interests dictated. Meanwhile, Henry VIII sent his troops to harry the Lowlands, and suborned Beaton's enemies to murder him: in 1546 he was successful, for in May of that year the Cardinal was assassinated in his own castle of St. Andrews, and his corpse was defiled. Thereafter, the object of the English was to seize the young Queen, but although in 1547 they won the battle of Pinkie, their prize escaped them, chiefly owing to the arrival of strong French forces in Scotland. In 1548 Mary was taken to France to marry the Dauphin, and two years later the ministers of Edward VI were forced to abandon all the fortresses held by England on Scottish soil.

The international complications resulting from the somewhat anomalous position of Mary, Queen of Scots, have already been discussed. If Elizabeth's policy towards Scotland was less brutal than that of her father and brother, though equally cynical, it was because she had less to fear from the North. For years there was no danger that Philip would aid Mary or her supporters, and when Spain and the Guises were at length reconciled, James VI could be relied upon not to pursue a policy hostile to England, the accession to whose throne depended not a little upon the goodwill of Elizabeth. So the situation remained until 1603, when the whole of the British Isles finally and peacefully came under the rule of the same sovereign.

H

CHAPTER X

FRANCE AND HER NEIGHBOURS, 1589–1624

WHEN Henry IV ascended the throne of France he found himself heir to a great tradition, but to a very poor legacy. For many years his country had played a sorry part in European politics, and during the Wars of Religion she had fallen steadily lower in the scale of nations, until she seemed to be well on the way to becoming a second Italy, that is to say a plaything tossed to and fro among the monarchs of Europe. It was the stubbornness of the Dutch, and the craft of Elizabeth, not the patriotism of Frenchmen, which had then thwarted the ambitions of Spain. Henry had done something to restore the situation during the earlier years of his reign, but the Treaty of Vervins had represented nothing more than the conclusion of the first round in the struggle between Bourbon and Habsburg.

In spite of that settlement the position of France was by no means secure, and her frontiers were very different from what they were later to become. In the South the provinces of Cerdagne and Roussillon still owed allegiance to the Catholic King at Madrid, as did the greater part of Flanders, Artois, and Hainault in the North, while Spanish soldiers mounted guard at Lille. In the East, Lorraine was independent under its own dukes, and neither Alsace nor the Franche Comté was yet French. In short, France was confined within narrow limits, and the recent war had shown how exposed was Paris to attack from the Spanish Netherlands. On every side Henry's dominions were surrounded by those of the Habsburgs, for although the thrones of Spain and the Empire had not been occupied by the same member of that family since the abdication of Charles V, the Emperor and the King of Spain worked very closely together, so that Spanish troops could still march through friendly territory from the Spanish duchy of Milan to the Spanish Netherlands. It is true that the sea-route across the Bay of Biscay and through the Channel had become increasingly difficult for Spain by the defeat of the Armada and the development of Dutch naval power, but these waters were only safe for France so long as she remained friendly with England and the United Provinces.

At the moment this condition was being fulfilled. Ever since

the Dutch had risen against Spain they had looked to France for
support, and when they wanted a flag they came to Henry IV,
who gave them the colours of the French Royal House. They constituted a permanent threat to the Spanish Netherlands on land,
while their naval power could be a useful check on England at sea.
The day was still very far distant when France and the United
Provinces would be at war, and for the present they were bound
closely together by fear of the Habsburgs. With England relations
were less cordial than they had been, for although Elizabeth had
aided Henry against Philip and the Holy League, she was an uncertain ally, and the English had proved that if they were invited
into a country they were extremely difficult to get out again. Of
other allies to whom the new King could look, there were always
the Turks, but they were in a period of decline, and for moral
reasons the Sultan's friendship was always something of a liability.
With Denmark and Sweden there still existed the Treaties of
Fontainebleau and Sceaux, while Henry's immediate predecessor
had for a brief space sat on the throne of Poland.

The strength of a chain is that of its weakest link, and this was
the case with the chain of Habsburg possessions which surrounded
France. The weak link was the Milanese, which lay open to
attack from Savoy; for any threat to Lombardy was a menace to
the whole Habsburg land communications, and these had become
of paramount importance since the defeat of the Armada. It was
therefore to Savoy that the French King turned his attention.

In the Middle Ages the Dukes of Savoy had been far more
French than Italian: their dominions stretched to the Rhône, and
they had disputed with the King of France the control of Provence
and Dauphiné. More recently, they had been gradually pushed by
their powerful neighbours towards Italy, but their real importance
lay in the fact that they held the gates of both France and Italy.
As the Duke of Savoy decided, so could the French troops pour
through his mountain passes into the plains of Lombardy, or the
Spanish armies invade the valley of the Rhône. At the same time
a single misreading of the political barometer might have fatal consequences, and the pursuit of a consistent foreign policy was impossible. Accordingly, the Savoyard rulers relied upon sheer op-
portunism as between the Great Powers by whom they were surrounded, espousing the cause of first one and then another as their
immediate interest dictated. This policy served them well for
several centuries, and they were far from abandoning it when

they became, first Kings of Sardinia, and finally Kings of Italy.

From the French invasion of the Italian peninsula in 1494 they had of necessity followed this tortuous path. During the expeditions of Charles VIII and Louis XII they had been on the side of France, but they had later espoused the Imperial cause, for which they had paid by a French occupation of their territory for twenty-five years. By the Treaty of Cateau Cambrésis, it will be recalled, the then Duke, Emmanuel Philibert, was restored to his duchy with the provision that a number of fortified places were to remain in French hands. During the Wars of Religion the opportunity to regain these fortresses was too great to be resisted by Charles Emmanuel I, who succeeded his father in 1580, and he therefore allied himself with the Guises and the Holy League. In 1588 he occupied Saluzzo, and invaded Provence with the help of the Spaniards. The Treaty of Vervins referred the restoration of Saluzzo to the arbitration of the Pope, but this provision remained a dead letter, thus providing Henry with an excuse for action when he thought fit to avail himself of it.

The opportunity occurred in 1600. The French King had obtained a divorce from his first wife, Marguerite de Valois, the sister of his three predecessors on the throne, and had married Marie de Medici, the daughter of the Grand Duke of Tuscany, by which he considerably strengthened his position in Italy. With this support he over-ran Savoy, and then concluded in January, 1601, the Treaty of Lyons with Charles Emmanuel. By this arrangement Saluzzo was handed over to the Duke of Savoy, while in exchange France received the two small duchies of Bresse and Bugey. Considerable astonishment was felt by contemporaries at what seemed to be an unnecessary surrender on the part of Henry, but he was looking ahead. He realized the importance of Savoy in the coming struggle against the Habsburgs, and he was determined to have the duchy on the French side. Saluzzo was a bone of contention between Savoy and France, as the Spaniards fully appreciated, and in French hands it was a standing menace to Turin. In these circumstances the concessions contained in the Treaty of Lyons are the measure of Henry's statesmanship.

The close connection between domestic and foreign policy which had come into existence during the latter part of the Wars of Religion also manifested itself in the relations between France and Savoy at this time, and was, indeed, one of the reasons which prompted Henry's attack on the duchy. The French nobility, long accustomed to the licence of civil war, soon grew restive under the strong rule of the new dynasty, and two of their leaders, the Marshal of Biron and the Duke of Bouillon opened negotiations with Spain and Savoy for a partition of France. When Henry struck, he struck hard, and in 1602 Biron was sent to the scaffold, a fate which Bouillon only avoided by escaping to Germany. There were thus strong domestic, as well as international, arguments in favour of winning over Savoy, though many years were to pass, and much blood was to be shed, before the French nobility learnt its lesson.

Sully, the leading statesman of Henry's reign, in his *Mémoires* has attributed to his master the Great Design for a general settlement of European problems. According to this the Habsburgs were to be humbled, the Turks were to be expelled from Europe, and the frontiers of France were to be extended to the Rhine. At the same time there was to be an arbitration court which should represent a confederacy of states, and there was to be religious toleration. That the French King, whose outlook was essentially realist and in no way Utopian, ever seriously entertained such a scheme is highly improbable, however much it may have beguiled his leisure moments, but it should be noted that the Great Design implied the hegemony of France, and those who most nearly put it into execution were Louis XIV and Napoleon I, who were, if possible, even less Utopian in their calculations than Henry IV.

However this may be, the French monarch was always on the look-out for a chance of weakening the Habsburgs, whether in Vienna or Madrid, and one duly presented itself in 1609. In that year there died without children John William, the Duke of Cleves, Jülich, and Berg, and the succession to his territories was at once claimed by two German princes. The first was the Elector of Brandenburg, John Sigismund, whose wife was the child of the eldest daughter of William the Rich, the brother and predecessor of the dead duke; he rested his wife's claim partly on her descent from the elder branch, and partly on a will made by William the Rich in which he gave the descendants of the elder daughter preference over those of the younger. The second claimant was the Count Palatine of Neuburg, who had married a younger daughter of William the Rich, and his wife claimed the inheritance as nearest of kin, but she made over her claim to her son, Wolfgang William. The question at issue was thus in the main the old one of the eldest by descent against the nearest of kin, and was in theory eminently a matter for the Imperial courts to decide.

Nevertheless from the beginning it was clear that legal considerations alone would not be allowed to solve the problem; for too much was at stake, and if a general war were avoided it would only be with the greatest difficulty. First of all there was the geographical position of the duchies; they lay along the lower Rhine, and Jülich and Cleves marched with the United Provinces. Thus if they passed into Imperial hands, or into hands favourable to the Habsburgs, they would constitute a serious threat both to the Protestants of North Germany and to the Dutch. Nor was this all, for there were also religious complications. The population of the duchies was Catholic, but both the claimants were Lutherans, and the Peace of Ausgburg in 1555 had accepted the principle of *cujus regio ejus religio*; if, therefore, the disputed territories went to a Protestant, there was every chance that they might become Protestant themselves, and even carry with them the archbishopric of Cologne, which they nearly surrounded. This, in its turn, would upset the whole Balance of Power in the Reich, and, quite possibly, in the whole of Europe. The death of this comparatively obscure German duke thus set all Europe by the ears.

The Emperor, Rudolf II, had no intention of letting his interests go by default, and he at once claimed the right of administering the duchies until the question of the succession was settled: in support of this contention he sent a force to occupy Jülich. Henry seized the opportunity which now presented itself. He declared himself the champion of the rights of the two claimants, thus following the policy which had been adopted by Henry II, and was to be so successfully practised by Richelieu and Louis XIV, namely that of supporting the lesser German princes against the Emperor. He secured the co-operation of England, the United Provinces, the German Protestant Union, Venice, and Savoy, and three French armies were assembled. One of them was to expel the Imperialists from Jülich; a second was to attack Cerdagne and Roussillon; and the third was to invade Italy. In connection with this last scheme Henry concluded, in April, 1610, the Treaty of Bruzolo with Charles Emmanuel I, by which in the event of victory the Duke was to obtain the Milanese (with the exception of Cremona, which was to go to the Republic of Saint Mark) and Montferrat, together with the title of King, while his eldest son was to marry Henry's daughter.

The ink was hardly dry on this treaty, and the first shots had hardly been fired in a struggle which presaged ill for the House of Austria, when, in May, as Henry passed through the streets of Paris, only two days before the date fixed for his departure for the campaign, he was stabbed to death by a Catholic fanatic named Ravaillac. The Dauphin, now Louis XIII, was a boy of nine, and the Regent, Marie de Medici, at once reversed the policy of her dead husband. In these circumstances it is hardly surprising that the only step taken towards the realization of the Great Design was the expulsion of the Imperialists from Jülich by Maurice of Nassau with the aid of a small English contingent.

With the death of Henry IV any hope of an immediate settlement of the problem of the duchies was at an end, and several years elapsed before one was reached. In the meantime the position was still further complicated by the conversion of the Count Palatine of Neuburg to Catholicism and of the Elector of Brandenburg to Calvinism. Eventually, by the Treaty of Xanten in 1614, subsequently modified in 1630, a division of the duchies between the two claimants was agreed upon: by this Jülich, Berg, and Ravenstein fell to Neuburg, while Brandenburg took Cleves, Mark, and Ravensberg. The Hohenzollerns had acquired their first territory in Western Germany, though, like Prussia in the East, it was isolated from the bulk of their possessions in Brandenburg. The continued attempt of successive Electors and Kings of the House of Hohenzollern to make these territories one connected whole was to be a prominent feature of European politics in the following century.

French relations with England deteriorated during the last years of Elizabeth, and there were several reasons for this. The Anglo-French alliance had served its purpose of thwarting the ambition of Philip II, and the rapid revival of France under Henry IV was beginning to frighten many Englishmen for the future of the Balance of Power. Then, although an increasing number of Elizabeth's ministers were inclining towards a settlement with Spain, the Queen herself by no means relished the way in which Henry had "basely sacrificed his friends and made common cause with the enemy" at Vervins. Elizabeth's view was that she had gone to war in the national interest, that is to say with a view to maintaining the integrity of the French monarchy as the bulwark of English freedom, but that by the desertion of Henry all she had done was to save France, and transform England into one of the principals in the war. As a modern historian has written: "This was an untoward and disconcerting result, not merely because it was a blow to our honour, but because it was a result contrary to all the canons of English diplomacy". Nor was this all, for there were serious commercial differences between the two countries, and Elizabeth was pressing Henry for the repayment of money lent to him in the days of his adversity. On his part the French King was extremely suspicious of English intentions, and he had a shrewd idea that Elizabeth wished to embroil him with Spain for her own purposes; nor was he mistaken in this supposition, for one of her last acts was to urge him, after the discovery of the Biron conspiracy, to purge his country of its evil humours by a foreign war. What Henry not unjustifiably feared was that if he again became involved in hostilities with Spain the English Queen would use this fact to raise her price to Philip III, and make a peace which would leave him in the lurch. It is true that by 1610 the French were ready for war, but this was not the case six years earlier. Time was required to put the outlying provinces in a proper condition of defence, for the Spanish attack would naturally fall on such parts as Brittany, Guyenne, Provence, and Languedoc. Also, there were ideological considerations to be taken into account. To wage offensive war against Spain, involving, as it would, a close alliance with England and the United Provinces, might easily upset the equilibrium in France itself, for it would of necessity create difficulties with Rome. In short, it would virtually mean a return to the divided France of the days when Henry was seeking to push his fortunes by means of a Protestant *contre-ligue*.

There were at this time only two possible cases in which the French King could embark on a war with any confidence. One was the unlikely event of the Spanish Netherlands calling in his help, and the other was if some obvious threat to French interests was created by the Habsburgs, such as was later constituted by the occupation of Jülich by the Imperialists. As neither of these conditions appeared likely to materialize, no attempt of Elizabeth to induce France to break the Treaty of Vervins could possibly succeed. Accordingly, even when confronted with the Biron conspiracy the King preserved an enigmatic attitude: he was apparently willing to consider war, but he never advised Elizabeth against peace with Spain if she could obtain it upon reasonable terms. Above all, Henry realized the danger of embarking upon a war in partnership with an aged Queen whose successor, being of a different dynasty, might not feel himself bound to continue the agreement. The union of England and Scotland under the same crown was, indeed, to have serious repercussions for French diplomacy, for it put an end to that "auld alliance" which had so often proved useful to France, yet French statesmen were to fish, not unsuccessfully, in the troubled waters of Scottish politics for another hundred and fifty years.

That Henry was fully justified in his cautious attitude was proved as soon as James VI of Scotland also became James I of England, for one of that monarch's first acts was to make peace with Spain. The war had served its purpose, and had reached a stalemate. England had beaten off an attempt at invasion and she had deprived her enemy of the mastery of the sea, but she was quite unable to engage in a Continental war, and even in the waters of the New World the chance of valuable prizes was considerably diminished since the Spaniards had adopted the system of convoy for their treasure-ships. James insisted that the negotiations should take place in London, and after some delay Philip III agreed to what was tantamount to an acknowledgment of defeat.

The first meeting of the plenipotentiaries was held on May 20th, 1604, and James signed the completed treaty on August 19th. Both parties proved eager for peace, but all the same there were one or two contentious points to be settled. The Dutch, although allies of James, were not a party to the negotiations, and the British representatives would not admit any terms prejudicial to them; thus they refused to acknowledge that the Dutch were rebels or to restrain British subjects from serving in their armies. A stipulation that either of the contracting parties would undertake to force open any ports of the other which were blockaded was inserted by the Spaniards in the hope of causing trouble between James and the Dutch, but it was accepted by the British without any thought of performance. No agreement in respect of the Americas proved possible, for the Spaniards would not admit the right of the British to trade there even with independent peoples, while the British refused to acknowledge that such trade was in any way illegal; so the matter was left out of the treaty, and for many years to come Englishmen and Spaniards were to cut each other's throats in the New World while their sovereigns were at peace in the Old. Another difficult point concerned the religious freedom of British subjects in Spanish ports, and this was settled on the understanding that they should not be molested so long as they caused no public scandal.

During the remainder of Henry's reign Anglo-French relations were not subjected to any special strain, and, as we have seen, James readily co-operated with France in face of the Imperialist occupation of Jülich. When, however, Henry had been murdered and Marie de Medici had indicated her intention of reversing his policy, the English King withdrew, as he was determined not to be drawn into a Continental war as a principal. Later, he did work with France to bring about the Treaty of Xanten.

As soon as Marie de Medici became Regent, she not only reversed Henry's policy, but she undid, both at home and abroad, most of what he had accomplished. She announced her intention of withdrawing altogether from the war, and of making an alliance with Spain by the double marriage of her daughter, Elizabeth, to the Prince of the Asturias, and of Anne of Austria, the eldest daughter of Philip III, to Louis XIII. Confronted with this defection, the allies of France had no option but to make peace. The German Protestants and the Dutch concluded the Truce of Willstedt with the Emperor in October, 1610, and the Duke of Savoy had to come to terms with Madrid: the key of Italy was once more thrown away, and all that remained to show for the reign of Henry IV was the acquisition of Bresse and Bugey.

Marie de Medici remained the dominant force in French politics for the next seven years, and during that period France counted for little in the counsels of Europe. She was experiencing one of those eras of eclipse which have been so frequent a feature of her history, and, in consequence, the Habsburgs, both in Madrid and Vienna, had a fresh lease of life. Louis XIII was declared of age in 1614, and two years later the double marriage with Spain was celebrated. In 1617 the domination of Marie came to an end, but this did nothing to clarify the internal situation, and in 1620 there was a widespread Huguenot rising in the South of France. Abroad, the Thirty Years' War was beginning, and it was generally felt that a strong hand was needed at the helm of state: in 1624 this need was satisfied by the arrival of Richelieu at the head of the government, and from that day a new era dawned for France and for Europe. Until 1870, when Europe exchanged a mistress for a master, France was to be the leading Power on the Continent.

CHAPTER XI

ORIGIN OF THE THIRTY YEARS' WAR, 1556–1618

THE disintegrating effect of the Reformation upon the Holy Roman Empire has already been noticed. Had Charles V been able to confine his attention to the Reich, that is to say had he not been the heir of Ferdinand and Isabella as well as of Maximilian I, he might either have crushed Protestantism at birth or have come to terms with it before it had realized its strength, but his commitments elsewhere prevented him from pursuing either policy. Furthermore, the reformed religion in its original manifestation was advocated by Luther in a form peculiarly congenial to the German princes, who were always inclined to view Imperial claims with the gravest suspicion, and so from the beginning it had the support of the traditionally centrifugal forces in the Reich. Above all, the Reformation was by no means a purely German affair, and when its repercussions led to war it was only to be expected that neighbouring Powers should intervene in the conflict for ideological or national reasons, or for a mixture of both. So it came about that the Thirty Years' War, which commenced as a revolt of the Bohemians against the Habsburgs, developed into an international conflict of which one result was the aggrandisement of France for two centuries, and the other was the abasement of Germany for the same period.

The *terminus a quo* of the struggle was the Peace of Augsburg in 1555, by which the principle of autonomy in ecclesiastical matters was definitely recognized. It had then been laid down that in future all religious disputes should be settled by peaceful means, and to this end, in all causes between a Catholic and a Lutheran, the Imperial Chamber was to be composed of an equal number of assessors from either party. The principle of *cujus regio ejus religio* was also established, and this stipulated that every secular prince or Imperial City should be allowed to decide which of the two religions should be adopted within their jurisdiction, and that those who would not conform should be allowed to depart with their goods. A compromise was also reached with regard to the secularization of ecclesiastical property within the jurisdiction of secular princes, and it was decided that all such property as had been secularized before the Treaty of Passau in 1552 should remain so, but that no further exercise of this right was to be allowed.

The Protestants had also demanded that the ecclesiastical princes should be placed on the same footing as the secular, that is to say they should be allowed to establish what religion they pleased within their own jurisdiction, and that any ecclesiastical prince or bishop who became a Lutheran should retain his dignities and his revenues. The Catholics strongly resisted this, and a somewhat unsatisfactory compromise was at length reached by which it was enacted that if any ecclesiastic should hereafter abandon the Catholic religion he should relinquish his office, with the revenues and patronage appertaining thereto. The Lutherans agreed to the insertion of this clause only under protest, and they announced that they did not consider the reservation binding on them; they also obtained the concession that those subjects of ecclesiastical princes who had already become Lutherans should be unmolested, and that those who might subsequently embrace Lutheranism should be allowed to emigrate.

Such were the terms of the Peace of Augsburg, which it was hoped would put an end to the troubles to which the Reformation had given rise in the Reich, but from the beginning it contained within itself the seeds of failure. In the first place, it only applied to the Lutherans, for at the time of its conclusion the Protestant princes of the Empire were all Lutherans, and they only thought of securing their own interests. Thus Calvinism had no rights whatever, and had still to win legal recognition. Then, again, differences had arisen concerning lands secularized since 1552, for in spite of the provisions of the Peace of Augsburg the Protestants had secularized a good deal of Church land, and the princes had found it of great value for the endowment of younger sons and other necessitous relatives.

The greatest difficulty of all, however, was in respect of what was called the Ecclesiastical Reservation, that is to say the case of a bishop or abbot who became a Lutheran.   As we have seen, it had been laid down that in these circumstances he was to vacate his dignity, but the Protestants maintained that this Ecclesiastical Reservation was only intended to apply where a bishop or abbot, who had been elected by a Catholic Chapter as a Catholic, became a Protestant, and did not affect those cases where a Chapter which had itself become Protestant elected a Protestant to be its bishop or abbot. In virtue of this contention eight of the great bishoprics of North Germany, and many abbeys throughout the country, became practically secularized. The Protestant bishop or abbot made no pretence of performing spiritual functions; he was merely a territorial prince who enjoyed an ecclesiastical title, instead of that of duke or landgrave, but his right neither to title nor to property had ever been admitted by the Imperial courts or by the Diet.

Meanwhile, the Counter-Reformation had made great strides, and by the beginning of the seventeenth century the reaction in favour of Rome was in full flood. Protestantism was largely a thing of the past in Poland, in the hereditary lands of the House of Austria, and in Bavaria, where Maximilian had succeeded as duke in 1596. The Catholics were thus in a much stronger position than they had been when the Peace of Augsburg was originally concluded; their opponents were also divided into two warring camps, while they could themselves in the last resort rely upon the Spanish *tercios* in Flanders and the Franche Comté.

The first rumblings of the coming storm were heard in 1607. In that year a Catholic procession was insulted at Donauworth, a free city on the Danube where there was a large Protestant majority. The Reichskammergericht, whose duty it was to deal with such matters, was inoperative owing to the religious divisions, and so the question was referred to the Reichshofrath, better known as the Aulic Council, which was entirely composed of the nominees of the Emperor. This body pronounced the ban of the Empire against Donauworth, and entrusted the execution of the sentence to Maximilian of Bavaria. He then occupied the town with his troops, but, not content merely with restoring order, he handed over the parish church to the Catholics on the ground that it had only been used for Protestant worship since the Treaty of Passau, and was therefore not protected by the Peace of Augsburg.

The treatment meted out to Donauworth alarmed the Protestants and encouraged the Catholics all over Germany. Christian of Anhalt, one of those turbulent spirits who come to the fore in troubled times, persuaded the Protestant states of the Rhineland in 1608 to form the Calvinist Union, and in the following year it was joined by free cities of the importance of Strasbourg, Nuremberg, and Ulm. The Elector Palatine was acknowledged as its head, and Christian of Anhalt and the Margrave of Baden-Durlach were appointed its generals. On the Catholic side too the ranks were being closed, for in 1609 the Catholic League was formed among the Catholic bishops of South Germany, under the leadership of Maximilian, to defend Catholic interests, while the Pope gave his approval and Spain promised assistance should necessity arise.

At this point it seemed as if the religious differences in the Reich were to be merged in the struggle of Bourbon and Habsburg, owing to the question of the succession to the duchies of Cleves, Jülich, and Berg. Had this happened it would have gone ill for the Emperor, since, although there was no immediate threat from the Turks, Rudolf was having trouble in his hereditary dominions, in Bohemia, and in Christian Hungary. However, the murder of Henry IV postponed the crisis, and another factor operating in the same direction was the death of Rudolf II in 1612; he was succeeded as Emperor by his brother, Matthias, who on account of his age and temperament was unwilling to push matters to extremes. Compromise was, if only temporarily, in the air, as was shown by the conclusion of the Treaty of Xanten in 1614. The new Emperor also tried to conciliate the Protestants by promising to reform the Aulic Council, to restore the privileges of Donauworth, and to redress various grievances of which they complained, but suspicion was too deep on both sides for these attempts to be successful, and the Protestants displayed as little confidence in Matthias as they had shown in respect of his predecessor.

In adopting this attitude they were evincing considerable foresight, as it proved, for the Emperor it was who was destined to precipitate the catastrophe. The heir of the Austrian Habsburgs, the Archduke Ferdinand of Styria, was not in the direct line, but came of a cadet branch, and a considerable amount of diplomacy was clearly going to be necessary if he was to succeed to the family possessions. It therefore became the cardinal point in the policy of Matthias to secure the succession of Ferdinand not only to these territories, but also to the Empire. So far as the hereditary dominions of the Habsburgs were concerned this presented no great difficulty, and the succession to them was soon established with the full consent of Philip III. Hungary and Bohemia, however, were another matter, for in both kingdoms the crown was elective. Nevertheless the Emperor at first had his way. The Estates of Hungary duly elected Ferdinand to be the successor of Matthias, and he was crowned at Pressburg (Buda was in Turkish hands) without a murmur of opposition being heard.

Even in Bohemia the Emperor experienced no immediate difficulty. The Estates of that kingdom, which was largely Protestant at the time, were called together in 1617, and were required to acknowledge Ferdinand as the lawful successor to Matthias by hereditary right, for evidence was produced that on previous occasions they had admitted the hereditary nature of their monarchy. Boldness won the day, and the Estates conceded what was demanded of them, so Ferdinand was crowned as King of Bohemia. Second thoughts, however, were not long in coming, and the Protestant nobles realized that they had made a rod for their own backs by their surrender of the elective principle. They found a leader in Count Henry of Thurn, a man who, like Christian of Anhalt, was not likely to let any scruples stand in his way where the embarrassment of the House of Austria was concerned. A meeting of the Protestant members of the Estates was accordingly called, and a petition was sent to the Emperor protesting against the change in the constitution. Matthias replied by justifying all he had done, and declared the present assembly to be illegal.

This was in the early spring of 1618. On May 23rd Thurn and a band of armed supporters rushed the palace at Prague, and burst into the room where the regents were sitting. Bitter words were spoken, and then the regents, with their secretary, were thrown out of the window by the insurgents. Such was the defenestration of Prague. Thurn hoped by this violent deed to render impossible peace between Bohemia and the Habsburgs; what he did was to give the signal for a war which was to last thirty years, and was to leave its mark on Germany for all time.

While these events were taking place in Central Europe a situation was developing in Scandinavia which was to have the most profound effect upon the history of Christendom during the whole of the seventeenth century.

Christian III of Denmark had died in 1559, and he was followed to the grave by Gustavus I of Sweden in 1560; with their deaths began a new era for the Northern kingdoms, which for the ensuing five generations were to emerge from their seclusion and to play an important part on the stage of European history. Gustavus I left four sons, namely Eric XIV, who succeeded him on the throne, John, Magnus, and Charles. Of these, Magnus soon developed signs of an insanity which removed him from the political scene, while Charles was a boy of ten at the time of his father's death. The differences between these brothers were powerfully to affect the cause of Scandinavian history. In Denmark the new monarch was Frederick II, who was the first cousin of Eric XIV, of whom he was destined also to be the lifelong rival.

There had, as has been described in a previous chapter, existed considerable tension between Denmark and Sweden during the late years of Christian III and Gustavus I, but a definite rupture had always been avoided, and it was not until the accession of their sons that the struggle, known to history as the Scandinavian Seven Years' War, actually broke out. There were many causes of this. Frederick could never forget that his predecessors had ruled Sweden, and he persisted in retaining the three crowns on his escutcheon, to which his Swedish cousin retaliated by quartering the arms of both Denmark and Norway on his own. More serious was the alarm caused in Copenhagen by the policy of Eric in the Eastern Baltic. The Teutonic Order, which had ruled in Prussia and the Baltic Provinces, was in a state of dissolution owing to the spread of the Reformation, and its territory was coveted both by Poland and Russia. The Tsar, Ivan IV, possessed himself of Narva, whereupon Reval made overtures to Gustavus I, but the old King hesitated to embark upon what he felt might prove to be a dangerous course. His son had no such scruples, and by the end of 1561 the Swedes were firmly installed in Esthonia.

In taking this step Eric laid the foundations of the Swedish empire in the Baltic, and there can be little doubt that in doing so he was largely influenced by the threat to Finland, then a Swedish possession, which would develop if either the Tsar or the Poles got control of Esthonia. On the other hand, this increase of Swedish power was by no means to the liking of the Danes, especially because they had claims of their own on Esthonia dating from its conquest by Valdemar II in 1219.

A further inducement to Frederick to undertake aggressive action against his cousin was the state of Swedish-Polish relations. Gustavus I had left Finland to his son John, but one of Eric's earlier acts was to get a Riksdag at Arboga in 1561 so to limit the power of his brother in his own province that he had little else to do save to collect and spend the revenues due to the crown. John professed to acquiesce in this treatment, but he was biding his time, and he thought that in the dissolution of the Teutonic Order he had found his opportunity. In 1562, without obtaining the consent of Eric, he went to Poland and married the sister of the reigning monarch, Sigismund II. By this time relations between Sweden and Poland were already strained over the progress of events in Esthonia, and Eric took the view that his brother was conspiring with the enemies of his country, and he prevailed upon the Riksdag to declare John guilty of treason and to confiscate his estates. John held out for some time, but in August, 1563, he was forced to surrender, and he and his wife were imprisoned in Gripsholm Castle. Eric might have increased his own power by the overthrow of his brother, but he had accentuated the hostility of Poland; and in the autumn of that same year, 1563, Sigismund concluded an offensive alliance with Frederick.

By this time Denmark and Sweden were already at war, for the beginning of the year had been marked by an event which had finally precipitated the long-awaited hostilities. Eric was desirous of enhancing his position by a spectacular marriage, and he paid court in turn to Elizabeth of England, Mary of Scots, and Christina of Hesse. To secure the hand of this last-named lady he despatched a particularly dazzling embassy, but on its way through Denmark it was detained by Frederick, who, in the summer of the same year, followed this up by instructing his men-of-war to prevent any munitions reaching his rival and, finally, by a formal declaration of war.

In the struggle which ensued Sweden was without allies, while Lübeck, which had old scores to pay off, as well as Poland, rallied to the side of her enemy. Russia, on the other hand, maintained an uneasy neutrality. Ivan IV was equally suspicious both of Poland and Sweden, but he was more frightened of Poland, and he therefore held his hand. In the fighting, which was marked by extraordinary ferocity, the Swedes were the more successful by sea and the Danes on land, and several attempts at mediation, notably by France, which had treaties with both the principal combatants, failed. In 1568 Eric XIV was deposed by his subjects on account of his manifest insanity, and two years later the Emperor Maximilian II succeeded in assembling a peace conference.

In December, 1570, agreement was reached by the peace of Stettin. Both monarchs renounced all claim to one another's territory. The fort of Elfsborg was restored to Sweden on payment of a sum of money, and in exchange for the provinces of Jemtland and Herjedalen. These terms were more favourable to Denmark than to Sweden, and this may well account for the fact that the rest of Frederick's reign was both peaceful and prosperous. Indeed, with the assistance of a number of able ministers, the King

I

raised his kingdom to the rank of a Great Power. Frederick II died in April, 1588, and was succeeded by his son, Christian IV.

It was far otherwise with Sweden, where John III was now reigning in place of the deposed Eric. Once the Danish war was over the Swedes found themselves embroiled with Russia, and Ivan gradually forced them out of Esthonia, which he was enabled to do the more easily as the policy of Poland was vacillating and indecisive. By 1577 the Russians were besieging Reval, the last Swedish stronghold in Esthonia, but they were not destined to capture the place, for the new King of Poland, Stephen Bathory, realized what was at stake, and concluded an alliance with Sweden. The allied forces defeated the Russians at Wenden in October, 1578, and before another three years were past the Swedes had not only recovered most of the ground they had lost in Esthonia, but they had also made fresh conquests in Carelia, Ingria, and Livonia, including the fortress of Narva.

This connection between Sweden and Poland, born of a common fear of Russian ambitions, was to be rendered even closer. In 1586 Stephen Bathory died, and out of the various candidates, including four Archdukes and the new Tsar, Feodor, the Poles chose Sigismund, the son of John III. The Articles of Kalmar, signed by both monarchs, were at once drawn up to regulate the future relations of the two countries when, in process of time, Sigismund should succeed his father as King of Sweden. The kingdoms were to be perpetually allied, but each of them was to retain its own laws and customs. Sweden was also to enjoy her religion, subject to such changes as a General Council might make, but neither Pope nor Council was to claim or exercise the right to release Sigismund from his obligations to his Swedish subjects. During Sigismund's absence from Sweden that country was to be ruled by seven Swedes, of whom six were to be chosen by the King and the seventh by his uncle, Charles. No new tax was to be levied in Sweden while the King was away, and the country was not to be administered from Poland. Any alteration in these articles was only to be made with the consent of the King, Charles, and the Riksdag.

So long as John III lived the position of his son on the Polish throne did not give rise to any insuperable difficulties, although in some circles there was disquiet as to what would happen when Sigismund also became King of Sweden. This concern was specially felt by the more extreme Protestants and by those who had been enriched by the plunder of the Church: at their head was Charles, who possessed to the full all the Vasa ability and ambition, as well as the lack of scruple characteristic of so many members of his family, but who definitely inclined to Calvinism in his religious views. Sigismund was a Catholic, and the Counter-Reformation was gaining ground all over Europe, so that Charles had no difficulty in building up a formidable party pledged to pursue at home and abroad the policy of his father, Gustavus I.

John III died in November, 1592, and in due course Sigismund was crowned at Upsala, after which he returned to Poland, leaving his uncle Charles to govern Sweden. The principal act of the new government was the conclusion of the war with Russia, which had been raging intermittently since 1570. By the Peace of Teusin, which was signed in May, 1595, the Tsar, Feodor, recognized the right of Sweden to Esthonia and Narva, while the Swedes ceded to Russia the province of Kexholm in Finland.

In Swedish domestic politics the inevitable development was taking place. Charles persuaded the Riksdag, in spite of the opposition of Sigismund, to make him regent, and he then proceeded to pack all the more important offices with his own supporters. The Catholics might be supposed to favour the King, so they were subjected to a rigorous persecution with the object, at the same time, of reducing their numbers and influence and of increasing their unpopularity with the bulk of the nation. By the summer of 1598 breaking-point had been reached, and Sigismund landed with an army to recover the kingdom which was so rapidly slipping from his grasp. He was, however, defeated by Charles at Stängebro in September, and then left Sweden for ever, though the civil war continued until March, 1600. In that month the Riksdag declared that Sigismund and his descendants had forfeited the Swedish throne; the rights of John, the second son of John III, were passed over; and the regent was recognized as King under the title of Charles IX. Thus came to an end the dual monarchy of Poland–Sweden, and in view of the ambition of Charles and the religious differences between the two countries, their separation was inevitable; had they remained united the subsequent history of Northern and Eastern Europe might have been very different, and there might have been no Partition of Poland. The ultimate beneficiaries of what did take place proved to be Russia and Prussia.

The not unnatural consequence of the seizure of the Swedish

throne by Charles IX was a war with Poland for her overseas possessions, and the hostilities which began in 1600 were still in existence at the time of his death eleven years later. In addition, the
temporary eclipse of Russia during the early years of the seventeenth century had caused the relations of Poland and Sweden to
be further complicated by Russian internal politics, and six
months before his death Charles had entered into negotiations for
his son to be recognized as Tsar. In that same year, 1611, the
Swedish King found another war on his hands, this time with
Christian IV of Denmark: the causes of disagreement between the
two Scandinavian Powers were many and of long standing, but the
principal at the moment was the endeavour of Sweden to secure
possession of Lapmark and other districts in the North of Norway,
with a view to obtaining access to the Arctic fisheries. On his
coronation Charles IX took the title of "King of the Lapps of
Nordland", and the privileges conceded by him to the citizens,
who were mostly Dutch, of the newly founded city of Gothenburg
included the right to trade and fish in the disputed districts. The
King of Denmark was by no means prepared to be conciliatory,
and in April he signed his formal declaration of war.

Charles IX was succeeded in 1611 by his son, Gustavus II,
better known as Gustavus Adolphus, then in his seventeenth year.
His cousin, John, son of John III, had publicly resigned his rights
to him, and Sigismund had been excluded from the succession.
The legacy which Gustavus inherited from his father was no easy
one. Sweden was at war on three fronts. The Danes held the two
chief fortresses of the kingdom, and the heart of the country lay
open before them. The apparent break-up of Russia had tempted
the Swedes to embark upon a career of aggrandizement for which
their resources were wholly inadequate. The Poles were already in
possession of Moscow, and were preparing to eject the Swedes from
the Baltic Provinces. These were the liabilities which the young
King was called upon to assume, but he also enjoyed one considerable asset, and that was a regular army which Charles IX had
created. What this meant to Sweden was to be proved on many a
battle-field during the next hundred years.

With two other wars on his hands, Gustavus determined to
come to terms with Denmark, and from the moment of his accession he showed himself conciliatory, for he abandoned the offensive title of "King of the Lapps of Nordland". Christian, on the
other hand, was by no means so pacifically inclined, and he de-

finitely refused Dutch offers of mediation: when the representatives of the United Provinces reproached him for warring against another Protestant monarch, he replied, "*Non agitur de religione sed de regione*". His brother-in-law, James I of Great Britain, was more successful, and in January, 1613, peace was made. In all essential points Sweden gave way. She renounced her claims to the island of Osel and to Lapmark, conceded to the King of Denmark the right of placing the three crowns on his escutcheon, and promised to pay one million rix-dollars in six equal instalments, while the fortress of Elfsborg and the towns of Gothenburg, Old and New Lödöse were mortgaged to Christian until this indemnity was paid. All other conquests on both sides were to be restored, and Sweden's immunity from the Sound tolls was specially recognized. Thus once more and for the last time, Denmark vindicated her right to be regarded as the greatest Scandinavian Power, for if Christian had not subdued his Swedish neighbour he had certainly humiliated her.

However this may be, it is difficult to see that Denmark derived any permanent advantage from the Peace of Knäred, for the resentment caused in Sweden was to do her little good. Moreover, a common distrust of Danish ambitions began to draw the Swedes and the Dutch together, and in 1614 Gustavus became a party to an alliance between Lübeck and the United Provinces which was really aimed at Denmark.

A month after the Peace of Knäred had been concluded, Michael Romanoff became Tsar, and this event was in due course to bring to an end the Russo-Swedish war, which was another heritage from Charles IX. So far it had, as has been shown, not gone too badly for Sweden, and Swedish statesmen were thinking, not unjustifiably, in terms of a trans-Baltic empire extending from Lake Ilmen northwards to Archangel, and eastwards to Vologda. The accession of Michael put an end to this dream, for the new Tsar soon rallied his subjects to the defence of their country. Twice Gustavus himself took the field, but although the Swedes won a number of battles they were never in sight of final victory. Once more the good offices of James I were invoked, and a peace conference met at Dederina. However, so dilatory were the Russian methods of negotiation, that the discussions lasted for over eighteen months, and they only came to a conclusion when the Swedish delegates threatened an immediate resumption of hostilities.

Finally, peace was signed at Stolbova in February, 1617.

Russia ceded the provinces of Kexholm and Ingria, including the fortress of Nöteborg (the subsequent Schlüsselburg) on the Neva, which was the key to Finland. She further renounced all claims on Esthonia and Livonia, and paid an indemnity of twenty thousand roubles. In return for these concessions Sweden surrendered Great Novgorod, which she had captured, and recognized Michael as Tsar. The Treaty of Stolbova, unlike that of Knäred, represented a triumph for Swedish diplomacy, for it excluded Russia from the Baltic. "I hope to God", said Gustavus, "that the Russians will feel it a bit difficult to skip over that little brook". The fulfilment of this aspiration depended upon the relative strength of the two countries remaining what it was when the Treaty of Stolbova was signed, and this was not to be.

With Poland a settlement proved far more difficult, as Sigismund claimed his cousin's throne, and fighting went on spasmodically, without any decisive advantage to either side, until 1629, when a six years' truce was concluded at Altmark, by which Sweden was allowed to retain provisionally her Livonian conquests together with Elbing, a considerable portion of the delta of the Vistula, Braunsberg in West, and Pillau and Memel in East, Prussia. Moreover, Gustavus was accorded the right of levying tolls at Pillau, Memel, Danzig, Libau, and Windau, from which he drew a large sum of money much needed for the prosecution of those designs in respect of the Reich which were now occupying his mind.

CHAPTER XII

THE BEGINNING OF THE THIRTY YEARS' WAR, 1618–1632

THE international repercussions of the defenestration of Prague were far from being immediate; indeed, for some months it appeared as if the King of Bohemia and his rebellious subjects would be allowed to fight the matter out between themselves. John George, Elector of Saxony, and Maximilian of Bavaria, respectively leaders of the Lutheran and Catholic parties in the Reich, refused to interfere, while Philip III promised help but failed to send it. Matthias and Ferdinand had only fourteen thousand men at their disposal under Bucquoi, a Spanish general who had served with distinction in the Netherlands. Had Count Henry of Thurn and his colleagues displayed more initiative, and had they realized that a rebellion on the defensive has already failed, they might have consolidated their position and dictated terms to the Habsburgs. As it was, they soon proved that although they might be successful conspirators they were singularly inept politicians.

Nevertheless, for a brief space fortune favoured them. Charles Emmanuel of Savoy, Catholic though he was, had by no means either forgiven or forgotten the humiliations to which he had been subjected by the House of Austria after the death of Henry IV, and the Bohemian revolution seemed to offer him an opportunity of having his revenge. He had two thousand mercenaries in his employ under Count Ernest of Mansfeld, and he offered these to the Bohemians provided he did not himself appear as a principal in the negotiation. The man selected for this rôle was the young Frederick V, Elector Palatine, who was married to Elizabeth, the daughter of James I. Frederick had already expressed his approval of the progress of events at Prague, and his attitude, together with the mistaken belief that he was supported in it by his father-in-law, greatly encouraged the Bohemian insurgents. Mansfeld arrived at the scene of war in September, and by the end of the year the whole of Bohemia was lost to the Emperor except for the beleaguered town of Budweis.

The year 1619 thus opened inauspiciously for the Habsburgs,

and in March the Emperor Matthias died. Thurn determined to make what profit he could out of the ensuing Imperial vacancy, and he marched straight on Vienna, where Ferdinand had a mere handful of troops with which to resist him; however, reinforcements arrived in the nick of time, and the attempt of the Bohemians to end the struggle by a spectacular *coup d'état* had failed. In August the House of Austria scored another success with the unanimous election of Ferdinand to the Imperial throne. At first this had appeared to be far from likely, and John George of Saxony had taken formal objection to the exercise by Ferdinand of the Bohemian vote until it had been decided whether the crown of Bohemia was really his. The way had thus been opened to the Calvinist representatives, namely the Elector Palatine and the Elector of Brandenburg, to postpone the election of Ferdinand, but Frederick was too jealous of John George to accept this plan. The result was that when the day of the election came the Calvinists had neither a candidate nor a policy, while all that they had accomplished by their activities was to attach the Elector of Saxony firmly to the Emperor's side.

Nevertheless, while Ferdinand was winning one crown at Frankfurt he was losing another at Prague, for the month which witnessed his election as Emperor also saw his deposition as King of Bohemia and the choice of the Elector Palatine in his place. After a very brief period of hesitation Frederick signified his acceptance, and on November 4th he was crowned in the cathedral of Prague.

Events soon proved that the Bohemians had made a mistake which was to cost them dear. Frederick was far from being a strong character, and he was in the hands of men like Christian of Anhalt and Mansfeld, who were mere adventurers. He brought no real assistance to the Bohemian cause, for although in some quarters it had been hoped that he would have the backing of his father-in-law, this was ere long demonstrated most clearly not to be the case; James knew too much about rebellions in the British Isles to have any sympathy with them in Central Europe, and in any event he was working for an Anglo-Spanish understanding which would certainly not be effected if he displayed any sympathy with Frederick and his ambitions. Nor was this all, for, as S. R. Gardiner wrote, "Up to that time the Bohemian cause stood upon its own merits. But if one prince of the Empire was to be allowed, on any pretext, to seize upon the territories of another, what bulwark was there against a return of the old fist-right, or general anarchy? Frederick had attacked the foundations on which the institutions of his time rested, without calling up anything to take their place."

By 1620, therefore, the character of the struggle had changed. It was no longer a mere revolt of the Bohemians against the House of Austria, but it had become a German war; the only question was how long it would be before it developed into a general European conflict.

Maximilian of Bavaria was one of the first to realize exactly what was at stake, and he placed his services at the disposal of the Emperor. His price was the electoral hat, which was to be transferred from Frederick, and the right of occupying Upper Austria as security for his expenses. In March, 1620, under his auspices a meeting of the Catholic League was arranged with the Elector of Saxony at Mülhausen, and an agreement was reached by which the League undertook not to attempt to recover the lands of the Protestant bishops and administrators in North Germany so long as they remained loyal to the Emperor. This arrangement was not, it is true, a solution of the problem of the ecclesiastical lands, but it secured at any rate for a time the neutrality of John George and the other Lutheran princes. When this had been accomplished, the Pope made a substantial contribution in cash to the funds of the League, and Philip III promised to invade the Palatinate from the Spanish Netherlands.

Frederick's opponents were also fortunate in their generals, for in Tilly and Spinola they had at their disposal two of the finest soldiers of the day. In June the campaign began, and with Tilly's victory at the battle of the White Mountain outside Prague in November it finished. The Spaniards had occupied the Palatinate, and the Winter King, as Frederick was contemptuously called by his enemies, was a fugitive dependent upon the charity of Maurice of Nassau at The Hague. Full advantage was taken by the Emperor of this remarkable change in his fortunes. The leaders of the revolution were executed and their property was confiscated; Frederick was placed under the ban of the Empire, and his lands and titles were forfeited; the Protestant clergy were for the most part banished, and before another generation had passed away Bohemia was definitely ranged among the Catholic countries of Europe. After some more sporadic fighting, in February, 1623, Maximilian had his reward, for the Emperor transferred Frederick's electoral hat to the Bavarian for his life at a meeting of the

Diet at Regensburg, and also gave him the administration of the Upper Palatinate as additional security for the expenses of the war.

The transference of the electorate to Maximilian of Bavaria marks the close of the first, or Bohemian, stage of the Thirty Years' War, and for the Reich it was a tragedy that the conflict was not then terminated. Had Germany been an island in the middle of the sea this might have been possible, but, on the contrary, she was surrounded by a number of Powers with conflicting interests, but all of whom found in her misfortunes an admirable opportunity for pursuing their own objects. So the war simmered on through the years 1623 and 1624, until in 1625 it burst once more into flame.

The reason for this was a change in British foreign policy. Ever since James had made peace with Spain in 1604 he had endeavoured to work on amicable terms with that Power, and to this end he had even sent Sir Walter Raleigh to the scaffold. Whether he would have continued this policy had Henry IV not been murdered can only be a matter of speculation, but the weakness of France during the regency of Marie de Medici was hardly likely to tempt him to adopt an anti-Spanish line. British public opinion and the King's own inclinations demanded that something should be done to restore the Palatinate to Frederick, and as the use of force was out of the question, James resorted to diplomacy. His hope was to secure the marriage of the Prince of Wales, later Charles I, to a Spanish Infanta, after which the new King of Spain, Philip IV, was to persuade the Emperor to restore to Frederick his hereditary dominions. With this end in view, Lord Digby, who had represented James in Madrid on a previous occasion, was created Earl of Bristol, and sent to the Spanish capital to conduct the negotiations for the marriage.

These, however, proceeded slowly, and in February, 1623, Charles and his father's minister, Buckingham, themselves set off to Madrid in the hope of expediting matters. In this they were soon disappointed, for Philip IV and Olivares saw no Spanish interest to be served by bringing pressure to bear upon Ferdinand II to restore Frederick; on the other hand, they were by no means averse to protracted negotiations out of which some advantage for their own country might be gained. The Pope also pressed the Spanish Government to take advantage of this opportunity to secure better treatment for Catholics in the British Isles, and he declared that only in return for this would he grant a dispensation for the marriage. That James was right in his desire for an understanding with Spain in respect of German affairs is hardly open to question, but the problem at issue was as much religious as political, and a settlement involved concessions to his Roman Catholic subjects which no King of England at that time dare have promised.

A further complication arose at this point, for at the beginning of July the Pope died, and there was some delay before a successor was elected in the person of Urban VIII. The new Pope was no less desirous than his predecessor of turning the proposed marriage to the advantage of the British Catholics, and he brought all the pressure he could to bear upon both James and Charles. He wrote to the latter, "You, who desire so greatly to wed a Catholic maiden, should surely take to yourself that bride, by whose beauty Solomon, that wisest of Kings, boasts that he was taken captive", and added, with unconscious irony, "Consider how that at the court of Spain you are now made a spectacle for God and man". Urban directed that articles should be inserted in the contract providing that the children of the marriage should have Catholic nurses, and that Catholic churches should be erected in each county. Whatever may have been the real attitude of the Spanish Government towards the marriage, there is no reason to question the sincerity of the Pope, and the impossibility of these conditions is evidence, not of Urban's bad faith, but of his ignorance of Protestant feeling in the British Isles. By August it was clear that the negotiations had failed, and October, 1623, found Charles and Buckingham back in England.

James was not prepared to allow this failure to affect his policy towards Spain, but he was an old man, and he proved unable to control the situation. Charles and Buckingham were resentful of what they regarded as the shameful treatment with which they had met in Madrid, while the British Parliament, in a frenzy of patriotism and Protestantism, was clamouring for the most extreme measures against Spain and the Emperor. Before this opposition James gave way, and allowed his son and his minister to negotiate a general alliance to win back the Palatinate for Frederick: he himself received Mansfeld graciously in London, and allowed him to enlist twenty thousand men for service in Germany, while he obtained permission from the French Government for this force to march through France. In March, 1625, James I died, and his successor, Charles I, was free to follow his own inclinations with regard to the Thirty Years' War: in this connection it should not be forgotten that until the birth of a Prince of Wales, later Charles II, five years later the heiress presumptive to the English throne was Elizabeth, wife of the unfortunate Frederick.

In pursuit of the new British policy envoys were sent both to Sweden and Denmark to persuade those Powers to march against the Emperor. Gustavus Adolphus was too much occupied with Polish affairs to listen to the arguments of Great Britain, but Christian IV proved much more amenable. He was fearful that the Swedish monarch might supplant him as leader of the German Protestants, and he also hoped that intervention in the Thirty Years' War might give him control of the Elbe and the Weser, as well as lead to the acquisition of some more of the secularized bishoprics of Northern Germany in addition to Verden, which he had already acquired. Accordingly, Christian was by no means unwilling to come to terms with Charles I, and in May, 1625, an agreement was reached by which the British Government promised a subsidy of £30,000 a month, and agreed to send a naval expedition against the coasts of Spain.

From the beginning everything went wrong with the Danish plans. In the previous year Louis XIII, who did not relish the prospect of a march across France by Mansfeld's ill-disciplined forces, had found an excuse for withdrawing his permission, with the result that the men had been sent to the United Provinces, where they were dying in large numbers from disease and neglect. In October, 1625, an English attempt to capture Cadiz failed miserably, and before long quarrels broke out between Charles and his Parliament which effectually prevented the payment of the promised subsidies to the Danish monarch. Above all, there appeared on the Imperialist side one of the greatest generals of the Thirty Years' War in the person of Wallenstein.

The combination of Tilly and Wallenstein was too formidable for the Danish King. His ally, Mansfeld, was defeated at Dessau in April, 1626, and, having failed to retrieve the situation by a dash at Vienna itself, he died in the following November while struggling through the mountains of Bosnia in the hope of obtaining assistance from the Republic of Saint Mark. In the meantime Christian had taken the offensive by advancing into Thuringia, only, however, to be decisively defeated at Lutter in the last days of August by Tilly. The Danes left eight thousand dead and all their artillery on the field of battle, as well as two thousand prisoners in the enemy's hands. Tilly then overran the duchy of Brunswick, quartered his men for the winter along the lower Elbe, and sent a force to occupy Brandenburg.

The next year, 1627, the tide of Imperialist victory rolled on. Wallenstein, who had been created Duke of Friedland, marched into Silesia in overpowering strength, and sent fifty standards to Vienna as evidence of his prowess. He then joined hands with Tilly on the lower Elbe, and the united armies poured into Holstein; they then occupied continental Denmark, and Christian himself was forced to take refuge in the islands. In February, 1628, Ferdinand put the Dukes of Mecklenburg-Schwerin and Mecklenburg-Strelitz to the ban of the Empire for the assistance they had given to the Danes, declared their lands forfeited, and ordered Wallenstein to occupy and administer the duchies. The result was that by the end of the year the Imperialists were in effective possession of the whole Baltic coast from Danzig to Lübeck, with the exception of Stralsund, which Wallenstein had failed to take in spite of a long siege. So far as Christian was concerned matters may be said to have reached a deadlock, for he dared not venture on the mainland, while the Imperialists, not possessing a fleet, could not follow him to the islands.

In these circumstances a negotiated peace between the Emperor and the King of Denmark was inevitable, and neither party had any interest in prolonging the struggle. Much of continental Denmark was a smoking wilderness, while Wallenstein was extremely desirous of coming to terms with Christian before trying conclusions with Sweden, where the attitude of Gustavus was every day becoming more disquieting. Accordingly the representatives of the two parties met at Lübeck in January, 1629, but the first terms demanded by the Emperor proved unacceptable to the Danes, for he required the cession of Schleswig and Holstein, the surrender of Jutland to the Elector of Saxony, the abandonment of the North German bishoprics, the payment of the expenses of the war, and the closing of the Sound against any enemy of the House of Austria. Further negotiations, however, secured a modification of these conditions, and in May the Treaty of Lübeck was formally concluded; by its provisions the kingdom of Denmark, as well as Schleswig and Holstein, were returned to Christian, who, in his turn, renounced all claim to the North German bishoprics, and promised to refrain in future from any interference in the affairs of the Reich. So ended the second, or Danish, phase of the Thirty Years' War.

Ferdinand now determined to utilize the victories which had been gained by his armies in the field to consolidate his position. For the past two years the ecclesiastical electors and Maximilian had been urging him that the time had come to assert the rights of the Church under the Peace of Augsburg, and in March, 1629, he issued the Edict of Restitution, which restored to the Church all land secularized since 1555. On legal grounds there could be little serious criticism of the Emperor's act, though he has been accused of straining the letter of the law in violation of its spirit; politically, it was more open to question. A very considerable amount of property was involved, and the Edict automatically ranged its holders among Ferdinand's opponents. Nor was this all, for it provided them with the argument that not they, but the Imperialists, were the real revolutionaries in the struggle, and this shook the loyalty of many a German who until then had supported the Emperor as the embodiment of tradition and the representative of the rule of law.

This was the moment chosen by the Swedish King to intervene in the war, and, as is usually the case in such circumstances, his motives were mixed. He certainly did not regard his intervention solely in the light of a Protestant crusade, as has sometimes been represented, and there can be little doubt but that he viewed the whole business, as was only natural, from a predominantly Swedish point of view. The King himself, in his correspondence with his Chancellor, Axel Oxenstjerna, has left it on record that he was greatly influenced by fear lest the Emperor should use his newly-acquired command of the Southern shores of the Baltic to build a fleet which would constitute a threat to Sweden. For the same reason he rejected the Chancellor's alternative of a defensive war at sea; merely to blockade the German ports with the Swedish navy was impossible with the ships at his disposal. As war was in any case inevitable it was better that it should take place anywhere but in Sweden, whose long coastline and numerous harbours would render it very difficult to prevent invasion. Gustavus believed his country would only be safe if the Baltic were a Swedish lake; he had fought the Tsar for this reason, and he was now prepared to fight the Emperor. No doubt he was also much influenced by religious considerations, and he was greatly attracted by the idea of taking the field as the champion of Protestantism, as well as by the prospects of the power which would accrue from this, but religion was not, for him, the decisive factor.

Whatever may have been the motives of the Swedish monarch, the task which he undertook was sufficiently formidable, for it was nothing less than to range a nation with a population of one and a half million against a victorious military Power, whose armies were estimated at a hundred and fifty thousand men. The real assets of Sweden were, of course, her King, her generals, and soldiers trained in the long wars against the Danes, the Poles, and the Russians; to these were soon to be added much fine fighting material from abroad, not least from the British Isles.

One advantage Gustavus was to enjoy upon which he had certainly not counted, and that was the absence of Wallenstein from the command of the Emperor's forces. The truth was that he was becoming too powerful for a subject. He had been strongly opposed to the Edict of Restitution, for his goal was a peace imposed by himself and his army upon the fanatics of both sides, and he believed that religious equality was the only possible basis for the reorganization of the Reich. His aim was to consolidate Germany into a national state under the House of Austria. It was only to be expected that these views would encounter the opposition of Maximilian and the Catholic League, and they were too bold for the somewhat narrow Ferdinand. Accordingly, a few weeks after the Swedish King had landed on the coast of Pomerania the Emperor dismissed the only general who was capable of making head against him.

Gustavus disembarked on the island of Usedom in June, 1630, at the head of an army of thirteen thousand men, which was raised to forty thousand before the end of the year. It was well for him that Wallenstein was about to be dismissed, for little help was forthcoming from the German Protestants, and at any rate in the earlier stages of their campaign the Swedes would clearly have to depend on themselves. The Elector of Saxony most carefully avoided committing himself to anything resembling an alliance with Gustavus, while the Elector of Brandenburg sent an envoy to the Swedish monarch to induce him to go back, or at least not to advance any farther, and at the same time he offered his mediation with the Emperor. Only those who had little or nothing to lose rallied to the Swedish flag in these early days.

Nor was this in any way surprising. The position of Ferdinand seemed invincible, and the fate which had overtaken Christian was not an encouragement to join Gustavus. The Edict of Restitution might have alarmed many, but by the dismissal of Wallenstein, at the instance of the cautious Maximilian, the Emperor was giving proof of his distaste for extreme measures. Then, again, there was widespread suspicion of a foreigner, even if he came in the guise of a liberator, for the day had not yet arrived when the average German was lost to all sense of nationality, as was to be the case later in the century. What had been denied to Henry II of France was not yet to be accorded to Gustavus II of Sweden, and the Protestants showed themselves as distrustful of the designs of the Swede as were the Catholics of those of the Czech Wallenstein.

On the other hand, owing to the changes in the Imperialist high command and the transfer to Tilly of such of Wallenstein's troops as were not disbanded, Gustavus found himself for six months practically unopposed, and he utilized this period to establish bases on the Baltic coast as well as to increase the strength of his forces. In January, 1631, he received a most welcome accession of strength in the shape of an alliance with France. Richelieu had regarded with growing distaste the aggrandizement of the Habsburgs in consequence of the victories of Wallenstein. He was not ready to intervene openly in German affairs, but he was quite ready to get the Swedes to do his work for him. Earlier negotiations had failed, since Richelieu had found Gustavus more stubborn than he had expected, and he had to realize that if he wanted the King of Sweden's help it must be on the King of Sweden's terms. Accordingly the Treaty of Bärwalde was concluded in January, 1631, by which France promised to pay Sweden two hundred thousand rix-dollars for six years on condition that Gustavus maintained an army of thirty-six thousand men, promised to respect the Imperial constitution, observed neutrality towards Bavaria and the Catholic League in so far as they observed it towards him, and left the Catholic religion untouched in those districts where he found it established.

The year 1631 was destined to be decisive in the history of the Thirty Years' War, but in spite of the treaty with France it did not open too well for the Swedes. Magdeburg, one of the few towns which had declared for Gustavus, was captured by Pappenheim in May, and put to the sack in a manner which horrified contemporary opinion, but which the twentieth century would not have considered in any way abnormal. The failure to relieve Magdeburg was a serious blow to Swedish prestige, but the damage was

almost immediately repaired by a serious blunder on the part of
Ferdinand. The Emperor believed that he was on the eve of final
victory, and he ordered Tilly to secure the demobilization of the
Saxon forces. John George resented this interference with his independence, and refused, whereupon the Imperialists seized Leipsic
and proceeded to ravage Saxony. At last John George determined
to make common cause with the Swedes, and at the beginning of
September a treaty was signed between the King and the Elector,
whereby the Saxon placed himself absolutely at the disposal of the
Swede. Gustavus had achieved his first object; he was no longer a
foreign invader, but the recognized leader of the Protestants in the
Reich.

The fruits of this alliance were soon gathered. On September
17th, 1631, the Imperialists under Tilly met the combined
Swedish-Saxon army on the wide plain of Breitenfeld to the North
of Leipsic; Ferdinand's forces were the weaker, numbering about
thirty-two thousand men to their enemy's forty-one thousand, but
the Saxons proved extremely unreliable when put to the test.
Where Gustavus had the real advantage was in the strength of his
artillery and in the skill with which he employed it. The result was
a victory which was to be decisive in the history of the Thirty
Years' War. No fewer than seven thousand of Tilly's men are said
to have fallen on the field, another five thousand were taken
prisoner, and a great many more were massacred by the Saxon
peasantry during their flight.

The battle of Breitenfeld decided that Germany was not to become a Catholic Power united under the House of Austria. Ferdinand had sacrificed his first chance of unifying the Reich when he
dismissed Wallenstein; now Gustavus had robbed him of his
second. What was still uncertain was whether the Swedish King
could unite the country on a different basis, or whether the end of
the long struggle was to be the triumph of the centrifugal forces.
For twelve months the answer to this question remained uncertain.

The battle of Breitenfeld was followed by a rapid diminution in
the power and prestige of the Emperor and the Catholic League.
Gustavus began the new year with fresh victories: the end of
March, 1632, witnessed his triumphal entry into Nuremberg; the
middle of April saw another defeat of Tilly, when the old marshal
received a mortal wound; and by the close of the first week in May
the Swedish King was riding through the streets of Munich. Even

K

the Saxons had marched unopposed into Bohemia, and John George was in possession of Prague. Faced with this reversal of fortune, Ferdinand turned to Wallenstein, the only man who could stem the tide which was flowing so strongly against him. Wallenstein, who had for a moment toyed with the idea of co-operating with Gustavus, agreed to come to the Emperor's assistance, but on his own terms, which he was now able to enforce, for the Swedish victories had drawn the teeth of Maximilian and the League. No army was to be allowed in the Empire except under his command, and he alone was to have the right of pardoning offenders and confiscating property; furthermore, the Edict of Restitution was to be withdrawn. Ferdinand had no option but to agree, and Wallenstein became dictator of that portion of the Reich which still acknowledged the Habsburgs. The mere magic of his name raised an army in an incredibly short space of time, and he was ready to meet Gustavus.

It is not often that two commanders of the first rank have taken the field against one another, but this was the case during the latter part of the year 1632. Strategically, the advantage lay in the end with Wallenstein, who had foiled his antagonist before Nuremberg and had invaded Saxony. On the other hand, in November the Swedish King forced Wallenstein to fight a pitched battle at Lutzen, which was against his wishes. The Swedes emerged victorious, but Gustavus was killed in the fighting, and all the fruits of victory accrued to Wallenstein.

The death of Gustavus Adolphus not only marked the end of another phase, the Swedish, of the Thirty Years' War, but it changed the character of the struggle altogether. The battles of Breitenfeld and Lutzen had settled the fate of Germany for two centuries; she was not to become a unitary state, and she was to be the playground of her neighbours' ambitions. Two years after the death of Gustavus his rival, Wallenstein, was murdered, and although the war dragged its disastrous course for another fourteen years no real principle was involved, and the devastation of the Reich continued merely that the French might annex Alsace or the Swedes seize Pomerania.

CHAPTER XIII

POLICY OF RICHELIEU, 1624–1642

THE position in which Richelieu found France in 1624 was in all respects worse than it had been when Henry IV was murdered fourteen years before. Not only was the country definitely the poorer for want of competent leadership, but it was weaker in respect of its neighbours. The House of Austria appeared in 1610 to be in deadly peril, and it was equally threatened from within and from without: now it was on the crest of the wave of its successes in the opening period of the Thirty Years' War, and Ferdinand II held a stronger position in the Reich than any of his predecessors since Charles V. Still more serious was the revival of Spanish power, for the troops of Philip IV were in possession of the Lower Palatinate, whence they threatened the independence of the United Provinces, while it was still uncertain whether the heir to the British throne might not marry a Spanish princess. To such an extent had the situation deteriorated since the dagger of Ravaillac put an end to the Great Design.

However, an opportunity soon occurred which enabled Richelieu to demonstrate that the destinies of France were in very different hands from those of his immediate predecessors. The League of the Grisons had for many years occupied the Valtellina, the broad valley which runs North-West into the heart of the Rhaetian Alps from the top of Lake Como. The Grisons were Protestant, while the population of the Valtellina was Catholic, and in 1620 it rose, massacred as many Protestants as could be found, and called in the assistance of the Viceroy of Milan. The geographical situation of the valley rendered it an important link in the chain of Habsburg communications, and the Viceroy was only too ready to respond to the advance made to him. The upshot thus was that Spanish troops moved into the Valtellina, where they built a fort, and the Grisons were compelled to admit an Imperialist garrison at Chur.

Richelieu at once realized what was at stake. First of all he took advantage of the resentment of the Prince of Wales and Buckingham at the treatment with which they had met in Madrid to arrange a marriage between Charles and Henrietta Maria, the sister of Louis XIII, whereby he hoped to secure the assistance of the British fleet. In Italy he co-operated with Venice and Charles Emmanuel I of Savoy with such success that early in 1625 the Papal troops, who had replaced the Spaniards in the Valtellina, had been driven out, and the valley was once more in the hands of the Grisons. On the other hand, a Franco-Savoyard attempt in the direction of Genoa proved a failure, and even resulted in a Spanish invasion of Piedmont. At this point Richelieu found himself called upon to face a Huguenot rising, so he was not unwilling to come to terms with Spain. By the Treaty of Monzon in March, 1626, it was agreed that the Valtellina should be returned to the Grisons, but with an autonomous administration, and that only the Catholic faith was to be practised. This was in many ways a compromise, but the Spaniards were out of the Valtellina, which was the original object of the French intervention.

Richelieu and his master were now convinced that if France was to have a consistent foreign policy, then she must be secured from a Huguenot stab in the back when she was engaged elsewhere. The Edict of Nantes in 1598 had constituted the Huguenots a state within the State, and in view of their aristocratic affiliations this was highly dangerous. As long as Henry IV was on the throne, willing and able to enforce the Edict, the compromise worked fairly satisfactorily, but when he was dead the chances that it would be permanent diminished daily. The Huguenots, partly in self-defence, and partly in pursuit of political aims, which the Edict had fostered, attempted to form into a semi-independent federation the towns entrusted to them, and thus began to constitute a threat to the unity of the State. Given the prevalence of centrifugal tendencies in the France of the day, it was only a step from this to an alliance with the foreigner to achieve their purpose.

In 1620 the Huguenots had struck out for an independent republic in the South, and it was not until after two years of war that they were subdued. By the Peace of Montpellier, which brought the conflict to a close in 1622, religious toleration was secured to the Huguenots, but they were forbidden to hold political assemblies of any kind whatever. All the fortifications recently raised by them were to be demolished, and La Rochelle and Montauban were for the future to be the only towns in their possession. This was the first step in the direction of abolishing the special privileges which the Huguenots had enjoyed in virtue of the Edict of Nantes, and which had been so abused that their continuance in the original form had become a menace to the unity of France. Richelieu gave it as his opinion that when he took office the Huguenots shared the government of the country with the King, and it was only a question of time when the issue would be finally decided. In the interval the ordinary Frenchman began to harden his heart against this aggressive minority which intrigued with the foreigner and the aristocratic opposition. Not the least important of the many reasons for the collapse of Protestantism in France as a political force was its unpatriotic behaviour in the hour of crisis. What the League had been in the days of Henry III and Henry IV, the Huguenots were in those of Louis XIII.

The Peace of Montpellier proved to be a mere armistice, and in 1625 the Huguenots rose again, and the King and the Cardinal decided that the time had come to eliminate this particular menace once for all. They were confirmed in this resolution by the fact that external war followed so closely upon internal complications, for the Huguenots called upon Charles I of England to assist them. It was true that he had only recently been married to the sister of the King of France, but the English Parliament was as avid of glory as it eventually proved averse to paying for it. Charles at this stage of his career, under the influence of Buckingham, was by no means unwilling to play the part of a Protestant hero, and so in 1627 he came to the assistance of the Huguenots. In spite, however, of the efforts of Buckingham to raise it, the siege of La Rochelle was pressed, and the city, after a most heroic resistance, was finally forced to surrender in 1628. Its municipal privileges were abolished, its fortifications destroyed, and its government was placed in the hands of royal officials. Liberty of conscience was indeed guaranteed to the citizens, but the last vestige of independent authority was abolished.

Once La Rochelle had fallen the conquest of the rest of Huguenot France was comparatively easy. Louis commanded his army in person, and marched through Languedoc and the district of the Cevennes, capturing towns and destroying castles. The Peace of Alais in 1629 brought the struggle to its conclusion, and henceforth the Huguenots had no political power. Their guaranteed towns were handed over to the Government, their fortresses were razed to the ground, their organization was destroyed, and their right of meeting was taken away, but their liberty of worship remained unimpaired.

Richelieu was a statesman above all else, and having secured national unity, he cared nothing about national uniformity. By the Peace of Alais he transformed the Huguenots from a formidable political party into a harmless religious sect, and they repaid his tolerant attitude by becoming loyal subjects of the Crown. During all the disturbances of the Froude they never stirred a finger, and Louis XIV would have done well to reflect on this before he committed the one really first-class blunder of his reign.

The year 1629 was also marked by the termination of the war with England. Charles had no desire to pursue a struggle which merely increased his dependence upon Parliament, and Buckingham, who had become so determined a Gallophobe, was dead. Richelieu, on his side, had nothing to gain by a prolongation of hostilities, for his interests were becoming centred in Italy and the Thirty Years' War, so in April peace was made between Britain and France at Susa. No territories, it may be added, had to be returned, for none had been conquered.

Peace with England had not been concluded before Richelieu was once more involved in Italian affairs, this time in connection with the Mantuan succession.

Vincenzo of Gonzaga, who had succeeded two of his brothers as Duke of Mantua and Marquis of Montferrat, died without issue in December, 1627. His nearest male heir was Charles of Gonzaga, Duke of Nevers and a French subject, who was actually governor of Champagne; but although female succession was excluded in Mantua, it was lawful in Montferrat, and so, to prevent a division of his territories, the late duke had married his niece, Mary, to the Duke of Rethel, the son of Nevers. In January, 1628, the Duke of Nevers took possession of his inheritance, to which his legal claim was unquestionable, but Philip IV and Olivares took a different view. They had no desire to see France securing a foothold in Italy once again, and with their encouragement a number of claimants to the heritage of the dead Vincenzo made their appearance, among others the Duke of Guastalla, who put forward the ingenious argument that the Nevers family had forfeited its rights by having borne arms against the Emperor. At this point Ferdinand II, urged on by his Spanish relative, asserted his right as suzerain to adjudicate upon the matter, and in the meantime ordered the territory in dispute to be handed over to his representative.

The new Duke of Mantua, trusting in French support, refused to obey the order, which the Spaniards then proceeded to enforce, for they regarded Montferrat as one of the outer defences of the

Milanese. Philip secured the support of Charles Emmanuel of Savoy by territorial concessions at the expense of Mantua, which the Spaniards and Savoyards then over-ran. This exercise by the Emperor of obsolete and doubtful rights, together with the victories of Wallenstein in Germany, alarmed the Italian princes, and the Pope, Urban VIII, together with the Republic of Saint Mark, invited Louis XIII to intervene. Both the King and his minister were only too willing to do this, and in January, 1629, a large French army crossed the Alps. So successful was its progress that within two months the Duke of Savoy had been compelled to sign the Treaty of Susa. By its terms he promised to give the French passage through his dominions, and also to provide supplies for the relief of Casale, which was besieged by the Spanish forces: as security for the fulfilment of this undertaking, Susa was to be left in French occupation.

Thereafter the fortunes of war varied. Richelieu discovered that the last embers of the Huguenot revolt took more time to extinguish than he had anticipated, and French power in Italy was the weaker in consequence; on the other hand, the overthrow of Christian IV had left the Emperor with a number of troops to spare, and he used them to further his pretensions in the Italian peninsula. Before long, however, the landing of Gustavus Adolphus redressed the balance, and Ferdinand had urgent need of his soldiers' services much nearer home.

The question of the Mantuan succession was finally settled at Cherasco in 1631. The Duke of Nevers received the Imperial investiture of the two duchies, but France compelled him to sell the greater part of Montferrat to the new Duke of Savoy, Victor Amadeus I. This represented compensation for French occupation of Pinerol, which Richelieu was particularly anxious to retain owing to its strategical position in relation to the Alpine passes. This settlement was from every point of view advantageous to France, and it foreshadowed the policy of Louis XIV, namely the domination of Italy, not by direct conquest, as in the days of the Valois, but by control of the Italian princes, of which the establishment of a Frenchman in Mantua was the beginning. The acquisition, too, of Pinerol represented a weakening of the Habsburg chain which ringed France.

It was, indeed, time that Richelieu should have his hands free in view of the recent course of the Thirty Years' War. With the arrival of Swedes it had ceased to be a civil, and had become an international, conflict, where the latest theories in politics and strategy were put to the test at the expense of the unhappy Germans. The most recent foreign participants were the Spaniards, for Philip IV and Olivares were determined to take advantage of the death of Gustavus, for the re-establishment of the Imperial power in Germany would perpetuate the encirclement of France, which was the basis of Spanish policy, and also prove a standing menace to the Dutch. Accordingly, Philip's brother, the Infante Don Fernando, the governor of the Spanish Netherlands, was sent to the aid of the Emperor with eighteen thousand of the incomparable Spanish infantry. The stroke was brilliantly successful, for at Nördlingen in September, 1634, the Swedes and the German Protestants were routed, leaving eight thousand dead on the field, and four thousand prisoners in the hands of the enemy. The battle of Nördlingen was one of the decisive engagements of the Thirty Years' War, for just as Breitenfeld had rendered impossible the conquest of North Germany by the Emperor and the success of the Edict of Restitution, so did Nördlingen put an end to Protestant hopes of the control of South Germany.

This defeat was a serious blow to Richelieu, but the Spanish success rendered it more imperative than ever that France should break the bonds which imprisoned her. Hitherto, she had not taken a direct part in the Thirty Years' War, but had acted through the Swedes and the German Protestants. Nördlingen made it essential that she should intervene directly, or see the Habsburg hegemony in Europe more firmly established than ever. Thus, in May, 1635, the Cardinal declared war against both Spain and the Emperor, and he encouraged the Dutch to attack Don Fernando in the rear.

The entry of France into the conflict did not at first arrest the course of Imperialist successes, for the French armies in the reign of Louis XIII were not what they were to become in that of his son. Flanders, Germany, and Northern Italy were the scenes of the fighting, and in these three theatres hostilities dragged on with varying fortunes, though on the whole the Spaniards had the best of it. In 1636 Philip's armies threatened Paris itself, and two years later Lombardy was completely cleared of the French, who had occupied it, while successive efforts on the part of the latter to invade Spain were unsuccessful. It was not until 1638 that the tide began to turn, for it was then that Bernard of Saxe-Weimar, rather in his own despite, conquered Alsace for France. Within twelve months he himself died, most opportunely from the point of view of Richelieu, leaving both his conquests and his army in the possession of the French. This constituted a serious threat to the land-route from Italy to the Spanish Netherlands.

In the following year a more deadly blow befell the House of Austria, for the line of communications by sea, which had been menaced ever since the defeat of the Armada, was finally cut. A large Spanish fleet had succeeded in reaching the Channel, but off Gravelines it met the Dutch under Tromp, and was signally worsted in the fight that ensued. The Spaniards thereupon sought shelter in English territorial waters. Richelieu had more than one old score to pay off against Charles I, so he told Tromp to take no notice of English neutrality. Nothing loth, the Dutch admiral sailed against the Spanish fleet, and almost completely destroyed it, for barely ten ships succeeded in reaching Dunkirk.

By this time Richelieu was nearing the end of his life, but the last two years of it were to crown his policy with success, for in 1640 the dominions of Philip IV began to disintegrate under the strain to which they were subject. There had been signs of impending trouble nine years before, when Biscay had risen in revolt against what the inhabitants of that province held to be a violation of their privileges by the proposed creation of a salt monopoly, but this was as nothing compared with the rebellions in Catalonia and Portugal. For years there had been trouble between the Catalans and Madrid over financial matters, as well as over the billeting of Spanish troops, and it was this latter grievance that precipitated the outbreak. The Castillian and foreign soldiers were in arrears with their pay, and they proceeded to live on the country in the same manner as they did in Italy and the Low Countries. The Catalan peasants retaliated, and the disorders spread to Barcelona, where, in June, 1640, a rising took place in which the Viceroy was killed.

The insurgents at once realized that they could not stand alone, and they invoked the aid of France. Richelieu was not the man to neglect so favourable an opportunity for striking an effective blow at the Habsburgs, and he gave the Catalans the choice of establishing a republic under French protection, or of recognizing Louis XIII as Count of Barcelona in place of Philip IV. It was the second alternative that was finally adopted. The Spaniards did everything in their power to nip the rebellion in the bud, but, after reaching Barcelona in triumph, they were routed at the battle of

Montjuich in January, 1641. French troops thereupon poured into Catalonia, and by the end of 1642 the outlying provinces of Cerdagne and Roussillon had been lost to Philip, in spite of the gallant defence of Perpignan by its Spanish garrison. Thereafter the fortunes of war began to vary, and in the sieges which form the inevitable concomitant of campaigning in the Peninsula the French were not always successful, for the Duc d'Enghien, soon to be known as "The Great Condé", failed to take Lérida. The Catalans, too, soon came to the conclusion that they did not really like the French any better than the Castillians, and when France was distracted by the Fronde, the King of Spain was enabled to regain most of what he had lost. All the same, the Catalan revolt had proved that Spain was as vulnerable on land as the English and Dutch had already shown her to be on sea.

The same moral was pointed by the revolt of Portugal, which had now formed part of the Spanish Empire for sixty years, though the old jealousy between the Spaniards and the Portuguese had in no way diminished as the result of their allegiance to a common crown. On the conquest of the country Philip II had done his best to conciliate his new subjects, and had kept his word to preserve all their national privileges, to respect their autonomy, and not to burden them with Spanish taxation: official posts were filled entirely by Portuguese, and the nobles of Portugal were always made welcome at the Spanish Court. Philip III followed his father's policy, and almost his last act was to attend a meeting of the Portuguese Cortes. Indeed, had these conciliatory methods continued to be employed, it is possible that the union of the two countries might have endured, but with the accession of Olivares to power all discretion was thrown to the winds.

In the first place, his followers were installed in the more lucrative Portuguese posts, for there were not enough Spanish sinecures to satisfy their greed. Then, again, the wars in which Spain was continually engaged were definitely harmful to the interests of Portugal, which saw her old possessions in America, Africa, and the East harried by enemies with whom she had no sort of quarrel, while at home Cadiz was taking away from Lisbon much of its commerce. This was the moment chosen by Olivares to introduce, in 1636, the Spanish tax of five per cent upon all property, movable and immovable, and a rising was the result. This was suppressed, but instead of taking the warning to heart, Olivares imposed a fresh special tax upon the Portuguese as a punishment, at the same time announcing a plan for abolishing the Portuguese Cortes and bringing the members to sit in the Cortes of Castille, of which kingdom Portugal was in future to be a province.

The strongest claimant to the Portuguese throne was the Duke of Braganza, and his popularity among his fellow-countrymen was great. As the rule of Spain became more unpopular, all eyes were turned towards him, and at the instigation of the Archbishop of Lisbon an organization was formed for the purpose of placing the crown upon his head. The Regent for the King of Spain was Margaret, the widowed Duchess of Mantua, but although she knew that the storm was brewing, she had not the necessary resources at her disposal to do anything, and when the revolution did take place, at the beginning of December, 1640, it was carried through with consummate ease. The conspirators, not above four hundred in number, rushed the palace in Lisbon, and compelled the Regent to surrender the citadel, with the result that the Duke of Braganza, after a three hours' revolt in which he had himself done nothing, found that he was King of Portugal under the title of John IV.

The Spaniards, it may be added, did not lightly or easily relinquish their claims, and although their efforts were unsuccessful, the war dragged on for another twenty-eight years. In the meantime every enemy of Spain could be certain of Portuguese help. Finally, with foreign assistance, the Portuguese in 1665 won the decisive victory of Villaviciosa, and three years afterwards, by the mediation of Charles II of England, there was concluded the Treaty of Lisbon, by which Spain recognized the independence of Portugal and her colonies at the price of the cession of Ceuta.

In the state of the Peninsula at this time separation was highly contagious, and hardly had Portugal thrown off her allegiance to Castille than Andalusia attempted to follow her example. The Duke of Medina Sidonia was not only the greatest landed proprietor in that province, but he was the brother of the new Queen of Portugal. His project was to make himself King of Andalusia with Portuguese help, but he was not a man of much initiative, and he lacked the resolution necessary to carry out his project. The details of the plot leaked out, and Olivares, determined to prevent a repetition of the Portuguese revolution, heavily reinforced the garrison of Cadiz. Medina Sidonia thereupon made his submission, and although his life was spared, he was not allowed to return to Andalusia.

Thus, during the last years of Richelieu's life, fortune at last seemed to be smiling on France, but the Cardinal did not allow his good luck to blind him to the need for eternal vigilance where his neighbours were concerned, as his attitude towards the troubled politics of the British Isles very well proves.

Since peace had been concluded with England in 1629 relations with that country had been upon an outwardly friendly footing. Charles I had commenced his reign with a spirited foreign policy for which his Parliament soon proved most unwilling to pay; thereafter he was condemned to keep the peace with his neighbours, for war meant a Parliament, which was sure to prove highly critical of the existing order in Church and State. Although he had married a French princess, Charles had proved no friend of France, and Richelieu had no more forgotten the English attempt to relieve La Rochelle than he could blind himself to Henrietta Maria's intrigues with her mother and the other opponents of the Cardinal at home. To keep England weak and divided had thus once again become the preoccupation of France, as in the days of Louis XI.

The traditional French method of achieving this was by an understanding with the Scots, who had rarely been averse from invading England when she was giving trouble to France. Since the union of the crowns in the person of James I and VI a generation earlier this policy had become difficult to pursue, but the Scottish opposition to the religious reforms of Charles I and Laud once more brought it into the sphere of practical politics. The extent to which Richelieu deliberately fomented trouble between the Scots and their King is a matter of dispute, but the late Sir Richard Lodge was clearly justified when he said that "French agents and French money had no small part in stirring up that Scotch rebellion which was to prove the undoing of the House of Stuart. And when the expenses and failures of the war forced Charles at last to summon the Long Parliament, Richelieu did not hesitate to establish relations with the opposition party. . . . No doubt the Great Rebellion would have arisen if Richelieu had never lived, but he had some share in moulding the actual events which led to it. It was even reported and believed that when Charles endeavoured to seize the five members, the warning which enabled them to escape came from the French ambassador." In short, the minister who did more than any other man to establish monarchical authority in France dealt it a mortal wound in England. Great statesmen are rarely particular about the political company they keep.

Thus, in 1632 as in 1610 the House of Austria seemed threatened with disaster, but on the later occasion as on the earlier the death of its foremost opponent afforded a respite. On November 4th, 1642, Richelieu died, and it is eloquent of the difficulty of the task which he so successfully accomplished that in that very year he had to deal with the Cinq-Mars conspiracy, which looked to Spain for support. He had indeed left France a great deal stronger than he found her. French armies were encamped on the Rhine and the plain of Piedmont; French governors were established in Alsace and Lorraine; and Roussillon, Cerdagne, and the passes of Savoy were in French hands. It has been well said that when the Cardinal died "he had got his hand upon the throat of his huge antagonist and was choking her."

With the disappearance of the Cardinal from the political scene France relapsed into another of those recurrent periods of weakness and disorder which have been so marked a feature of her history. The situation was further complicated by the death of Louis XIII in the following year, and by the regency of his widow, Anne of Austria, for the four-year-old Louis XIV.

CHAPTER XIV

THE END OF THE THIRTY YEARS' WAR, 1632-1648

THE real issue at stake in the Thirty Years' War, namely the future of Germany, was decided by the battles of Breitenfeld and Nördlingen: the Reich was not to take its place with the nations which had attained unity. More than two centuries were still to elapse before that goal was reached, and the delay was to be fraught with the most calamitous consequences for the whole world. In the meantime, although the war was in fact finished, it was far from being concluded, and its character degenerated with every passing day. The by no means ignoble ideals for which Protestants and Catholics had in many cases taken up arms were forgotten, and henceforth French and Swedes on one side, and Austrians and Spaniards on the other, were occupied in rending the corpse of the moribund Holy Roman Empire. What had been a clash of principle had merged into the quarrel between the Houses of Bourbon and Habsburg, and into the contest there threw themselves all who hoped to share in the spoils.

The degeneration of the war, which had not been remarkable for its humanity from the beginning, was described by the late S. R. Gardiner in a passage that is well worthy of quotation. "On both sides all trace of discipline had vanished in the dealings of the armies with the inhabitants of the countries in which they were quartered. Soldiers treated men and women as none but the vilest of mankind would now treat brute beasts. 'He who had money', says a contemporary, 'was their enemy. He who had none was tortured because he had it not'. Outrages of unspeakable atrocity were committed everywhere. Human beings were driven naked into the streets, their flesh pierced with needles, or cut to the bone with saws. Others were scalded with boiling water, or hunted with fierce dogs. The horrors of a town taken by storm were repeated every day in the open country. Even apart from its excesses, the war itself was terrible enough. When Augsburg was besieged by the Imperialists, after their victory at Nördlingen, it contained an industrious population of seventy thousand souls. After a siege of seven months, ten thousand beings, worn and haggard with famine, remained to open the gates to the conquerors, and the great commercial city of the Fuggers dwindled down into a country town." Gardiner was writing at the close of the nineteenth century, which may serve to explain his horror at behaviour which four decades later would not have been considered in any way abnormal in the conduct of a war.

On the death of Gustavus the supreme direction of Swedish affairs passed into the hands of Oxenstjerna, whose main object it was to carry out the policy of his late King, but he was not a soldier, and in any event he lacked the necessary authority. Before long it became apparent that the man, namely Richelieu, who was paying the piper also intended to call the tune, and not only the Swedes but also "the princes of Southern and Western Germany, whether they wished it or not, were reduced to the position of satellites revolving round the central orb at Paris".

There was one German prince in particular who did not approve of this trend of events, and who was determined to dissociate himself from it, and that was the Elector of Saxony. He had joined Gustavus only with great reluctance and under considerable provocation, and since the Swedish monarch's death he had been in negotiation with Wallenstein as to the possibility of a settlement which should be acceptable to all parties. With the murder of Wallenstein at the beginning of 1634 these negotiations ceased, and the uneasiness of John George increased. He was a conservative and a patriot, and he had no desire to assist in the dismemberment of the Empire for the benefit of the King of France and the Queen of Sweden.

It is in no way surprising, therefore, that in May, 1635, the Peace of Prague should have been concluded between the Emperor and the Elector of Saxony. The question of the ecclesiastical lands was settled by taking the year 1627 as the test year. Whatever belonged to Protestants at that time was to remain Protestant, and whatever was then Catholic was to continue Catholic. This arrangement secured nearly all the Northern bishoprics to Protestantism, while Lusatia was to be made over to Saxony, and Lutheranism in Silesia was guaranteed by the Emperor. It was also agreed that Lutheranism was still to remain the only privileged form of Protestantism. When the Peace of Prague was signed it was hoped that it would serve as the basis of a general pacification, and quite a number of cities and of the lesser princes so accepted it. The fundamental weakness of the settlement, however, lay in the fact that it provided no security for the Calvinists, and that it made no provision for foreign invasion.

So the struggle continued for another thirteen years, while the French secured Alsace, and the Swedes established themselves in Western Pomerania. Nevertheless, the desire for peace, at any rate within the Reich itself, gained ground as the old protagonists passed away. The Emperor died in 1637, to be succeeded by his son, Ferdinand III, and three years later he was followed to the grave by George William of Brandenburg, who was succeeded by Frederick William, one day to be known as the Great Elector. Weary of the apparently unending conflict, the new Elector of Brandenburg in July, 1642, made a separate treaty with the Swedes, which practically withdrew his electorate from the war, and in August, 1645, John George of Saxony followed his example, but on far worse terms. It was not, however, until 1648 that a general settlement was reached, and this was in the main due to the alarm of the Emperor at the success of the French arms, and to the pacific counsels of Queen Christina of Sweden.

The Peace of Westphalia was signed on October 24th, 1648, that is to say exactly thirty years after the defenestration of Prague. The religious difficulty in Germany was met by the extension to the Calvinists of all the rights enjoyed by the Lutherans under the religious peace. The first day of the year 1624 was taken as the test day by which the question of the ecclesiastical lands was to be settled. All that was in Catholic hands on that day was to remain Catholic, all that was in Protestant hands was to remain Protestant. Roughly speaking, the line thus laid down was the line which answered to the facts. It preserved the bishoprics of the South, which were avowedly Catholic, to the Catholics; and the secularized lands of the North, such as Bremen and Verden, Halberstadt and Magdeburg, where the Protestants were in a large majority, to Protestantism; and it secured to Catholicism the victories of the Counter-Reformation in the hereditary dominions of the House of Austria, in Bohemia, in Bavaria, and in the Upper Palatinate. Finally, the treaty provided for the equal division of the two interests in the Imperial Court of Justice. The fact was that after thirty years of warfare both parties had been forced to the conclusion that they could not destroy one another, and so toleration was of necessity forced upon them.

BOUNDARY in 1492
BOUNDARY in 1713

NETHERLANDS

DUNKIRK
CALAIS
ARTOIS
LILLE
PICARDY
ARRAS
AMIENS
ST QUENTIN
NOYON · LAON
CLERMONT · SOISSONS
ROUEN · SENLIS · REIMS
CHERBOURG
HARFLEUR
BAYEUX · CAEN
NORMANDY
PARIS
CHAMPAGNE
LORRAINE
LOST 1697
VERDUN · METZ
NANCY
BREST
BRITTANY
1491
RENNES
ALENÇON
MAINE
CHARTRES
TROYES
BASLE
NANTES
LE MANS
ORLEANS
BURGUNDY
ANJOU
ANGERS
DIJON
BESANÇON
POITOU
TOURS
BOURGES
BERRY
AUTUN
CHAROLLES
GENEVA
POITIERS
LA MARCHE
BOURBON
SAVOY
LIMOGES
CLERMONT
LYONS
SAINTES · ANGOULÊME
AUVERGNE
VIENNE
GRENOBLE
PÉRIGUEUX
VALENCE
DAUPHINE
SALUZZO LOST 1601
BORDEAUX
GUIENNE
LE PUY
EMBRUN
GASCON
AGEN
MONTAUBAN
ORANGE
AVIGNON
PROVENCE
BAYONNE
AUCH
TOULOUSE
NIMES · ARLES · AIX
PAU
LANGUEDOC
BEZIERS
SPAIN
NARBONNE
MARSEILLES
ROUSSILLON · PERPIGNAN

FRANCE 1492~1713

ACQUISITIONS of HENRY II 1547~1559   1558   1559
~''~   HENRY IV 1589~1610   1589   1601
~''~   LOUIS XIII 1610~1643   1632   1641   1642
~''~   LOUIS XIV 1643~1715
                            1648 1659 1668 1670 1678 1684 1697 1713

LP

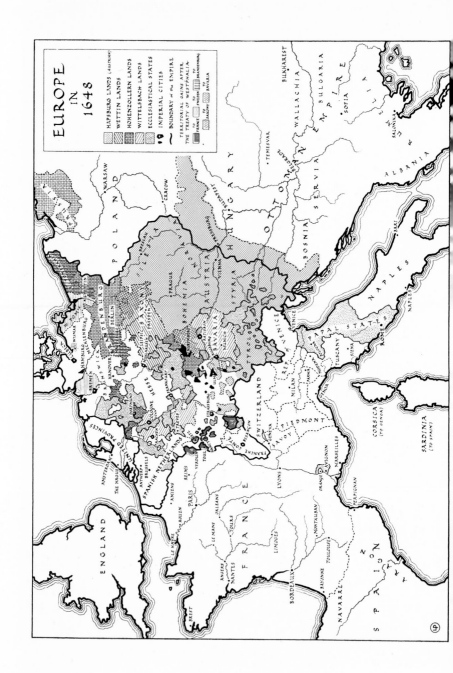

EUROPE
IN
1648

HAPSBURG LANDS (AUSTRIAN)
WETTIN LANDS
HOHENZOLLERN LANDS
WITTELSBACH LANDS
ECCLESIASTICAL STATES
IMPERIAL CITIES
BOUNDARY of the EMPIRE
TERRITORIAL GAINS AFTER
THE TREATY OF WESTPHALIA.
TO FRANCE
TO SWEDEN
TO SAXONY
TO BRANDENBURG
TO BAVARIA

The territorial arrangements were as follows:—

1. Maximilian of Bavaria retained the electorate, which was made hereditary in his family, and the Upper Palatinate was added to his dominions.

2. A new electorate was created for Charles Louis, the eldest son of Frederick V, and the Lower Palatinate was restored to him.

3. Sweden received Western Pomerania, including the mouth of the Oder, and the bishoprics of Bremen and Verden, which gave her not only a commanding strategic and commercial position on the German river system, but also the right of being represented in the German Diet.

4. Brandenburg was compensated for the loss of Western Pomerania by the acquisition of the bishoprics of Halberstadt, Camin, Minden, and the greater part of Magdeburg; she was also confirmed in her possession of Eastern Pomerania. In addition, she now finally obtained control over the duchies of Cleves, Mark, and Ravensberg, which had been ceded to her by the Treaty of Xanten, but which during the war had been in Spanish or Dutch hands.

5. France obtained possession of Austrian Alsace, including Breisach, and the right to garrison Philipsburg, but the free city of Strasbourg was expressly reserved to the Empire. The three bishoprics of Metz, Toul, and Verdun, which had been in French hands since the Treaty of Cateau Cambrésis, were formally annexed, and the French occupation of Pinerol was recognized.

6. Saxony retained Lusatia, and acquired a part of the bishopric of Magdeburg.

Earlier in that same year, 1648, the Treaty of Münster had been concluded between Spain and the United Provinces, by which the independence of the latter was recognized by Philip IV. This settlement was incorporated in the Peace of Westphalia.

It is no exaggeration to say that with the Treaties of Utrecht, Vienna, and Versailles the Peace of Westphalia is one of the great landmarks of modern history. Henceforth the Habsburgs turned to the East, and when, a generation later, the Ottoman Empire began to decay, they embarked upon the congenial task of obtaining compensation on the Danube for what they were losing upon the Rhine. This meant the acquisition of vast territories inhabited

L

by people of very mixed races, and when, in the fullness of time, nationalism was added to the other problems of Europe, the end of the Habsburgs was at hand: meanwhile the leadership of the Reich upon which they had turned their backs passed into the hands of the Hohenzollerns. In the interval there was a period during which Germany, exhausted by the Thirty Years' War, was leaderless, and at the mercy of her neighbour to the West. That period lasted during the life of Louis XIV (and for many years afterwards), and these circumstances contributed not a little to the greatness of France.

Outside the frontiers of the Reich the Peace of Westphalia marked a definite stage in the history of the Papacy and of Sweden. The Pope refused to sanction the settlement, but his protests were ignored by Catholics and Protestants alike, and from that time his direct influence in international affairs may be said to have ceased. On the other hand, for Sweden the Peace of Westphalia was the high-water mark of her prestige in Europe. She was recognized as a Great Power; her supremacy in the Baltic was admitted; and the domination of North Germany was placed within her grasp. The task, however, was to prove beyond her capacity, and she slowly declined before the advancing power of Brandenburg and Russia, until, with the lapse of two more generations, it had become abundantly clear that the Peace did not mark the permanent inclusion of Sweden among the leading Powers of Europe.

The great merit of the Westphalia settlement was that it recognized facts. Thirty years of war had proved that Germany could not be unified either on a Catholic or a Protestant basis; the Empire was becoming increasingly more Austrian; the princes were achieving territorial independence; and France and Sweden were taking an active interest in the affairs of Central Europe. These were incontrovertible facts, and allowance was duly made for them. That was the great merit of the settlement and the reason for its endurance.

CHAPTER XV

THE EARLY YEARS OF LOUIS XIV, 1643-1665

Although the deaths of Louis XIII and his great minister were to usher in a period of renewed weakness, in which Spain was enabled to make one last effort to retrieve her position, there was at first no sign of any such development, and the momentum given by the dead cardinal carried the French armies to victory. In the North the year of his death had been by no means auspicious, for Don Francisco de Mello, a Portuguese nobleman faithful to Spain, had captured Lens, and inflicted a crushing defeat upon the French at Honnecourt. Emboldened by these successes, the Spaniards in the following year, after a feint on Picardy, entered Champagne through the Ardennes, and laid siege to Rocroi. At this place a few days after Louis XIV ascended the throne in May, 1643, was won the first, and by no means the least important, of the great victories which were to mark his reign.

Condé determined to attack the besiegers, in spite of the fact that the bulk of them consisted of the veteran Spanish infantry which was still acknowledged to be without a rival in the world. The French won the day by the adoption of new tactics. The solid mass of pikemen, which constituted the military strength of Spain, wedged together in close formation, could resist all cavalry attack by their stubborn endurance, and by sheer weight could bear down all opposition. If, however, the mass became once disorganized, it could never re-form. Gustavus had shown at Breitenfeld how it could be broken by artillery, and Condé applied the lesson at Rocroi. He alternated his squadrons of cavalry with musketeers, and used the one or the other against the Spanish phalanx as the situation demanded. Time after time the Spaniards drove the French back, but at last their formation broke, and they were slaughtered where they stood. In itself Rocroi may not have been of the first strategic importance, and the Spanish menace to France was by no means at an end, but the battle was prophetic of what lay ahead: never again were the armies of Spain to go into action with that feeling of superiority which had been theirs for a hundred and fifty years, and which all Europe had freely recognized.

The immediate effect of Rocroi was the French penetration of the Low Countries. Condé lost no time in entering Hainault, and he pushed his scouts almost as far as Brussels. He then turned to the East and captured Thionville, but his further progress was stopped for the moment by a victory of the Spaniards and the Imperialists over the French at Tuttlinghen, which threatened to open the Alsace frontier to invasion. Nevertheless, the succeeding years saw the loss to Spain of a great part of Western Flanders, and of Dunkirk, while in 1648 Condé won another resounding victory at Lens. In Northern Italy, too, the Spaniards lost ground, and were driven out of Mantua, Tuscany, and the islands of Porto Lanzone and Piombino.

It was not, however, only in the North of Italy that Spain was sustaining reverses, for in Naples there took place one of the most famous insurrections in history, namely that led by Masaniello. This revolt had been preceded by several earlier disturbances, for Philip III was hardly seated upon his father's throne when, in 1600, the peasants of Calabria rose at the bidding of a mystic called Campanella, but the movement was suppressed. In 1621 there were riots in Naples itself owing to the rise in the cost of living, but these, too, were put down. By 1646 the cost of Spanish participation in the Thirty Years' War made it necessary to impose fresh taxation upon Naples, and the Viceroy put a gabelle upon fruit, the staple article of Neapolitan diet.

This provoked an explosion in the following year, and Masaniello, a fishmonger, became the symbol, rather than the leader, of the agitation which followed. The Viceroy had but few troops at his disposal, and, being himself of a timid nature, he conceded all the demands of the insurgents. The consequence of this was mob-law both in town and country, and in the anarchy Masaniello, whose arrogance had become insufferable, was murdered. At this point a Spanish fleet arrived and bombarded Naples, but this, far from inducing the insurgents to surrender, drove them to abandon the last pretence of loyalty to Spain. With Condé winning victories in the Low Countries, and with Portugal and Catalonia in revolt, Philip IV was in no position to coerce Naples, and he must have lost that kingdom had the Neapolitans not been so fickle, or had they received adequate support from France. Henry, Duke of Guise, did come to Naples, where he passed as the heir of the Angevins, and at first he met with an enthusiastic reception. The new master of France, Cardinal Mazarin, was unable to give him

any serious assistance owing to the Fronde, and Guise soon quar-
relled with the Neapolitans, who wanted him to be a kind of Stadtholder on the Dutch pattern, while he was determined to be King.

In these circumstances all who had anything to lose saw that
the only hope of restoring order lay in the re-establishment of
Spanish rule, and the revolt soon afterwards collapsed. The
Spaniards returned without conditions, and when the new Viceroy
reduced the gabelles, the Neapolitans allowed him to hang the
leading rebels without protest. The Duke of Guise, it only remains
to add, made another attempt in 1654, but he received no support
on this occasion, and for the remainder of the reign of Philip IV,
as well as during the whole of that of his son, the history of Naples
was uneventful.

The Peace of Westphalia did not terminate the struggle between France and Spain, although it brought to an end the war
between France and the Empire. At one time, however, there was
a distinct possibility that both branches of the House of Austria
might be included in the general pacification, for Mazarin was
desirous of exchanging Roussillon and Catalonia, which were in
French hands, for the Spanish Netherlands and the Franche
Comté. This proposal was unacceptable to Spain, but it had much
to do with the conclusion of the Treaty of Münster: it alarmed the
Dutch in respect of French ambitions in the Low Countries, and
as the years passed they began to incline towards their ancient
Spanish enemies away from their old French friends.

From 1648 to 1653 France was distracted by the Fronde, and,
even though it was for the last time, the Spaniards fought back with
no inconsiderable success. They took advantage of the opportunity
to recover Catalonia and much of the ground they had lost in the
Netherlands, while when Condé turned against his own country
Philip was enabled to place one of the best generals of the day at
the head of his troops. In 1653 Condé invaded France, and once
more the Spaniards threatened Paris, but the capital was saved by
the admirable strategy of Turenne. Slowly but surely the French
recaptured the Spanish conquests, yet as late as 1656 Condé inflicted a severe reverse on Turenne, who was besieging Valenciennes. It was an uphill struggle, although Spain was in full decline, and when Mazarin found that he could not get the terms he
wanted he began to look round for allies. He had not long to wait
before he secured an English alliance.

In spite of the close relationship between Louis and the Stuarts, the republican régime in Britain had been recognized by France as soon as its stability seemed to be assured, and Mazarin himself would appear to have come to the conclusion that the monarchy would never be restored. As for Cromwell, he had some difficulty in making up his mind between the two Continental Powers, and before he threw in his lot with France a body of New England colonists had in 1654 actually invaded the French possession of Acadia. His motives in concluding an alliance with France in spite of this event were various. The English republican ambassador in Madrid had been murdered by the supporters of the Stuarts: there were complaints of the maltreatment of English subjects by the Inquisition; and there was the desire to compel Spain to open her American possessions to English trade. The attitude adopted by Cromwell is sufficient evidence that he looked at Europe with the eyes of an Elizabethan, and saw in Spain only the champion of the Inquisition and the Counter-Reformation that she had been in his youth. He did not realize that while he was battling with the Cavaliers at home the world had changed. Rocroi had marked the end of Spanish military supremacy, while the Peace of Westphalia had ushered in a period in which religion was to count for progressively less, and politics and economics for progressively more.

It is true that England was to play a bigger part in international affairs than at any time since the reign of Henry V. Her fleets were victorious in the North Sea, the Mediterranean, and the Caribbean; her army won the admiration of Europe on the battlefields of Flanders; and her diplomacy was successful where it had never made itself felt before. Yet the foreign policy of the Commonwealth was a failure. The Lord Salisbury who was Prime Minister once wrote that "the commonest error in politics is sticking to the carcases of dead policies", and it was an error of which Cromwell was certainly guilty. As one of the leading modern authorities on the period, Miss James, has written, "the foreign policy of the Commonwealth and Protectorate was spirited, but, from an economic point of view, disastrous. It was the attempt of a half-starved man to dominate his neighbours when he ought to have been filling his stomach."

It is, however, perhaps unjust to blame Cromwell overmuch for his mistake. The France of the Fronde did not look like the future mistress of Europe: Spanish weakness was not fully revealed until the death of Philip IV; and it was not easy for contemporaries to realize that the frontier between Rome and Reform had already been fixed where it was to remain, with but slight modification, for the next three centuries. Nevertheless, whether the Lord Protector's blunder was venial or not, there can be little doubt that the economic crisis which followed was the principal cause of the return of Charles II to the throne of his ancestors.

In the year before Condé defeated Turenne at Valenciennes, namely in October, 1655, a treaty of peace and friendship was signed between Great Britain and France. By this the two Powers undertook not to assist each other's rebels, and they agreed to name arbitrators who should assess the damages due to subjects of either state for losses as shipowners or merchants; these arbitrators, who were never in fact appointed, were also to decide whether the forts in Acadia taken by the English ought to be restored to the French. There were other articles of a commercial nature, and by a secret clause the future Charles II and his brother, the Duke of York, as well as seventeen of their leading supporters, were excluded from France. The policy which inspired this treaty recalls that of Henry VII, and the object was the same as that which the first Tudor so often had in view in his negotiations with Continental Powers, namely to deprive his opponents at home of effective assistance abroad.

Two years later, in March, 1657, matters were carried a stage farther, for the apparent stability of the republican régime in England encouraged Mazarin to convert the treaty of peace and friendship into a definite alliance, and the advisability of such a step had been impressed upon him by Condé's victory. By the terms of this latest agreement the two Powers decided to join in an attack on Gravelines, Dunkirk, and Mardyke by sea and land; France was to contribute twenty thousand men and England six thousand, who were to be paid by the French Government; and that when taken Gravelines should belong to France, and Mardyke and Dunkirk to England, but if Gravelines were taken first, then the English were to hold it as security for Dunkirk. The English troops, it may be noted, were to act with the French, but they were to have their own commander, while in any towns which they might capture the free exercise of the Roman Catholic religion was to be permitted.

The terms of this alliance well illustrate the need which either party had, or thought it had, of the other's support, for both gave away something to which they had hitherto strenuously adhered, for the English assisted in a French conquest of the Low Countries, while the French showed themselves ready to plant the English flag once more on the eastern shore of the Channel.

The appearance of England on the side of France soon proved to have rendered the cause of Spain hopeless: Turenne won the battle of the Dunes in June, 1658, and then captured Dunkirk, which was handed over to England in accordance with the terms of the treaty. In Italy, too, Philip's armies were being worsted by the combined forces of France, Savoy, and Modena. Such being the case, it is in no way remarkable that negotiations should have been set on foot for the conclusion of the long war between France and Spain.

These were conducted directly between Mazarin and the Conde de Haro, and they took place on the Isle of Pheasants, which was in the middle of the Bidassoa, and was not considered to belong to either Power. On this island was built a pavilion, which had two doors, one for the French and one for the Spaniards: in the middle of the room there were two tables and two chairs, for the Cardinal and Haro respectively, and they were so arranged that the two statesmen could carry on their business without either of them being obliged to leave his own country. As a rule they negotiated alone, but sometimes Lionne accompanied Mazarin and Haro brought Don Carlos Colonna. The other diplomats seem to have had very little to do save entertain one another, which they appear to have done with great content, and under the influence of these festivities the animosities of years were soon forgotten.

Mazarin and Haro not unwisely took their time, and they had twenty-five meetings between August 13th and November 12th, 1659. When the Treaty of the Pyrenees, for so it was termed, was concluded, it proved to be one of the most satisfactory ever made on behalf of France. Spain surrendered Roussillon and Cerdagne, and also all Artois except St. Omer and Aire. Gravelines, Bourbourg, St. Venant, the Sluys, Landrecies, Quesnoy, Thionville, Montmédy, Damvilliers, Irovy, Marienbourg, Philippeville, Rocroi, Chatelet, and Limchamp remained in the hands of the French, while Dunkirk was ceded to the English republic. The fortresses in Burgundy were returned to Spain, as well as several towns in Flanders, and France renounced all claim to Catalonia. In face of considerable opposition on the part of the Cardinal, the Spanish representative insisted that Louis should not only pardon

Condé, but also fully reinstate him. Finally, the French King was to marry the Infanta Maria Teresa, who was to waive her right of succession to the Spanish throne on condition of receiving a dowry of five hundred thousand crowns. This last stipulation was, it is said, suggested by Lionne, who knew that Philip could not find the money, and that thus the question of the succession would remain open.

The Treaty of the Pyrenees undoubtedly strengthened France, but it did not enable her to break the circle of Spanish possessions by which she had been surrounded ever since the days of Charles V. The peace was, in effect, little more than an expression of the lassitude of the two countries which had been at war for so long. Spain came to terms because Philip IV, though not old, was an invalid. France was glad of the opportunity to profit by an advantageous military situation that might change, and also because, in the event of the King of Spain dying without male heirs, she wished to make in peace the necessary preparations to grasp the Spanish heritage. Thus the Treaty of the Pyrenees did not mark finality. The governors of the Catholic King continued to command in Lille and Besançon, while his viceroys held the Two Sicilies and the Milanese, and could, in case of need, effect a junction with the Emperor. In short, France still possessed no guarantee of security except the financial impoverishment and military weakness of the government at Madrid.

A few months after the conclusion of the Treaty of the Pyrenees, namely in May, 1660, the British monarchy was restored, and this event took Continental statesmen by surprise. Mazarin had certainly done nothing to recommend himself or France to Charles II. With that cynical realism which marked the whole of his foreign policy, as it had marked that of his predecessor, Richelieu, he had made his alliance with Cromwell, and forced the male Stuarts to leave French territory; nor did his attitude change with the fall of the Protectorate. In December, 1659, he was approached by Charles with the suggestion that the exile should marry his niece, Hortense Mancini, but the Cardinal would have none of it. Engrossed in the negotiations relative to the Treaty of the Pyrenees, he had not studied the course of events in England, and he adhered to his belief that the monarchy would never be restored. It must be admitted that there was something to be said for this point of view, for Charles himself was by no means optimistic, and he went to Fuenterrabia while the Franco-Spanish treaty negotiations were in progress in what proved to be the vain hope of persuading one or both of the Powers to do something for him. Within six months he was back at Whitehall without the assistance of either.

Subsequent events were to prove that the sudden collapse of a régime which appeared so stable as the English republic left an ineradicable impression upon Louis XIV. When, in 1688, the Stuarts were forced to take the road of exile once more, he felt that in due course history would repeat itself, and that after an interval there would be another restoration. This explains, in part at any rate, his attitude towards James II and his son. The first restoration had taken France by surprise, and she had got nothing out of it: Louis was determined that this should not happen again. At the same time it would be a mistake to leave out of account his natural magnanimity, which was fully exhibited in his dealings with the unfortunate Royal Family of England.

No sooner was Charles II back on his throne than Mazarin endeavoured to repair his blunder. Hortense was offered to the restored King together with a dowry of twenty million livres, but Clarendon, the English Chancellor, disapproved of the match on political grounds, and advised his master that it would be inconsistent with his dignity to marry a woman who had been refused to him in the days of his exile; the offer was accordingly declined.

This was one of Mazarin's last diplomatic acts, for at the beginning of March, 1661, he died. To the end he displayed that personal vanity which was so marked a feature of his career. A week before his death he had himself shaved, his mustachios trimmed, and his cheeks rouged, to give the illusion of perfect health. He then entered his chair and made a tour of the gardens, in spite of the cold February wind, to the great astonishment of the courtiers; the effort, however, was too much for him, and he had to be carried back to his apartments. Soon after his death the president of the ecclesiastical assembly waited upon the King to enquire to whom he was in future to address himself on questions of public business: Louis replied, "To myself".

In view of the influence which he was to exercise upon European diplomacy for the next fifty years, the character of Louis XIV is worth more than a passing reference. Lord Acton described him as "by far the ablest man who was born in modern times on the steps of a throne", and he went on to say: "He was laborious, and devoted nine hours a day to public business. He had an excellent memory and immense fertility of resource. Few men knew how to pursue such complex political calculations, or to see so many moves ahead. He was patient and constant and unwearied, and there is a persistent unity in his policy, founded, not on likes and dislikes, but on the unvarying facts in the political stage of Europe. Every European state was included in his system, and had its part in the game. His management of each was so dexterous that diplomacy often made war superfluous, and sometimes made it successful."

On the other hand, Louis was very susceptible to flattery, and he became increasingly so with the passage of the years, until the disasters of the War of the Spanish Succession brought him back to reality. He was inclined to take it for granted that the success of ministers and generals was due to his own inspiration, and the logical consequence of this was the employment towards the end of his reign of second-rate men both in the council-chamber and in the field; after all, if the King was the motive power in the State, then the capacity of his instruments mattered little. This line of reasoning was to cost France dear. Like so many men who are successful, Louis came to believe that things would always be as he wanted them to be, and he was proportionately the more astonished when he found that this was not the case. He was none too well educated in many departments of knowledge, and he sometimes joked about his own ignorance: indeed, the circumstances of his youth, passed amid the anarchy of the Fronde, would in any case have prevented him from receiving a good education in the academic sense. Yet he was avid of information. "My intention is," he wrote in 1663, "to be informed of all that is best and exquisite in all countries and in all branches of knowledge, and to make the best of such information for my honour, and service and glory."

One charge in particular has been brought against Louis XIV by historians of all shades of opinion, and it is that he plunged his country into a series of unnecessary and expensive wars from the very moment that he assumed the reins of power. It must be admitted that, like Napoleon I, he did not know where to stop, although his original efforts to break the Habsburg ring, by which France was hemmed in, were wholly justifiable. There must, in this connection, also be taken into account the attitude of the French people, which was bellicose and aggressive in the extreme. No ruler, however absolute, can neglect a determined public opinion, and that of France in the seventeenth century was very different from what it was to be in the middle of the twentieth. There is no indication that any of the wars in which Louis engaged, save possibly the War of the Spanish Succession in its later stages, was unpopular with his subjects, who were at least as desirous of martial glory as their ruler. In addition to being the embodiment of the French State, the King was a typical Frenchman of the period, and he shared to the full in the likes and dislikes of the vast majority of his fellow-countrymen.

To sum up, in the words of a contemporary, Lord Bolingbroke, Louis "had acquired habits of secrecy and method in business, of reserve, discretion, decency, and dignity in behaviour. If he was not the greatest King, he was the best actor of majesty, that ever filled a throne. He by no means wanted that courage which is commonly called bravery, though the want of it was imputed to him in the midst of his greatest triumphs; nor that other courage, less ostentatious and more rarely found, calm, steady, persevering resolution: which seems to arise less from the temper of the body, and is therefore called courage of the mind. He had them both most certainly, and I could produce unquestionable anecdotes in proof. He was, in one word, much superior to any prince with whom he had to do, when he began to govern."

Such was the monarch who took control of France from the dead Cardinal Mazarin, and at the first full meeting of the Council after that statesman's death the King announced that he would have "other principles . . . in foreign policy from those of the late cardinal". Events in London and Rome were soon to show that this was no idle boast.

It was at that time customary to give an ambassador a solemn reception upon taking up his post. He made what was called his "entry," and the other ambassadors went to meet him in their coaches, and then escorted him to his house. At the end of September, 1661, a new Swedish ambassador arrived in London, and during his "entry" there was a fight for precedence between the household of the Conde de Watteville, the representative of Philip IV, and that of the Comte d'Estrades, who represented Louis XIV. The Spaniards had the best of the struggle, during which several people were killed. According to Pepys, "all the City did rejoice" at this result, for "we do naturally all love the Spanish, and hate the French".

Louis took a very serious view of the incident, not least on account of the damage to his prestige in English eyes. He at once gave instructions for the Spanish ambassador in France to be given his passport, and for the French ambassador in Madrid to be recalled: he also demanded from Philip an apology proportionate to the offence, as well as an undertaking that in future French ambassadors were to enjoy precedence in all the Courts in Europe. After some negotiations Louis gained his points in full, and on March 24th, 1662, the Spanish ambassador, in a formal audience at the Louvre, in the presence of his fellow-diplomats, announced that Philip had conceded all the French King's demands. It is to be noted that it was only then that Louis officially informed his father-in-law of the birth of the Dauphin, which had taken place in the previous November. Louis had further instructed d'Estrades to secure the punishment of those Londoners who had assisted de Watteville, but, not for the last time, he found that Charles II was unamenable to such pressure.

In Rome the French King's determination to assert his rights was no less pronounced. The French ambassador to the Holy See, the Duke of Créqui, had made himself very unpopular, and, in revenge for what the Romans considered his intolerable pride, the Corsican guards of the Pope, egged on, it was said, by the reigning Pontiff's brother, made an attack upon the Duchess of Créqui one day, as she was returning to her palace. In the uproar which ensued a page was killed, and many servants were wounded; thereupon the French ambassador, in real or assumed fear for his life, left Rome. At first Alexander VII seemed resolved to hold his ground, but Louis proceeded to extreme measures. He seized Avignon, and began assembling an army with the avowed intention of occupying Rome itself. The Pope then gave way, but, even so, it was some time before the French King was mollified, and the terms which he dictated were sufficiently severe. He compelled Alexander to banish his brother, to disband his Corsican guards, and to erect a monument in Rome as a permanent memorial of his own disgrace. The lesson was not lost upon the rulers of the other Italian states.

While Louis was utilizing these incidents in London and Rome to impress upon Europe the fact that France had supplanted Spain as its leading Power, he was also studying the international situation very closely indeed. The Treaty of the Pyrenees had improved the position of France, but she was still surrounded by the Habsburg dominions, and Louis was determined to break that ring.

The situation required extremely careful handling, because it was essential at this stage not to rouse English or Dutch suspicions, while there was also the prospect that at any moment the branch of the Habsburgs reigning in Madrid might die out, and France must be ready to avail herself of the opportunity to secure the whole or part of the inheritance. The question of the Spanish succession, in one form or another, dominated the reign of Louis from the Treaty of the Pyrenees to that of Utrecht.

Once peace had been signed in 1659, Philip not unnaturally thought that he would be free to turn his attention to his Portuguese rebels, who had now been in arms against him for nearly twenty years, but this was not at all the idea of his son-in-law. Louis sent money to the Portuguese through Charles II, who was on the point of marrying Catherine of Braganza, though there were times when he was worried whether these subsidies were being applied to the purpose for which he intended them. This financial aid, together with the more material assistance secretly given in the shape of Schomberg and a number of French officers officially described as "volunteers", greatly contributed to the Portuguese victory at Villaviciosa, by which the independence of the country was finally re-established. Of course Philip knew what was happening, and he protested against this infringement of the Treaty of the Pyrenees, but he got no satisfaction. The real irony of the situation lay in the fact that forty years later Portugal, to secure whose independence from Spain the French monarch had displayed so much duplicity, took the field against him and his Spanish allies.

At the other end of the Mediterranean the new order in France also made itself felt. As will be shown on a later page, the Ottoman Empire was experiencing a revival, destined to be its last, under the inspiration of the Kiuprili family, and the Sultan had been tempted to treat the French ambassador with contumely. A few years before his predecessor had caused another French ambassador to be thrown into a dungeon and flogged, but times had changed, as the Porte was soon to realize. Louis sent the Duke of Beaufort, Grand Admiral of France, to the assistance of the Venetians, who were defending Crete against the Turks, and this nobleman found his grave in the island, while troops were also dispatched to aid the Imperial armies in Hungary. Under the command of Montecuculi the French contingent largely contributed to the great victory at St. Gothard in 1664, a battle which,

like that of Rocroi twenty-one years earlier, marked the passing of
a military hegemony owing to the superiority of the French. The
Osmanli, like the Spaniards on the earlier occasion, fought with
obstinate valour, but their tactics were out-of-date, and in Eastern,
as in Western, Europe men were forced to admit that France was
supreme in arms.

These were not the only successes that Louis won during the
years immediately following the death of Mazarin, for in 1662 he
bought Dunkirk from the English, thus strengthening the North-
Western frontier of France. Charles II proved, as always, a hard
bargainer, and it required a month's negotiations before the English came down from twelve, and the French rose from two, to five
million livres as the price of the town. It was finally agreed that
two millions should be paid in cash, and the rest in eight bills
spread over the next two years. This transaction aroused much ill-
feeling in England, though in actual fact Dunkirk was quite use-
less, and its retention would have been only too likely to embroil
Charles in the by no means unlikely event of another Franco-
Spanish war.

There was one other nation which never ceased to play an important part in the French King's calculations, and that was the
United Provinces. The intimate connection between France and
the Dutch during the reign of Henry IV has already been shown,
as has the strain put upon this alliance by the decline of Spain.
The controlling influence in the government of the United Provinces was at this time exercised by John de Witt, the Grand
Pensionary of Holland, and his attitude towards France has been
well summed up in the phrase *Gallum amicum sed non vicinum*. He
wished, in effect, to keep the Spanish Netherlands in some form
between his country and the dominions of Louis, and the recollec-
tion of Mazarin's project of acquiring them in exchange for Cerdagne and Roussillon did nothing to allay his suspicion of French
ambitions.

In spite of the old alliance, the Dutch were not popular in
Paris. Louis had no particular regard for them, and of his ministers, Lionne disliked them on political, and Colbert on commercial,
grounds. There were also outstanding difficulties about fishing-
rights, tonnage duties, and certain Dutch territorial claims. In
addition was the fact that one nation was Catholic and the other
Protestant. The wars of religion were over, it is true, but the
groundswell had not yet subsided, and religious differences were

always liable to cause trouble. Nevertheless, Louis was determined to keep on good terms with the Dutch as long as possible, and in 1662, by the Treaty of Paris, he concluded an offensive and defensive alliance with them. De Witt himself placed no reliance on French goodwill, but the treaty served the purpose of Louis, for it lulled the Grand Pensionary's colleagues into a false sense of security.

Such were the relations of France with her neighbours when, on September 17th, 1665, Philip IV died, leaving as his heir his son, Charles II, a half-witted boy of four.

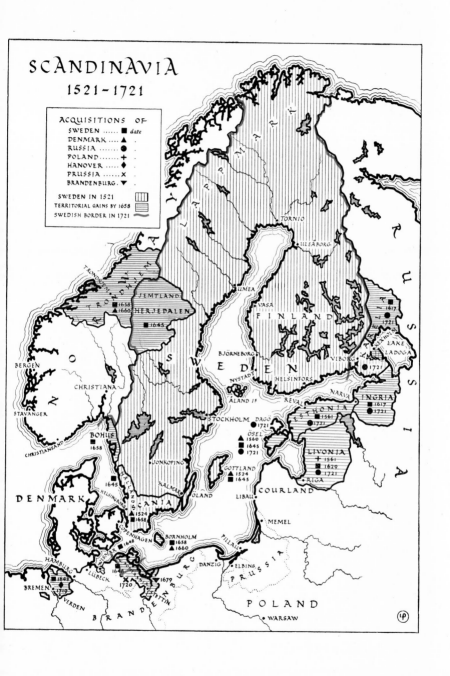

SCANDINAVIA
1521~1721

ACQUISITIONS OF
SWEDEN ...... ■ date
DENMARK .... ▲ .
RUSSIA ...... ● .
POLAND ...... + .
HANOVER ..... ◆ .
PRUSSIA ...... ✕ .
BRANDENBURG. ▼ .

SWEDEN IN 1521
TERRITORIAL GAINS BY 1658
SWEDISH BORDER IN 1721

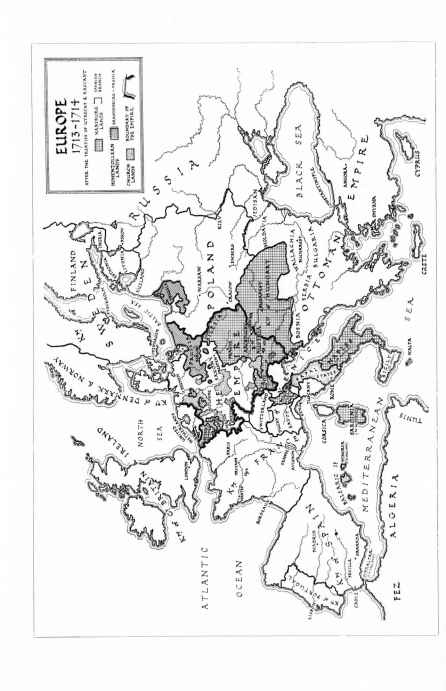

CHAPTER XVI

LOUIS XIV AND THE UNITED PROVINCES,
1665–1678

As soon as his father-in-law was dead Louis proceeded to turn the event to his own advantage, for he had long realized that it might be utilized to further his schemes for the rectification of the French frontiers. He therefore set up, on behalf of his wife, a claim to the Spanish Netherlands. He alleged that by the *Jus Devolutionis*, a local custom, Maria Teresa, as the only daughter of Philip IV by his first marriage, was the heiress of the Low Countries to the exclusion of the new King of Spain and his sister, who were the offspring of a second marriage. Louis also cited in his favour the precedent of the elder daughter of Philip II, the wife of the Archduke Albert, who had succeeded to Flanders upon her father's death.

Plausible as this argument sounded, more especially when it was supported by Lionne's able diplomacy, it could not in reality be sustained. The custom by which if a man married twice the succession went to the children of the first wife to the exclusion of those by a second, referred only to private property, and was, even so, not widely extended, for it was limited to Brabant, Malines, Namur, Hainault, and perhaps one other province. In Luxembourg, according to the custom which then obtained, two parts would have gone to Charles II, and one part to each of his sisters. In the Franche Comté the practice was gavelkind, that is to say upon intestacy the deceased's real estate was divided equally among his sons, or among brothers or other collateral heirs on failure of direct or nearer heirs. In these circumstances, even if it be admitted that Louis was justified in appealing to a local and private custom as holding good in his case, he was only entitled to take advantage of it in a few provinces, and not in the Low Countries as a whole.

There was a further argument against the French claim, and it was that Maria Teresa had renounced her rights at the time of her marriage; though to this it was replied that as her dowry had never been paid the renunciation was not binding. All these contentions, however, were mere quibbles, and if Louis was justified

M

in invading the Spanish Netherlands, it was not on legal grounds, but because it was imperative to break the Habsburg ring which still imprisoned France. Paris was constantly threatened from the North, and Louis was determined to put an end to that menace.

The moment was extremely favourable for putting these designs into execution. The hands of the Dutch were tied by the Treaty of Paris, while the Emperor was more apprehensive of the Sultan than of the French King. In March, 1667, Louis came to an agreement with Portugal by which the latter agreed to continue the war against Spain. As for England, whose interest in the Low Countries was traditional, she had been at war with the United Provinces since March, 1665, and France herself had recently become involved in the conflict; most unwillingly, it may be added, for it suited Louis admirably to have the English and Dutch wearing out one another's strength without his intervention.

Circumstances, however, had proved too strong for him. The British Government was determined to press the war by land as well as by sea, but since it had no troops of its own it hired those of the Bishop of Münster, who was content to receive payment by instalments. Christian Bernard von Galen was a prelate of unsavoury reputation, and although he was the son of a murderer who had died in prison, he had managed to become a canon of Münster. One night he gave a party at which all the other canons got so drunk that he had little difficulty in persuading them to elect him as their bishop. Innocent X not unnaturally refused to confirm the election, but his successor, Alexander VII, was less particular. Accordingly this unsaintly prelate raised thirty thousand men, and without encountering much opposition broke through Overyssel and Drenthe into Groningen with a view to co-operating with his English allies on the coast. This invasion enabled the Dutch to claim French help against aggression under the terms of the Treaty of Paris, so Louis sent six thousand troops, and he gave orders to the admiral in the Mediterranean to bring the Toulon squadron into the Atlantic for the campaign of 1666. In January of that year he declared war on England.

All this put the French King in an exceedingly strong position. The Dutch stood every chance of being crushed between the English and the Bishop of Münster without the aid of France, while Charles II could not win a decisive victory now that the United Provinces had the support of the French. Louis could prolong the Anglo-Dutch war, or bring it to an end, as might best suit his schemes for the annexation of the Spanish Netherlands. Mr. Hartmann has well said: "Louis XIV was not very keen on pursuing an active war against England. His object was to help the Dutch as little as he safely could, without being accused of trying to evade his engagements towards them, and at the same time to make war against Charles in such a manner that he would not alienate him permanently and drive him into a friendship with Spain". He admitted quite frankly afterwards that he had only declared war on Charles on paper. The English King, whose capital had been recently wasted by pestilence and fire, had neither the means nor the desire to engage in active hostilities against France, and so in March, 1667, he made the first of his secret treaties with Louis: by this he agreed not to oppose a French invasion of the Spanish Netherlands on the understanding that the French fleet did not help the Dutch. Diplomacy had now paved the way for force, and at the end of May the armies of Louis crossed the frontier. The War of Devolution had begun.

The successful progress of the French campaign in the Spanish Netherlands was uninterrupted. Lille held out for a month, and capitulated when the garrison had been reduced by a third. Hardly had the town fallen than a relieving force appeared, only, however, to be severely defeated. The other Spanish towns for the most part put up no greater resistance, partly on account of the weakness of their garrisons, but partly because of the skill of Vauban, whose methods of investing a fortress showed a great advance on those previously employed. The end of the summer of 1667 thus saw an important part of the Spanish Netherlands in the hands of Louis, and the rest clearly at his mercy. The winter was to produce even more surprises.

It was not only to the North that the frontier of France was unsatisfactory, for, as has already been mentioned, so long as the Spaniards were in possession of the Franche Comté there was always the possibility that they might bring troops from Italy to the Low Countries, or create a diversion in the East of France. Louis determined to utilize the present opportunity to free himself from this threat. Turenne had been in charge of the campaign in Flanders, for which he was well suited, but for a sudden blow Condé was clearly the general to put in command. No precaution was neglected which could ensure the secrecy of the operation, and that is doubtless why it was arranged for the winter, a season during which in those days military operations were suspended. Condé demanded fourteen thousand men, but Louis placed eighteen thousand at his disposal, and it was announced that some of them were to go to the Catalan frontier, and others to the Rhine. Even ordinary letters were sent to the wrong destinations so that no news should leak out regarding the French intentions.

On February 4th, 1668, Condé crossed the frontier, and so well had he made his plans that within a fortnight the lilies of France floated over the Franche Comté. Louis had himself played his part in these operations. During the month of January he danced in a masquerade, and gave the impression that he had no thought of anything save his own enjoyment. Two days before Condé moved the King left Paris, and in five days covered the hundred and fifty miles to Dijon, in spite of the badness of the roads and the time of year. There he received the submissions of Rochefort, Besançon, and Salins, while on February 13th he was present at the surrender of Dôle, the capital of the province. A week later Louis returned to Paris, leaving Condé in charge of his new conquest.

Much of this, however, is to anticipate, for in spite of the skill of Lionne the progress of the French arms had been so rapid as to alarm the whole of Western Europe, and there can be little doubt that the conquest of the Franche Comté was hurriedly undertaken in case the international situation should in the near future render it impossible. Before Lille had fallen the Anglo-Dutch war came to an end, for de Witt had soon realized that the immediate danger to the United Provinces was not from England but from France, while the hostile tariffs imposed by Colbert in 1667 had rallied public opinion to the side of the Grand Pensionary. As for the King of England, he was by no means unwilling to have his hands free, "for Charles had learnt that wars were expensive, and henceforward he regarded continental commitments solely in the light of whether they could be made to pay. Europe to him was a meadow-land of milch cows. His urgent need for money at home made it needful for him from time to time to visit such pastures." From this attitude he never departed, and during his reign England was not engaged in any major conflict of other than a maritime nature.

Louis never trusted his English cousin, whom he once accused of "drawing back with one hand what he tendered with the other", while of one proposal of Charles he said that it "would tie the King (*i.e.* himself) indissolubly to the interests of the King of Great Britain, but not His Britannic Majesty to the interests of the King".

Charles knew quite well that the English forces could not save the Spanish Netherlands from the French, but he was determined at all costs to prevent the naval power of France from becoming unduly strong in the Narrow Seas. So it came about that neither monarch ever placed any real reliance upon the other, in spite of the pacts, agreements, and secret treaties they made between them. The consequence was that Louis fell back on the policy of Richelieu thirty years before, and egged on the Puritans and Whigs to attack the English throne, while Charles never missed an opportunity of showing the King of France what a nuisance he could be unless he was properly treated. In this connection, too, account must be taken of the unpopularity of the French in England, as shown during the fight between the suites of d'Estrades and de Watteville. During the earlier years of his reign Charles was none too safe on the throne, and he had to keep a watchful eye on the prejudices of his subjects.

The opening months of 1668, therefore, witnessed some complicated manœuvring for position, in which war and diplomacy were intermingled. Before he launched Condé on the conquest of the Franche Comté, the French King had assured himself of the neutrality of the Emperor, who might otherwise have realized that his true interest lay in opposing the establishment of a French hegemony in Western Europe. The bait with which Louis caught Leopold I was a Treaty of Partition of the Spanish Empire. By this it was agreed that on the death of Charles II of Spain the Emperor was to have Spain, the Americas, the Milanese, and the *presidi*, while Louis acquired the Two Sicilies, the Spanish Netherlands, the Franche Comté, Spanish Navarre, the Philippines, and the Spanish possessions in Africa. This agreement was signed on January 19th, 1668, so that when Condé entered the Franche Comté no Imperialists took the field against him, and the Habsburg at Madrid in vain invoked the aid of the Habsburg at Vienna.

Hardly had Louis gained the Emperor than the Spanish Government, alarmed at the progress of the French arms, used the good offices of the King of England to conclude the Treaty of Lisbon with Portugal on the basis of the recognition of that country's independence. This was a severe blow, for only a few months before a revolution had taken place in Portugal which seemed to bring her definitely and permanently into the French orbit. It had its origin not so much in politics as in the dislike felt by the Queen, Isabella of Nemours, for her husband, Alfonso VI.

The King of Portugal, moreover, had a brother, Pedro, whom the Queen much preferred, and the arrival of a French squadron in the Tagus ensured the triumph of love and the interests of France, for Isabella and her brother-in-law had promised to get rid of Castel Melhor, the Anglophil minister of Alfonso VI. At first all went well; Pedro got himself made Regent, and Castel Melhor was dismissed; but a reaction soon set in, with the result that when Spain recognized her independence Portugal was lost to France in spite of the many infractions of the Treaty of the Pyrenees on her behalf.

There was, however, a worse blow still in store for Louis and Lionne, for Sweden ranged herself with England and the United Provinces. Since the death of Gustavus the diplomacy of France had been a little too prone to take it for granted that Stockholm must always follow the lead of Paris; in consequence the Swedes, like the King of England, were by no means averse from proving to Louis that they had a distinct nuisance value. At this period Sweden was governed by a council of regency, for the King, Charles XI, was a minor. The most prominent member of this body, Magnus Gabriel de la Gardie, was Francophil, but his policy was vacillating, while he and his colleagues did not pay sufficient attention to the armed forces of the country. In effect, Sweden was passing through a period of weakness, and foreign Powers were interfering in her internal affairs. For the moment the Dutch were able to carry the day against the French.

In this way there came into being, during the first four months of 1668, the Triple Alliance of England, Sweden, and the United Provinces. In the previous November the King of England had authorized Arlington to send Sir William Temple, at that time his representative at Brussels, to The Hague to open negotiations for a treaty, and so expeditiously did he get to work that by the end of January a convention had been signed. It consisted of three separate agreements. By the first of these Great Britain and the United Provinces concluded a defensive alliance, and specified what aid each was to furnish to the other in case of attack. By the second they agreed to call upon the belligerents to make peace on one or other of two alternatives with which Louis had declared in the previous year he could be satisfied, that is to say the retention either of his then existing conquests or of the Franche Comté. By the third, which was to be kept secret but of which Charles informed Louis, they agreed that if France refused these terms they

would co-operate to bring her back to the limits of the Treaty of
the Pyrenees. Sweden immediately associated herself with this
convention, though the Francophil party at Stockholm managed
to delay its formal ratification for a few weeks.

It is difficult to say whether the proposals of the Triple Alliance
aroused more resentment in Spain or in France. The Spaniards,
having come to terms with the Portuguese, flattered themselves
that they were now in a position to recover what they had lost,
and they saw no reason why they should be forced by a coalition
of neutrals to make such substantial concessions to so manifest an
aggressor. The advisers of Louis were divided as to the best course
to pursue. Turenne, Condé, and Louvois were for accepting the
challenge of the Triple Alliance and opinion in Paris was decidedly
warlike: Colbert and Lionne, on the other hand, urged that the
King should take what was offered to him. Louis at this stage of
his career knew when he had gone far enough, and he decided in
favour of peace. He was not prepared to stake everything on the
chance of success in a war against a coalition of Powers which was
certain to grow larger with the passage of time. Moreover, an
opportune show of moderation would do much to disarm the suspicion he had aroused, and, in any case, he had the agreement
with the Emperor in his pocket.

On May 29th, 1668, the Treaty of Aix-la-Chapelle was signed
between France and Spain. By it Louis restored the Franche
Comté, having dismantled the fortresses, and received Charleroi,
Binch, Ath, Douai, Tournai, Oudenarde, Lille, Armentières,
Courtrai, Bergues, and Furnes, with their districts. He never
seems to have hesitated between these towns and the Franche
Comté, and rightly so. The Franche Comté was clearly his whenever he chose to take it, while the boundary towns might not prove
so easy of capture on a second occasion, and their possession pushed
the Northern frontier farther from Paris. The Spaniards made no
objection, once they realized that some sacrifice on their part was
inevitable, for the farther Louis went in the Netherlands the
sooner he would come into conflict with the Dutch. It is an interesting commentary upon the changed position of Spain that
within a hundred years of the time when Philip II was endeavouring to suppress the Dutch, his successor upon the Spanish throne
had come to place upon those same Dutch his only hope of retaining some portion of his possessions in the Low Countries.

Although the Treaty of Aix-la-Chapelle settled nothing, and

soon proved to be little more than a truce, yet it marked the beginning of a new, and the end of an old, system of alliances. The War of Devolution revealed the weakness of Spain for all the world to see, and even the most conservative realized that there was no point in treating Charles the Bewitched as if he were Philip the Prudent. The Dutch drew away from their old French allies, and England showed unmistakably the direction in which she would move if her interests were seriously menaced. Furthermore, the mere formation of the Triple Alliance, temporary as was that coalition of Powers, was evidence of what would happen if Louis went too far. Even the attitude of the Emperor was prophetic of what was to come, for his abandonment of the old *rôle* of German champion against France, chiefly owing to his commitments in Eastern Europe, was to bring ruin on future generations of Habsburgs. Much that was latent in the settlements of Westphalia and the Pyrenees was patent in the Treaty of Aix-la-Chapelle.

Louis himself had no doubts regarding the true significance of what had taken place. His progress had been checked by a coalition formed by the Dutch. The task before him, therefore, was to break up that coalition so that he might have his hands free to deal with the Power that was now the principal enemy of France, namely the United Provinces. England could be won over—temporarily—at a price, though Charles was neither to hold nor to bind for long, and the nobles who composed the Swedish council of regency were venal in the extreme. Spain was too weak to prove of much assistance to the Dutch, while the Emperor could be relied upon to remain neutral, partly on account of the treaty, which Louis had made with him, and partly because of the Turkish activity on his Eastern marches. The isolation of the United Provinces from all potential allies was thus the immediate, and apparently by no means insuperable, task before French diplomacy: once that had been accomplished the French military machine could be safely left to do the rest, or so it seemed to Louis and his advisers.

The determination of the French King to overthrow the Dutch power has been attributed to various causes, but it is most probable that his motives were mixed. He was determined to obtain possession of the Spanish Netherlands, and recent events had clearly shown that this could only be done in spite of the Dutch; therefore the way to Brussels lay through Amsterdam and The Hague. Commercially, too, the French and Dutch were rivals,

and it has already been shown how Colbert's tariffs had exacer-
bated the relations between the two countries. Personal factors
also cannot be left out of account. Louis did not become any
more tolerant of criticism as he grew older, and the Dutch Press,
although in its infancy, was remarkably outspoken. Such cartoons
as that which represented the sun, the chosen emblem of the French
King, being eclipsed by a large Dutch cheese were hardly
calculated to promote better feeling.

On the other hand, it is doubtful whether religion played so
large a part as has sometimes been maintained. Louis was no bigot
until he came under the influence of Madame de Maintenon, and
that time was not yet. Indeed, where religion was concerned it is
not easy to determine his position at any given date, and in the
late sixties of the century he was still midway between the essentially political attitude of Richelieu and Mazarin, and the intolerance which came to characterize him as the husband of Scarron's
widow. In effect, Louis at the beginning of the Dutch War was
still far from the state of mind in which he revoked the Edict of
Nantes.

The first step in the isolation of the Dutch was to detach England from the Triple Alliance. The action of Charles II in concluding this alliance had at once surprised and irritated Louis, but
the French King was too experienced a statesman not to have a
wholesome respect for his English cousin for what he had done.
Charles always represented the Triple Alliance, not as deliberately
directed against France, but as a disinterested effort to preserve the
peace of Europe. Louis now took the English monarch at his word,
and adopted the standpoint that the Triple Alliance having served
its ostensible object there was no longer any justification for its
existence. The negotiations between Paris and London which then
ensued are described in Chapter XVII, and their upshot was the
signature of the Treaty of Dover on May 22nd–June 1st, 1670, by
which Louis secured the promise of English help against the
Dutch.

Nearly two years were yet to run before war began, and they
were marked by intense diplomatic activity on the part of Louis.
Lionne died, to be replaced at the Ministry of Foreign Affairs by
Arnauld de Pomponne, before the Swedes were detached from the
Dutch. This might have proved even more difficult had it not
been for the parsimony of the United Provinces, whose statesmen
had already earned in politics the reputation which a century and

a half later George Canning was to ascribe to them in commerce. Finally, Sweden was won over by a large sum of money down, and an annual subsidy together with a promise that Denmark was not to be included in the alliance. In return the council of regency pledged their country to hold the North German states in check, and to send an army into Pomerania. On this basis the Treaty of Stockholm was signed in April, 1672, a month before the attack on the Dutch began.

Germany, as usual, was a house divided against itself, and Louis had taken early steps to impress its princes and people with the armed might of France. Hardly was the ink dry upon the Treaty of Dover, which secured the French left flank, than Louis proceeded to strengthen his position by the occupation of Lorraine. The pretext which he put forward was that the Duke of that country, Charles IV, in defiance of the treaties which bound him to France, was conducting a Francophobe policy. No one came to his aid, and Créqui occupied his duchy without encountering any opposition worth the name. The unfortunate Duke retired to Cologne, but French diplomacy made his withdrawal from that city advisable, and he finally settled at Frankfurt to await the turn of fortune's tide. It never did turn so far as he was concerned, and he died in exile five years later. The effect of this blow on the other side of the Rhine was soon seen. Bavaria began that friendship with France which was to last intermittently until the return of Napoleon from Moscow; the Emperor signed a treaty of neutrality so long as Louis did not attack Spain; and the smaller states followed the Imperial example. Only Brandenburg showed any disposition to stand by the Dutch, with whom her Elector proceeded to conclude a defensive treaty.

Of all French statesmen, not excluding Napoleon himself, Louis displayed the greatest skill in his policy towards Germany. He fully realized that the old Germanic constitution was in decay, but he saw that the interests of France demanded that he should seek to profit by the fact, rather than create a fresh order on the other side of the Rhine. He sought to influence rather than to command, and to play upon the jealousies of the different states in order to keep the Reich disunited. It is, indeed, difficult to disagree with Mr. C. T. Atkinson when he says ,"If in his dealings with Germany Napoleon reached a pinnacle of power beyond that to which Louis XIV ever attained, it must nevertheless be admitted that the Bourbon shows to greater advantage in his dealings with Germany than does the Corsican", and the distinguished historian goes on to point out that Napoleon was "bent on a purely personal aggrandizement, consistent with neither the interests, the welfare, nor the ambitions of his French subjects. The Emperor's reforms removed many of the obstacles to German unity, while his oppressions and aggressions in the long run brought the Germans together in opposition to him." There was little to choose between Louis and himself in the importance they attached to their position, but the one was a Frenchman and the other an Italian, so it is perhaps hardly surprising that the King should have a greater knowledge of, and devotion to, the real interests of France than the Emperor. However this may be, it was not the Bourbons, but the two Napoleons, who complicated the European situation for France by assisting the creation of united Germany and united Italy.

A foreign policy without armed force to support it is bound to be ineffective, and concurrent with the diplomacy of Louis, Lionne, and Pomponne in the preparation of the war against the United Provinces was the work of Louvois and Vauban in the military sphere. Louvois worked unsparingly at the perfection of the military machine, and, with the exception of von Roon, there are few war ministers in history who are entitled to equality with him. Unfortunately, but not unnaturally, he became increasingly desirous of using the instrument he had created, and with this end in view he played upon the King's inborn love of glory. Colbert opposed him, but his position was weakened by the fact that France as a whole was avid of military success, and looked to the King to provide it. Vauban made his name a household word whenever the art of war was studied, and he was one of the greatest military engineers of all time. During his life he is said to have conducted fifty-three sieges, to have built thirty-three fortresses, and to have repaired three hundred. Yet he always regarded war as a means to an end, namely peace, rather than as an end in itself. He was also very careful of the lives of his men, and at the siege of Cambrai in 1672 he told Louis, "I would prefer to save Your Majesty a hundred men than to kill three thousand of the enemy".

At the beginning of 1672 the first rumblings of the storm became audible. The Dutch protested to Louis against his military preparations, which the French King in reply declared had been undertaken "to protect our subjects from the aggression which threatened them". Charles II of England was the first to declare war, which he did on March 17th, and Louis followed him on April 6th.

In its earlier stages the campaign was simply a triumphal march for the French troops, commanded as they were by Condé and Turenne, the two greatest generals of the age. Louis took the field in person, and the French marched down the Sambre and Meuse past Liége and Maestricht; the Rhine was crossed, and within a few weeks Louis was within striking distance of Amsterdam, the capture of which would end the war. A rapid victory was, moreover, essential, for notwithstanding the skill of the French diplomacy, it was clear that Europe would not indefinitely regard without protest the invasion of Dutch provinces by Louis. In spite of all this and of the remonstrances of Condé, the King drew back; he sent Turenne towards Rotterdam, and himself proceeded to besiege the petty forts on the Yssel. It is difficult to account for this fatal decision, for which in the first instance Louvois seems to have been responsible. It is true that a revolution was brewing in the United Provinces, and Louis may well have thought that his enemy was incapable of further resistance. However this may have been, the Dutch put a speedy end to such extravagant hopes by cutting their dykes, and before June was over Amsterdam had been saved by this means. Such a step took Louvois by surprise, although a similar procedure had been adopted when Leyden was besieged by the Spaniards a hundred years before, so that it surely might have been anticipated.

All the same, in spite of the inundations and of a naval victory over the English and French, the Dutch felt far from confident of victory, and they accordingly made proposals to Louis for peace. The United Provinces offered to cede Maestricht and the Rhine towns, as well as to pay a very considerable indemnity. When Louis refused to discuss these terms, the Dutch increased their offer: in exchange for the places which the French had taken in the provinces of Utrecht, Overijssel, and Guelderland they should have not only Maestricht and the towns on the Rhine, but also those held by the Dutch outside the seven provinces which originally rose against Spain, such as Breda, Bois-le-Duc, and Berzen-op-Zoom. They were also prepared substantially to increase the indemnity. Pomponne urged his master to accept, and had it not been for Louvois this advice might well have been taken, for the King's original intention had been to rest content with a moderate peace.

The terms offered by the Dutch would have given Louis everything for which he had gone to war. The United Provinces themselves would have been weakened, and the Spanish Netherlands, deprived of all hope of Dutch assistance, would have been at the mercy of the French King whenever he chose to take them. Unhappily, Louis on this occasion did not display the timely moderation which had marked his conduct four years before, and, influenced by Louvois, he made additional demands upon his opponents. The frontier of the United Provinces was to be withdrawn to the Waal, while all the fortified towns on that river were either to be dismantled or occupied by the French, while Defzijl was to be ceded to England. All legislation unfavourable to French commerce was to be revoked, and a treaty of commerce was to be concluded regulating the interests of the East and West India Companies of France and the United Provinces. Among the other stipulations was one to the effect that the indemnity was to be increased, and every year a deputation was to come to France to present Louis with a gold medal, on which was to be an inscription thanking him for having left to the United Provinces the independence which the Kings, his predecessors, had enabled her to acquire.

Such conditions were impossible of acceptance, and the States-General broke off the negotiations. Louvois and his master had committed a blunder of the first magnitude owing to their obsession that the Dutch were so reduced as to be ready to agree to anything.

Not the least important result of the intransigent attitude adopted by Louis towards the Dutch was a revolution in the United Provinces which substituted for de Witt as Grand Pensionary the young nephew of Charles II, that is to say William of Orange, as Stadtholder. In this way the two rivals, William and Louis, came face to face, and for nearly thirty years their enmity was to prove the most important factor in European politics. The Dutchman was not an attractive personality, but he was an admirable judge of character; indeed, few statesmen in the course of history have seen more closely into other men's motives than he did, and he played with those by whom he was surrounded as if they were pieces upon a chess-board. Calculating as Bismarck, unscrupulous as Walpole, and as pitiless as Napoleon, he became the incarnation of the opposition to France, which threatened the land of his birth.

The failure of Louis to conquer the Dutch, and his refusal to come to terms with them had the effect both of prolonging the war and of extending its scope. The other Powers became alarmed, though it must be admitted that the measures which they adopted were not very effective. In the summer of 1672 the Emperor made an alliance with Frederick William of Brandenburg, and three months later he made one with the United Provinces. Before, however, these agreements could achieve anything, Turenne, in June, 1673, forced Frederick William to make a separate peace. There was even an attempt at a general pacification, but it came to nothing, and the Emperor proceeded to form a new coalition. In the autumn of 1673 this was joined by Spain and the exiled Duke of Lorraine; in the next year by Denmark, the Elector Palatine, and some of the lesser German potentates; and, finally, by the Great Elector, who thus entered the war for the second time. In 1674 the English Parliament forced Charles to make peace with the Dutch, and with the spirit of '41 once more influencing public opinion in the British Isles, it was clear that Louis could not expect much support from his cousin at Whitehall.

In such circumstances it was for French arms to repair the blunders of French diplomacy, and for a time even the military situation looked none too good, since at the beginning of 1674 of all the Dutch conquests only two towns of any importance still remained in French hands. The position was, nevertheless, restored before long. The Franche Comté was again conquered, though after a more determined resistance than on the earlier occasion; Condé checked William of Orange at Seneff; and Turenne displayed the brilliance which justified Napoleon's high opinion of his generalship. The Great Elector was routed at Colmar, and the left bank of the Rhine was clear. After this the fortunes of war varied, though on the whole they favoured the French, in spite of the defeat of their Swedish allies by Frederick William. There was even an extension of the conflict to Sicily, which rose against Spain, and Louis sent some troops to the island, where, however, they did very little. By 1678 all the Powers were ready for peace.

Louis, not for the last time, showed himself greater in adversity than in success, and when, largely owing to his own fault, the Dutch war had disappointed his expectations by becoming an international struggle, he restored the situation by some very brilliant diplomacy indeed. France was becoming weary of the contest, and in some provinces the discontent was taking ominous forms. "Still, however, the superiority of the French soldier showed itself in battle, and both the Dutch and the Imperialists became as tired of fighting battles which they never won, as the French were of winning victories which they could not utilize." From England, in particular, there were dangers threatening Louis, but there was also the possibility of rapping Charles over the knuckles for his equivocal behaviour. So far France had spent a great deal of money on the King of England without getting anything like value in return. This was not a line of conduct that appealed to Louis, and he was by no means sorry for the opportunity of proving that he could be an unpleasant enemy.

The peace between England and the United Provinces had been followed by the marriage, in 1677, of William of Orange and Mary, the elder daughter of the Duke of York. English opinion was every day becoming more Gallophobe, and Charles, with the fate of his father before him, had no desire to come into conflict with his subjects. In the meantime he was determined to extract the maximum advantage out of a very delicate situation. While the wedding festivities were in progress, Charles, William, and Danby, the Lord Treasurer, decided on terms which were to be presented to Louis for the termination of the war. By them he was to restore Lorraine, but was to keep the Franche Comté and all his conquests in the Low Countries except Maestricht, which was to be restored to the Dutch, and seven frontier towns, which were to be given back to Spain. Louis, who had been subsidizing Charles to remain neutral even after England had made peace with the United Provinces, returned a polite, but emphatic, refusal, which was exactly what the English King had expected. Charles at once assumed a warlike attitude. He made a formal treaty with the Dutch, by which, as ten years before, agreed terms were to be forced on France and Spain; he ordered thirty ships to be equipped for sea, he prepared to send twelve thousand men to assist the enemies of France on land; and he summoned Parliament with the avowed intention of extracting a considerable sum of money for his compliance with its anti-French sentiments.

It was not at first any too easy for Louis to estimate how far all this was meant, how far it was bluff, and how far it was for the purpose of alleviating his cousin's domestic difficulties. He therefore determined to put Charles to the test by offering him £200,000 for a prorogation or further adjournment of Parliament, and by promising to cede three of the frontier towns to Spain.

When these terms were refused it was obvious that Charles was unable or unwilling to reverse his policy, and Louis at once proceeded to intrigue with the English Opposition, with whom he had already had negotiations. Barillon, the French ambassador, quickly made the necessary arrangements, for the Opposition leaders, loudly as they declared themselves in favour of war with France, had no real desire that the King should be put in possession of the men and money which would make him independent of them, and so the bargain was struck. The red herring of "No Popery" was drawn across the trail of the Royal foreign policy. It was the old game that Richelieu had played against Charles I, and once again it was successful. The carefully exploited divisions of England proved the salvation of France.

Much the same policy was employed in the case of the Dutch. William's repeated defeats had caused the republicans to raise their heads, and Louis played upon their dislike of the Stadtholder, representing to them that he was stronger than ever since his marriage with Mary Stuart. He supported these arguments by a military offensive, and when, in March, 1678, he took Ghent and Ypres, the Dutch were ready for peace. William, who was as careless of the lives of others as he was of his own life, wantonly fought a pitched battle near Mons in the hope of breaking off negotiations, but he was unsuccessful.

Finally, Louis succeeded in coming to terms with his enemies separately, which gave him an advantage he would not have enjoyed had he been compelled to treat with them all together. Accordingly, on August 10th, 1678, he made peace at Nimeguen with the Dutch, on September 17th with Spain, on February 2nd, 1679, with the Emperor, the Empire, and such of the German princes as were at war with him. Sweden and Brandenburg signed their treaty at Saint Germain in 1679, when Louis saw to it that his Swedish ally should lose nothing, and Sweden and Denmark made peace a few months later.

The Treaty of Nimeguen proved how successfully Louis had snatched victory from defeat, though the Dutch displayed remarkable ingenuity in making peace at the expense of their Spanish ally. It is true that Louis restored not only recent conquests such as Ghent, but also some of his gains at Aix-la-Chapelle like Charleroi, Ath, Courtrai, and Oudenarde, yet on the balance the French were the gainers. To them went Cambrai, Bouchain, Valenciennes, Condé, Aire, and Saint Omer, as well as Ypres,

Cassel, Maubeuge, and Charlemont, and the Franche Comté. The differences of Louis with the Emperor were not deep-rooted as yet, though, characteristically enough where Vienna was concerned, the delicate question of the French claims to the Imperial towns in Alsace was left in abeyance.

Louis obtained by the Treaty of Nimeguen all that France had fought for since the Peace of Westphalia. The Pyrenees and the Alps were secure frontiers to the South and South-East; a powerful navy defended the sea-board alike in the Mediterranean, the Atlantic, and the English Channel; the Spanish Netherlands had to no inconsiderable extent been absorbed, and the safety of Paris was assured by the possession of strongly fortified border towns; and now that the Franche Comté was in French hands the Spanish line of communication between the Milanese and the Low Countries had been cut. All that Louis had to do was to wait until the death of Charles II of Spain enabled him to force the division of the Spanish inheritance on his own terms. What he did was to set to work to carry the frontier of France to the Rhine, and in the process he passed the point where defence of French interests became defiance of other nations.

N

CHAPTER XVII

FOREIGN POLICY OF CHARLES II, 1660–1685

I N foreign, as in domestic, affairs the restored monarchy inherited more liabilities than assets from the preceding republican and dictatorial regimes. Oliver Cromwell, as we have seen, had looked upon international affairs with the eyes of an Elizabethan, and had allied his country with the rising power of France rather than, as prudence would have dictated, with the declining force of Spain. Furthermore, he had pursued a foreign policy which had placed an undue strain upon the national resources, with the result that if, at his death, the prestige of Britain in the councils of the world was high, this had been achieved at an excessive price. War had also taken place with the Dutch, and when Charles II was restored to the throne British relations with the United Provinces were among the most urgent of the problems that confronted him.

So long as Spain was the dominant Power in Western Europe a common fear of her ambitions had operated in favour of friendly relations between England and the United Provinces, but when the Spanish danger began to diminish, this friendship soon gave place to the most bitter rivalry. The first object of contention was the mastery of the Spice Islands. By an agreement made in 1619 the trade of these islands was divided between the Dutch and English East India Companies, but before long the Dutch Company, which possessed far greater local resources than the English, determined to expel its rival altogether. In 1621 the Dutch seized Pularoon and one of the Benda group, and two years later some Englishmen charged with conspiring to surprise the castle of Amboyna were arrested; they were then tortured to extract a confession, and were finally put to death. Both James I and Charles I repeatedly demanded redress in vain, but the English were driven from the Spice Islands, where the Dutch henceforth enjoyed a monopoly. The insult rankled, although circumstances made revenge impracticable.

The death in 1650 of William II of Orange, who had married a sister of Charles I, severed the tie between the Dutch and the Stuarts, but in spite of the fact that both the United Provinces and

Britain were henceforth subject to not wholly dissimilar republican regimes, relations between them continued to deteriorate. This was in no small measure due to the passage, in October, 1651, of the Navigation Act, by which no goods might be imported into Britain from Asia, Africa, or America except in an English ship or in a ship belonging to the English plantations and with a crew of which at least one half was English, and no goods could be imported from any European country save in a ship of that country or in an English ship. Such a measure was a direct attack upon the Dutch, in whose hands was the carrying trade of no inconsiderable part of the world.

The Navigation Act, however, was not the only cause of dispute between the two countries. The English still claimed the sovereignty of the seas surrounding Britain, and the Dutch objected equally to dipping their flag to the English and to being allowed only on sufferance to fish in the North Sea. Furthermore, English merchants who alleged that they had suffered wrongs from Dutchmen obtained letters of reprisal which enabled them to prey on Dutch shipping. Finally, the British Government held the doctrine then generally admitted that a neutral flag does not cover enemy goods, while the Dutch maintained that it covered everything except contraband of war. With such points as these at issue, the maintenance of friendly relations between the two Powers became a matter of great difficulty, in spite of the fact that Cromwell himself had no desire to proceed to extremes where a Protestant state was concerned. The crisis came in the summer of 1652, when the Dutch admiral Tromp encountered the English Blake in the Downs, and refused to salute his flag. A fight between the opposing squadrons then took place, with the not unnatural result of an official outbreak of war a few weeks later.

During the ensuing contest the English generally had the best of it for a variety of reasons. The republic had inherited a particularly fine fleet from the monarchy, and it was able to finance the war by confiscating the property of its political opponents. Then, again, the United Provinces was much the more vulnerable of the belligerents. England was an agricultural country, which could feed herself and supply most of her own requirements; she also had a relatively small mercantile marine to protect. The Dutch, on the other hand, enjoyed none of these advantages. The routes followed by their commerce, with the exception of that which led to the Baltic, passed along the English coast, and so lay open to attack from the English ports; thus, instead of waging war on strict principles of naval strategy, the Dutch admirals were compelled to divert much of their strength to the task of convoying large fleets of merchantmen through these dangerous waters. Above all, the Dutch territory was so small, and so large a proportion of the Dutch people lived by trade, that any interference with their command of the sea soon resulted in widespread distress at home.

The war dragged on till April, 1654, when it was terminated by a treaty according to which the Dutch so far acknowledged the English sovereignty of the seas that they promised to strike their flag to English ships, but they were not to be obliged to pay a rent for their North Sea fishery. Those responsible for the Amboyna massacre, who were probably all dead, were to be punished, and commissions chosen equally by both parties were to assess the damages due to the citizens of either for wrongs suffered in the East Indies or elsewhere. The two Powers further concluded a defensive alliance, and undertook not to harbour each other's enemies, but no agreement was reached on the vexed question of what was covered by a neutral flag.

Such was the state of Anglo-Dutch relations when Charles II came to the throne, and in the circumstances it was not difficult for Louis XIV to fan the flame of jealousy between Britain and the United Provinces. Nor was this all, for although both Charles and de Witt were peacefully inclined, English and Dutch were in fierce competition in Asia, Africa, and America, for peace in Europe by no means implied peace in the other continents. In 1664 the Dutch were ejected from their settlements in Guinea as well as from the New Netherlands in America, which was thereupon given the name of New York. War was formally declared in March, 1665, and it soon became, as we have seen, complicated by outside factors. Louis, somewhat unwillingly, was forced to come to the assistance of the Dutch, while such domestic difficulties as the Plague and the Fire of London handicapped Britain. A compromise peace was made at Breda in July, 1667, and by this England acquired New York, New Jersey, and the Delaware at the expense of Surinam and concessions in West Africa.

By this time Anglo-Dutch differences, which were not primarily political, had become merged in the wider issues at stake between the Western Powers, and in this connection the general attitude of Charles II towards foreign policy must be taken into account. In this, as in all matters, he was a realist, and he knew where his country's true interests lay. Britain was a maritime and commercial Power, and her strength lay on the sea, not on the land. So long as she was supreme in her own element it mattered little who was master of the Continent, and in taking this line Charles was anticipating the policy of British statesmen during the latter part of the nineteenth century. At the same time he was by no means above proving to his French cousin that he could not be ignored, all the more because this could be made to produce money which, in its turn, rendered him independent of Parliament. The clue, therefore, to the foreign policy of Charles II is to be found in his determination not to tolerate any threat to British maritime supremacy; for the rest, he would avoid anything that might involve intervention on the mainland of Europe on a large scale, for this would be contrary to the interests, as he saw them, both of his subjects and of himself.

In the light of this it is not difficult to understand why, having concluded peace with the Dutch in 1667, Charles should in the following year have been so largely instrumental in the formation of the Triple Alliance, or why he should have listened to the proposals of Louis after the conclusion of the Treaty of Aix-la-Chapelle.

The individuals chosen by the French monarch to conduct the negotiations which subsequently culminated in the Treaty of Dover were Henrietta, Duchess of Orleans, the sister of Charles, and Colbert de Croissy, the brother of the French statesman. At first progress was slow, for Charles was determined to get as much as he could, and he was not prepared to abandon his commitments under the Triple Alliance without obtaining substantial concessions in return. It was, in particular, clear from the beginning that there was going to be some hard bargaining over commercial and maritime matters. "The thing", declared the King of England, "which is nearest the heart of this nation is trade and all that belongs to it." In addition to other complications, there was that of religion. The attitude of Charles to his Maker is not easy to ascertain; but there can be little doubt that he did desire toleration for all sections of religious opinion in England: equally his sister was most anxious that he should become a Roman Catholic. He did not take this step until he was on his deathbed, but he gave Henrietta the impression that he was willing to do so at once. Louis was by no means unsympathetic, for he saw that it would increase his cousin's dependence upon France, while Charles appreciated the fact that the idea could be made to pay. Thus there came into the negotiations a new element, namely a declaration on the part of the Stuart monarch of conversion and universal toleration, in return for which he was to receive a cash subsidy from France.

The original English demands were impossibly high. Charles insisted that he should make the public declaration of his conversion before entering upon any war with the Dutch, and he asked for a sum of ten million livres in case his subjects rebelled: then he required help in money and men without limit. Furthermore, if Charles was to join Louis in a war against Spain he demanded as compensation nothing less than the whole of the Spanish possessions in the New World. Eager as the French King was for English aid against the United Provinces, particularly at sea, he was not prepared to do business on these terms. He wrote to Colbert de Croissy that he was amazed at the extravagance of the English proposals, and that Henrietta was as astonished as himself. Of course Charles had only put many of these claims forward as bargaining-points, but the minimum which he was prepared to accept appeared for several months so far from the maximum which Louis would grant that an agreement seemed hopeless. The English King was undoubtedly playing for time, since the Dutch were every day becoming more unpopular among his subjects, and this delay would make it easier for him to reconcile them to a reversal of the policy which had led to the Triple Alliance.

In due course Charles became more moderate, but he would not give way about the employment of the English Navy. Louis and Colbert thought that their own fleet could deal with the Dutch provided that it had the assistance of an English squadron, which was to be under the orders of the French admiral. Charles would have none of this. "It is the custom of the English", he wrote, "to have the command at sea, and if I were to order the commander of my fleet under pain of death to obey foreigners he would not do it." The truth was that he had no very high opinion of French seamanship, and he told Colbert de Croissy so as politely as possible. In this matter Charles remained intransigent, and if his wishes were not met the utmost that he would promise was to remain apparently neutral while secretly helping Louis as far as he could. When Colbert de Croissy endeavoured to modify the naval clauses in the French interest, Charles went off to Newmarket, and left the ambassador to treat with Arlington and Clifford, who proved no less resolute than their master. In the end, Colbert de Croissy informed Louis that he would either have to give in over the naval clauses, or else abandon, at any rate temporarily, the whole treaty. The French King decided to adopt the former course.

The main points of the resulting "secret" Treaty of Dover, signed in the summer of 1670, may be briefly summarized:

1. The King of England, being convinced of the truth of the Catholic religion and resolved to make a public declaration of it and to reconcile himself with the Roman Church as soon as he was able, was to receive from the King of France the sum of two million livres, half to be paid three months after the exchange of ratifications and the rest three months later, to aid him in making this declaration. The King of France also promised, if need be, to assist the King of England with six thousand troops to be raised and maintained at his own expense. The time of the King of England's declaration was left to his unfettered discretion.

2. Louis not to infringe or break the Treaty of Aix-la-Chapelle, thus allowing Charles to maintain it in conformity with the conditions of the Triple Alliance.

3. If new rights to the Spanish monarchy should accrue to the French King, Charles promised to help him with all his land and sea forces.

4. War to be declared on the United Provinces by both countries, and no separate peace was to be made by either Power.

5. France was to conduct the war on land with the assistance of an English force of 6,000 men paid by Charles, whose general was to be under the orders of the French commander-in-chief.

6. Charles was to undertake the conduct of the war by sea. He was to provide fifty capital ships and ten fireships, and Louis thirty, the least to carry forty guns, and a sufficient number of fireships up to ten if necessary. The French squadron was to be commanded by a French Vice-Admiral or Lieutenant-General under the Duke of York, who was to be appointed commander-in-chief by both monarchs; but the French Vice-Admiral was to take precedence over the

English second-in-command. In order to enable Charles to maintain his fleet Louis was to provide him with an annual subsidy of three million livres for the duration of the war. The English were not to be obliged to declare war until the French squadron had actually joined the English fleet at Portsmouth. If any Dutch territory was conquered, England was to receive Walcheren, the mouth of the Scheldt, and the island of Cadzand. The interests of the Prince of Orange in Holland were to be safeguarded in separate articles.

7. Efforts were to be made by both monarchs to persuade the Kings of Sweden and Denmark to join in the war against the Dutch, or at least to remain neutral. Similar representations were to be made to the Electors of Cologne and Brandenburg, the House of Brunswick, the Duke of Neuburg, and the Bishop of Münster. Everything possible was to be done to secure the neutrality of the Emperor and of Spain.

8. After Charles had made his Declaration, Louis was to choose, in consultation with him, the right moment for declaring war, which England was to do at the same time.

9. All articles in preceding treaties made with other countries by either monarch that were contrary to any of the provisions contained in this treaty were to be accounted void. It was agreed to conclude a commercial treaty as soon as possible.

There were also three additional articles dealing with points which had clearly arisen at the last moment, and by them it was agreed that if Charles could not supply six thousand troops, Louis was to be satisfied with four thousand; that if the Duke of York retired, an Englishman was to succeed him as commander-in-chief; and that the stipulation regarding the Prince of Orange was not on any account to prevent the declaration of war.

In this way Louis secured the help of England against the Dutch, but the price was high; indeed, it is a question whether it was not too high. The commercial rivalry between England and the United Provinces would almost certainly have caused the disintegration of the Triple Alliance before long, so that there is much in the argument that Louis merely paid Charles to do what he would have done anyhow. The religious clauses seem to have been inserted by the English King solely for the purpose of extracting money from the French treasury, for Charles did not become a member of the Church of Rome until he was dying. Henrietta was overjoyed at what she had accomplished, and she suggested that Turenne should come to London at once to concert measures against the Dutch: her brother was not unwilling, but Colbert de Croissy pointed out that such a step must inevitably arouse the suspicions of the potential enemy, and the project was abandoned.

Charles II has been the object of much hostile criticism on account of the Treaty of Dover, and Professor Trevelyan has gone so far as to say that had the Anglo-Dutch alliance been maintained "the career of Louis' ambition would have been checked at the outset, and Europe would have been spared an age of blood and destruction". It is, however, by no means certain that this was possible in 1670. The United Provinces constituted England's most dangerous foe on all seven seas, and the naval and commercial rivalry between the two Powers rendered any real friendship impossible until it had been decided which of them was the stronger. It is therefore difficult to resist the conclusion that there is much to be said for Mr. Hartmann's point of view, when he says, "In plain fact the alternative to the Anglo-French alliance at this time was not an Anglo-Dutch alliance, but an alliance between the French and the Dutch against England. If he could not secure the English alliance, Louis was prepared to make an arrangement with the Dutch to partition the Spanish Netherlands." In the recent war England had already had an unpleasant taste of what a Franco-Dutch alliance could mean, for it was the threatened arrival in the Channel of the Toulon fleet, and the consequent necessity of detaching Prince Rupert to intercept it, that had been the main reason for the Dutch success in the Four Days' Battle in June, 1666.

Viewed in this light, there must surely be some modification of the old view that the Treaty of Dover was a disgraceful and humiliating compact which made Great Britain a servile satellite of France. Charles once declared that there could be no real conflict between his interests and those of Louis, because England was only concerned with the sea, and there can be little doubt but that this statement gives the clue to his foreign policy. The Treaty of Dover reflects this determination to retain British naval supremacy. On the other hand, the danger from the United Provinces was very real, and that it was averted was in no small measure due to the astute, if tortuous, diplomacy of Charles.

The events which followed the conclusion of this secret arrangement between the Kings of England and France have been described in the preceding chapter. As soon as Charles realized that Louis and the United Provinces were irretrievably committed to war, his interest waned, while the rise of his nephew to power was also not without its effect upon him. Meanwhile Louis was re-insuring his position by negotiations with the Whigs. The consequences of this were extremely advantageous from the French standpoint, for the so-called Popish Plot and its repercussions paralysed England for several years, and it was not until his triumph over his opponents in 1681 that Charles was once more able to concern himself with international problems. He saw no threat to what he conceived to be the true interests of his country, for both the French and the Dutch were too jealous of each other to combine against Britain, which was what he really feared: the aggressions of Louis on the Rhine or in Italy concerned him not at all.

At the same time, France was never able to take the attitude of England for granted. While Charles II was on the throne national considerations would plainly be uppermost in the minds of the British Government, for although his foreign policy often lacked dignity, it was always, so far as circumstances would allow, conducted in accordance with the interests of the nation as a whole. The Commonwealth had produced an economic and financial crisis of the first magnitude, and when to this is added the effect of twenty years' civil war it is clear that the country required a period in which to lick its wounds and become convalescent. Charles provided his subjects with this needed respite, and during his reign there was a phenomenal rise in the national wealth. Louis never trusted him, and when Charles died in February, 1685, the French King probably thought that the change to James II was decidedly for the better. Events were soon to prove the opposite.

CHAPTER XVIII

LOUIS XIV AND WILLIAM III, 1678-1698

"I AM of the Prince's opinion," said Sir William Temple just before the conclusion of the Treaty of Nimeguen, "that he (the King of France) will make with a design of a new war after he has fixed his conquests", and so it proved. To Louis the security of his country appeared to be by no means established, and nothing short of the Rhine frontier would satisfy him. To the South he also became extremely active at this period, and both in the Italian peninsula and in the Mediterranean the weight of France was increasingly felt. The opportunity for further expansion was well chosen, since Louis had little to fear from his neighbours. Spain was sunk in a sleep which appeared that of death; England was in a state of virtual civil war; and the Emperor was already threatened by the Sultan, with whom he was shortly to be engaged in a life-and-death struggle. It was clear that once France had recovered from the effect of the previous war she could make another step forward with relative impunity.

The first measures which Louis took were legal rather than military. The Treaty of Westphalia had ceded to France the sovereignty of Upper and Lower Alsace, but there still remained a number of Imperial Cities of which the precise status was extremely vague. The method adopted to reopen a question which appeared to have been settled a generation before was at least ingenious. The Bishops of Metz, Toul, and Verdun were summoned to render homage to Louis, but they asked for the institution of a tribunal to adjudicate upon usurpations which had taken place during the course of time. A committee of the Parliament de Metz was accordingly set up to enquire into the matter, and it became the first of the *chambres de réunion*. Others were set up at Besançon, Breisach, and Tournai, and within a few years, by a combination of diplomacy, legal fiction, and some force, France had acquired almost as much territory as if she had won another war, for the *chambres de réunion* gave their decisions in accordance with the policy of the French Government. The most important of these decisions were those of the Breisach tribunal, which declared the absolute and exclusive sovereignty of Louis in Upper and Lower

Alsace, thus waiving aside any special privilege that might have been held to attach to the Imperial Cities or to those landowners who held directly from the Emperor.

This ruling was particularly welcome to Louis, as it provided him with a claim to Strasbourg, the possession of which was valuable on strategic grounds. He secured the removal of the Imperial garrison, and after communication with the outside world had been cut off Louvois ordered the occupation of the city at the end of September, 1681.

In Italy a similar forward policy was pursued, and the ground had been well prepared in advance. Although Spain still held the Milanese and the Two Sicilies, her decline was clear for all men to see, and, as in Germany, the various rulers looked to Paris. At first Louis had been content to exercise a general supervision over the Courts of Italy, but, under the influence of Louvois, he gradually began to interfere more directly, and his ambassadors thereafter were continually squabbling with the princes and their colleagues over questions of etiquette and precedence. Savoy was forced to send five thousand troops to serve with the French armies during the Dutch War, and Genoa to raise a regiment of Corsicans, while in the smaller states the French recruiting officers behaved as if they were in their own country. When Charles Emmanuel II of Savoy died in 1675 he left his youthful son, Victor Amadeus II, to all intents and purposes in the guardianship of France, and Cosimo III of Tuscany was bound to the French Royal House by marriage. Nor were successive Popes in any way exempt from pressure, and on one occasion not only did Louis seize Avignon, but he actually imprisoned the Papal nuncio in Paris. Thus, although France was not in possession of any territory in Italy, as in the days of the Valois, she was supreme in the peninsula.

Louis was not satisfied with this position from a military standpoint, and he was determined to possess himself of a foothold or two in the country comparable with the *presidi* on the Tuscan coast which enabled the Spaniards to throw troops into Italy when occasion demanded, or, in these latter days, when they had any to throw. The fortress of Casale, in the duchy of Mantua, was much coveted by France, and the reigning Duke was not unwilling to admit a French garrison for a suitable recompense. In due course the Duke met d'Estrades, the French minister to Savoy, at Venice, and was offered a pension for the control of Casale. The Duke's secretary, Mattioli, then visited France and arranged to sell the fortress for a hundred thousand crowns, with an extra ten thousand for himself. Pomponne could hardly credit such easy terms, and Marshal Catinat was sent to Pinerol to make the necessary arrangements to take over Casale, but with such secrecy that he pretended to be a prisoner and lived in a dungeon.

Months passed, and then the Duchess of Savoy told Louvois that Mattioli had betrayed him, that he had acted without the authority of the Duke of Mantua, and that he had revealed the whole arrangement to Venice and the Emperor. On hearing of this Louvois determined to punish Mattioli for his perfidy and at the same time to strike terror into his fellow-countrymen. With the connivance of the Duchess of Savoy, the Mantuan statesman was induced to meet d'Estrades at Turin, where the Frenchman, without letting him know he was suspected, said that if Mattioli would go to hold a personal interview with Catinat on the frontier he would be supplied with the money necessary to complete the negotiation regarding Casale. D'Estrades explained that the meeting must of necessity take place on the frontier, as Catinat could not conveniently leave the troops whom he commanded, and who were stationed in the neighbourhood of Pinerol.

On the appointed day, therefore, Mattioli and d'Estrades set out from Turin in the direction of Pinerol, but shortly before they arrived at the place where they were to meet Marshal Catinat they came to a broken bridge, which caused them to proceed on foot. When Catinat appeared he was accompanied by two officers and four men from the garrison of Pinerol. After some conversation Mattioli was informed by Catinat that he was a prisoner, and he was at once taken to Pinerol. From that moment he disappeared from history under his own name, though he is the likeliest of the many claimants to identity with the Man in the Iron Mask. At any rate Mattioli and this mysterious individual were about the same age, though why such secrecy should have been observed about the unfortunate Mantuan's incarceration when the fact of his arrest was widely known in North Italy is not easy to explain.

Mattioli's treachery caused a postponement of the French designs against Casale, but in 1680 the Duke of Mantua gave way to Louis in return for a pension and a cash payment. Materially, this strengthened the position of France, but it inspired a resentment among Italians comparable with that which was rising among the Germans owing to the seizure of Strasbourg. Louis was left in no doubt as to the feeling he was creating. "I assure Your

Majesty", wrote d'Estrades, "that there are few countries where
the French are less loved than in this one, or where Your Majesty's
power causes more apprehension and distrust, since you have taken
possession of Casale." Louis and Louvois entertained to the full the
traditional French contempt for Italians: *oderint dum metuant* was
their attitude where Italy was concerned, and of this they soon
gave further proof by their treatment of Savoy and Genoa.

For the best part of two generations France had been accustomed to treat the House of Savoy as vassals, and Louis saw no
particular reason why he should depart from this policy in the case
of young Victor Amadeus II and his mother. Accordingly he
played them off one against the other, and finally forced them to
agree to the presence of three thousand French troops in the
country. For the moment Louis had gained his point, but he had
raised up against himself in the young Duke of Savoy an enemy as
subtle and as determined as William of Orange. Victor Amadeus
knew that the time had not yet come when he could face Louis,
so he dissembled his real feelings, and compromised with the
French King, though without sacrificing anything of value of his
own. When Louis attacked the Vaudois in the Alpine valleys after
the revocation of the Edict of Nantes in October, 1685, he ordered
the Duke of Savoy to co-operate on his side of the mountains, and
when the Duke objected he threatened to send French troops to do
the work for him. Victor Amadeus had no choice but to obey,
though he took care to move so slowly that the Vaudois had time
to escape. When he finally broke with Louis there was no more
persecution of the Protestants, and the Vaudois fought gallantly
for him against the French.

Genoa experienced even more cavalier treatment than Savoy.
In her case Colbert seems to have been at least as responsible as
Louvois for urging Louis to extreme measures, for Genoa was the
commercial rival of Marseilles, and Colbert knew no mercy in
such circumstances: "sometimes", it was related of him, "he can
hardly contain his anger when he hears of the arrival of a rich fleet
at the port of Genoa". Although the old alliance between Genoa
and Spain had long since ceased to be effective, yet the scant
regard shown by the French ships for Genoese neutrality in recent
wars had done much to revive the old feelings, and the republic,
when France and Spain broke off relations again in 1683, began
to arm galleys for herself and Spain, as well as to allow Spanish
ships to anchor and refit in her harbours. Louis ordered the Geno-

ese Government to desist, and when he met with a firm refusal the French fleet bombarded Genoa in May, 1684. The city was under fire for ten days, eight thousand cannon-balls are said to have fallen, and a thousand buildings were destroyed. The French ships only withdrew when their ammunition was exhausted. In spite of the punishment thus inflicted on the unhappy city, Louis refused to make peace until the Doge and four senators had come to Versailles to ask his pardon.

The effect of these acts of aggression upon European public opinion is essential to an understanding of the diplomacy of the day, for it was such events as the seizure of Strasbourg and the bombardment of Genoa which rendered the French King a veritable ogre in so many places beyond his own frontiers. "No peace can be made with France", Matthew Prior was to write to Portland, "till King Louis be driven like Nebuchadnezzar from the society of all human creatures." Strasbourg and Genoa did much to create this bitterness. On the other hand, there can be little doubt that this forward policy of Louis was exceedingly popular among his own subjects.

In November, 1681, the French laid siege to Luxemburg, and the alarm throughout Europe became great. Yet there was little to be effected, in spite of the efforts of William to form a coalition against Louis. Leopold was too busy with the Turks, who were advancing on Vienna, and Charles II had no mind to imperil the fruits of his recent victory over the Whigs by summoning another Parliament, so nothing was done. As was generally the case, Louis played his cards with consummate skill, for he announced that in view of the Moslem threat to the common civilization of Europe he would abandon his designs upon Luxemburg. This did much to reassure the less uncompromising among his opponents, while the conclusion of agreements with Denmark and Brandenburg showed that he was far from being isolated in spite of the defection of his old ally, Sweden, which under Charles XI was inclining towards the United Provinces. The fact was that nobody wanted war. The opponents of France were not ready for it, and although Louis was prepared to fight if necessary, he preferred to consolidate his recent acquisitions in peace. Only the Spaniards were so ill-advised as to resort to arms, in December, 1683, but they were soon beaten, and lost Luxemburg.

In these circumstances, in August, 1684, the Truce of Ratisbon was concluded with Louis by Leopold and the Empire. By this arrangement it was agreed that for twenty years France should continue to hold not only Strasbourg but all the places assigned to her before August 1st, 1681, by the *chambres de réunion*. The Spaniards were compelled to make large concessions to France, including the transfer of many villages in Hainault and Luxemburg, and even the Dutch had to accept the truce. It is hardly remarkable that Saint-Simon should have said, "Here ends the apogee of the reign, and height of its glory and prosperity".

In the year following the conclusion of the Truce of Ratisbon, that is to say on October 22nd, 1685, the Edict of Nantes was revoked, and this event had international and diplomatic repercussions of so widespread a nature that it cannot be dismissed as a mere incident in French domestic history.

During the earlier part of the seventeenth century it was certainly more tolerable to be a Protestant in France than a Roman Catholic in the British Isles, but although the Huguenots had taken no part in the Fronde, public opinion was bitterly hostile to them, and was prepared to support any action, however drastic, against them. Louis himself had proved by no means intolerant in his earlier years, but after he came under the influence of Madame de Maintenon his attitude hardened. Furthermore, his Gallican views had brought him into conflict with Rome, and he wished to give convincing proof of the fact that, although he might be quarrelling with the Pope, he was nevertheless as devout a Catholic as ever. One good turn, too, deserved another, and as a reward for the support of the clergy against Innocent XI, the King yielded to their wishes in the suppression of Protestantism.

The first step was to send missionaries to the Protestant districts, which were still mainly in the South, and those who were converted to Roman Catholicism were financially rewarded. This method was soon considered too slow, and troops were quartered upon the recalcitrant Huguenots. The unhappy Protestants then saw their children taken from them to be forcibly baptized, while their wives and daughters were a prey to the lusts of the soldiery. Some of the Huguenots took up arms, and, as in the days of the Fronde, Frenchmen shed the blood of Frenchmen. When the Protestant leaders were caught they were tortured, broken on the wheel, and quartered as a warning to their co-religionists. Such was the persecution which acquired the name of the *dragonnades*.

The decree announcing the revocation of the Edict of Nantes, an action which was condemned by the reigning Pope, contained eleven articles, by the first of which all privileges granted to the Protestants by earlier monarchs were suppressed. The next two forbade the exercise of the reformed religion throughout France, while others commanded all Protestant clergymen to leave the kingdom within fifteen days, offered rewards for conversion, prohibited Protestants from holding schools, and enjoined parents to bring up their children in the Roman Catholic faith. Protestantism in France thus became, like episcopacy in Scotland a few years later, an illegal religion outside the pale of the law and proscribed by it. There was one small concession, namely that Huguenots could remain unmolested in their houses and property, provided that they altogether ceased to practise their religion openly. It will thus be seen that however hard Louis was on his Huguenot subjects, they were not subjected to indiscriminate spoliation merely because they were Protestants. Discrimination of this nature was a refinement of cruelty left to a later age.

If the *dragonnades* were a crime, the revocation of the Edict of Nantes was a blunder. The exodus of Huguenots from France was the first evidence of the mistake which had been made. For the previous twenty-five years they had been leaving the country in small numbers, but now what had been a stream was converted into a river. Over the exact figures there is a difference of opinion among the authorities. Basnage gives an estimate of between three and four hundred thousand, La Martinière prefers the latter figure, while Voltaire reckons the number at between two and three hundred thousand, and modern writers have generally been content to accept his statistics. Whatever the exact figure, the quality of those who fled abroad was out of all proportion to the quantity. Those who left were the most industrious citizens, and they carried with them to the rivals of France, that is to say to England, the United Provinces, and Brandenburg, the thrift and the skill which had made their native land the richest country in Europe. Those who were left behind eventually rose against their oppressors, and under the name of Camisards kept Marshal Villars and an army of veterans occupied in the days of the French King's greatest need, during the War of the Spanish Succession.

If the economic loss to France was great, the military and political damage she sustained was also on a considerable scale. Huguenot soldiers taught the English and Dutch armies much of the discipline and drill which had made the veterans of Louis irresistible, and among those who left the French service in conse-

o

quence of the revocation of the Edict of Nantes were Ruvigny and Schomberg. The exiles, too, fought against their persecutors with a fury which well expressed their resentment, and in more than one battle the generals of Louis had bitter cause to regret their master's intolerance. Nor was this all, for the *dragonnades* and the revocation roused feeling in the Protestant countries against France, and in England this had much to do with the Revolution of 1688. Suspicion of the French King's designs had been growing for years among the princes and statesmen of these Powers, but when the Huguenot refugees began to pour in, the ordinary citizen too became disquieted, and a public opinion was gradually formed which was bitterly hostile to France. The revocation revived religious hatreds all over Western Europe, and proved the prelude to the League of Augsburg.

Into the domestic causes of the English Revolution of 1688 it is unnecessary to enter here: what William saw in the growth of opposition to James II was an opportunity to bring Great Britain into a war against France, and Louis was under no illusions as to what was in his rival's mind. James, on the other hand, having suppressed Monmouth's rising with relative ease, was supremely self-confident. He rejected the suggestion of Louis that a junction of the French and English fleets should be effected in order to stop William's expedition, and he resented what he considered to be the patronizing air of the French monarch. Marshal Villars well described the state of opinion at Versailles: "The Court hesitated as to what should be its policy, whether it should give aid to King James about to be attacked, or should prevent the peace with the Turks, which was being made, and which would bring upon us the whole forces of the Emperor and the Empire. M. de Louvois, upon his return from Forges, where he had been taking the waters for some days, decided to take the second course. In effect nothing was more important for us than to secure so powerful a diversion in our favour as that of the Turks. Besides, what prospect was there that so great a revolution could take place in England without much trouble and discord? This suited us better than a settled government under King James; the more so that we had already seen England at peace and under the authority of King Charles II, a devoted ally, compel that sovereign to declare war against us." So the French armies marched on Philipsburg instead of Maestricht, and William was free to overturn his father-in-law's throne.

This miscalculation was to prove serious, for the easy victory of the Prince of Orange added England to the enemies of France, and in the end tipped the scales against her. In the East of Europe the French King also proved to be out in his reckoning, but in neither case can he really be blamed for lack of foresight. Louis believed that the Turks would take Vienna, and that in his extremity Leopold would turn to France: in this case Louis proposed to restore the situation on the Danube, and then, having saved Christendom, to claim as his reward the reversion of the Empire. He forgot John Sobieski, and the Turks were defeated without his aid. Thus both in the West and the East he sustained severe rebuffs as a result of the chances he had taken; yet it is difficult to resist the conclusion that the risks were legitimate ones for a statesman to run, and Louis had often before played successfully for equally high stakes.

Another decision which Louis took at this time, namely the devastation of the Palatinate, in pursuit of what a later age would have described as "a scorched-earth" policy, also proved to be a serious mistake, and did much to harden contemporary opinion against him. The district had been ravaged by Turenne in the previous war; but it was now subjected to even more drastic spoliation. The reason given was that, in view of the increase in the number of their enemies, it had become necessary for the French armies to concentrate, and strategy required that the districts evacuated should afford no sustenance to the opposing forces. The destruction was on a considerable scale, and it has been estimated that three or four small towns, more than fifty castles, and an immense number of villages were razed to the ground. To the credit of Louis it must be said that when Louvois wanted to go farther, and destroy Trèves, the King refused his consent.

The invasion of the Palatinate brought to an end the Truce of Ratisbon, and in 1689 there came into existence against France the Grand Alliance of the Emperor, England, and the Dutch: the war which ensued was known as that of the League of Augsburg, for such was the name given to the coalition which then took the field against Louis. It dragged on in the same indeterminate way that its predecessor had done. Louis had no generals now of the type which had led his armies to victory in the earlier years of his reign. Turenne and Condé were dead, and Villars and Luxembourg, though competent enough commanders, were not of their calibre, while Catinat and Villeroy were definitely second-rate. Fortunately for France, her opponents were even worse led, and a more consistently unlucky general than William of Orange it would be difficult to name.

The French attempt to distract William's attention by keeping hostilities going in Ireland was defeated at Aughrim in 1691, chiefly because Louis XIV made the same mistake as Philip II, and failed to provide enough troops for the purpose. At sea the French victory at Beachy Head in 1690 was followed by the French defeat at La Hogue two years later, and in Flanders one campaign after another proved that though the soldiers of Louis could still win victories in the field, his enemies were too numerous and his generals too indifferent for the French successes to be decisive. On the Rhine there was no event that calls for notice, while in Italy the French, though much weakened by the necessity of continually reinforcing the Flanders front, managed to hold their own under the command of Catinat against the Duke of Savoy, who had joined the Grand Alliance. Victor Amadeus was defeated at Staffarda in 1690 and at Marsaglia in 1693, and as his allies had done very little for him, he felt justified in utilizing the difficulties of Louis elsewhere to gain satisfactory terms for himself. In 1696, therefore, he came to terms with France, and not the least important of these was that he received the *trattamento reale*, while his daughter, Adelaide, became affianced to the Duke of Burgundy. When this had been arranged, Victor Amadeus, with a rapidity which took away the breath of his former allies, joined forces with his old enemy Catinat, and proceeded to invade the Milanese.

The unexpected then took place. When the Duke of Savoy went over to the French it appeared certain that Louis, with the troops thus released from Italy, would at once order an offensive in the Low Countries, which his opponents would have found it extremely difficult to resist. Instead, Louis showed an unexpected readiness to make peace. His reason for adopting this course was the approaching demise of the King of Spain, and his desire to come to an agreement with William as to the division of the Spanish Empire.

The actual negotiations between France and Great Britain began at Ryswick in May, 1697, under the mediation of Sweden, but, as so often happens on such occasions, the really decisive discussions took place elsewhere, in this case between Marshal

Boufflers and Lord Portland. One of the major difficulties in the way of a settlement resulted from the English Revolution, for William wanted from Louis a clear recognition of his title to the throne as well, if possible, as the expulsion of James II from France. Behind all was the problem of the Spanish succession, and what influence it exercised upon the negotiations can be gauged by a report from Boufflers to Louis in July in which he says, "Lord Portland let fall a word—I believe purposely, but without appearing to lay stress upon it—that, perhaps, when peace was once concluded, and the agitation of people's minds calmed, Your Majesty would not be sorry to have an ally, like the Prince of Orange, and, that then you would find him as faithful and conscientious in favouring the interests of Your Majesty, as he has hitherto been opposed to them."

The air having been cleared, the negotiations were once more transferred to Ryswick, and in September, 1697, the first treaty was signed there between France on the one hand and England, Spain, and the United Provinces on the other. Louis acknowledged William as King of Great Britain and Ireland, and promised not to abet any plots against him, while William abandoned his demand that James should be compelled to leave France. The French King restored all the places taken or claimed since 1678, including Luxemburg, and agreed to the garrisoning of certain strong places in the Spanish Netherlands by the Dutch, who also obtained commercial advantages to which the dead Colbert would never have assented. Another month elapsed before William was able to persuade Leopold to follow his example and put an end to the war. Once more Louis displayed unexpected moderation. He gave up all his conquests since Nimeguen, with the exception of Landau and Strasbourg, and he restored Lorraine to its Duke. By Christmas, 1697, Western Europe was again at peace.

CHAPTER XIX

SOUTH-EASTERN EUROPE, 1566–1718

THE turning-points of history are not infrequently more obvious to posterity than to contemporaries, and such was the case with the commencement of the decline of the Ottoman Empire. We know now that after the death of Suleyman the Magnificent in 1566 that empire was never again to be what it had been, yet it was not until five years later that its sea-power was broken by Don John of Austria at Lepanto, and in spite of that reverse the Porte shortly afterwards compelled the Republic of Saint Mark to cede the island of Cyprus. The Ottoman Empire was not built up by the energy and ability of a single autocrat in each generation, for there were many capable statesmen, administrators, and generals who also contributed to the achievements of their masters, the Sultans. Many such men survived the death of Suleyman I, and preserved the empire for a further period: indeed, it was not until considerably later that it began to shrink in extent, and for a time, as if from the momentum given to it by the great Sultans of the past, it actually continued to expand.

The Spanish Empire, as we have seen, declined very largely because Spain became saddled with responsibilities which were beyond her strength to bear; with the Ottoman Empire it was different, and her decay was rather due to the deterioration of the dynasty and of the army. The first ten Sultans had been men of great ability, and, with the exception of Bayezid II, they habitually led their armies in the field: indeed, it may be doubted whether, in the world's history, any other dynasty has produced so long a succession of men with such eminent and persistent qualities. With Selim II, significantly known as "the Sot," the only son of Suleyman who escaped the bow-string, a remarkable change came, and of the fourteen sovereigns who occupied the throne between 1566 and 1718, only one, Murad IV (1623–1640), possessed any real ability. One out of the fourteen was murdered, and four other were deposed: none led an army to victory; and most of them devoted to the pleasures of the bottle and the harem all the time they could spare from the neglect of their official duties.

The close connection between the throne and the army meant

that the decadence of the dynasty was soon reflected in the military forces of the empire, and particularly in the Janissaries. They began to make and unmake monarchs in a manner reminiscent of the Praetorian Guards of Imperial Rome, and like their proto-types they tended to lose their martial qualities in the process. No longer effectively commanded by their Sultans, and character-ized by an increasing lack of discipline, the Ottoman armies began to lose their terror for the enemies that came into conflict with them.

The preoccupation of Philip II with the affairs of Western Europe, and the decline of Spanish power under his successors, caused Spain to play a less important part in the affairs of the Mediterranean as the sixteenth century drew to its close; further-more, the relief of Malta and the battle of Lepanto in due course proved to have set the definite limit to the Ottoman advance in that quarter, though as late as 1609 it was considered advisable to expel the Moriscoes from Spain altogether on account of their intrigues with foreign countries. In future, opposition to the Turks in the South was mainly confined to the Republic of Saint Mark.

Until the rise of Russia in the middle of the eighteenth century the task of holding the frontiers of Christendom against the Osmanli devolved mainly on the Austrian Habsburgs. No doubt successive sovereigns of the House of Austria were not unin-fluenced in this contest by their position at the head of the Holy Roman Empire, but much more did they feel the necessity, as rulers of Hungary, Croatia, and Transylvania, to make themselves undisputed masters of the valleys of the Danube, the Drave, and the Save. With the Crescent firmly planted at Buda, and with the Turkish troops in striking distance of Zagreb, not only was Vienna in permanent danger, but the communications between Austria and Italy were liable at any moment to be cut. This was sufficiently inconvenient when the Milanese and the Two Sicilies were in the hands of the Spanish branch of the Habsburg house, but it became intolerable when, after the Treaty of Utrecht, they came under the rule of Vienna. Nor was this all, for the more the Emperor was deprived of leadership in Germany by the growth of the centrifugal forces in the Reich; and the more he lost his hold on the Rhine owing to the expansion of France; the more essential it was for him to retain his grip on the Danube. Thus, throughout the seventeenth century the history of South-Eastern Europe may be summarized in the duel between the Habsburgs and the Sultans for political and military supremacy on the Danube and the Save.

The struggle was a severe one, and the Moslems were driven back slowly, if steadily, for they fought far more strenuously for the command of the Danube than they were later to do for Greece or Bulgaria. Then, again, more than once there was a revival of Ottoman power, and before the tide finally receded it had threatened for the second time to engulf Vienna.

Attention has already been called to the fact that owing to the peculiar nature of their military organization the Sultans were unable to wage a simultaneous war on two fronts, and the closing decades of the sixteenth century were marked by an activity in Arabia and on the coasts of the Black Sea, as well as by a war with Persia, which effectively precluded any major offensive against Central Europe. In 1569, too, an armistice had been concluded with Maximilian II on the *uti possidetis* principle, and this lasted until 1593, when war once more broke out. In the meantime Murad III had been solicited by Elizabeth of England to aid her against Philip II.

Previous to 1579 there had not been any direct contact between London and Constantinople, but in that year three English merchants were sent to the Turkish capital, and in due course obtained from the Porte for their fellow-countrymen the same commercial privileges as were enjoyed by other foreigners. Four years later Elizabeth accredited an ambassador to Murad in the person of William Harebone, and as her relations with Philip II deteriorated she began to angle for Turkish assistance. She described herself as "the unconquered and most puissant defender of the true faith against the idolaters who falsely profess the name of Christ", and in November, 1587, the English ambassador addressed a note to the Sultan in which Murad was implored to send at least sixty or eighty galleys "against that idolater, the King of Spain, who, relying on the help of the Pope and all idolatrous princes, designs to crush the Queen of England, and then to turn his whole power to the destruction of the Sultan, and make himself universal monarch". The note goes on to point out that if Murad will assist in the maritime war against Spain, the "proud Spaniard and the lying Pope with all their followers will be struck down".

In this appeal Elizabeth was supported by Henry III of France, who went so far as to send an envoy to Constantinople in the spring of 1588 to warn the Sultan that if Philip conquered

England he would soon overwhelm the Turks. The Porte, in its turn, expressed itself favourably, but no action followed, possibly because the English Queen either did not bribe enough or bribed the wrong person.

The war between the Emperor and the Sultan, which broke out in 1593, was not conducted with any great vigour by either side, and was only remarkable for the Ottoman victory in October, 1596, in a three days' battle on the marshy plain of Cerestes. Hostilities continued for thirteen years in all, but much of the fighting was of a desultory nature, and during it the vassal rulers of Moldavia, Wallachia, and Transylvania allied themselves with the Habsburgs against their overlord at Constantinople. Peace was made at Sitvatorok in November, 1606, when the Sultan renounced his suzerainty over Transylvania, and in exchange for a lump sum surrendered the annual tribute of thirty thousand ducats which the Emperor had been paying him in respect of that part of Hungary which was in possession of the House of Austria. The Treaty of Sitvatorok is also notable in that for the first time the Sultan recognized the Emperor as an equal, thus putting him on the same footing as that enjoyed since 1535 by the King of France.

The Treaty of Sitvatorok ushered in a period of peace, which lasted for several decades and a variety of reasons. With the Thirty Years' War engrossing their attention it was certainly not to the interest of the Habsburgs to stir up trouble on their Eastern frontiers, and it was extremely fortunate for them that their Ottoman neighbours did not take advantage of an opportunity which was never to recur. Achmet I, Mustapha I, and Othman II, who occupied the throne between 1603 and 1623, were not the men to revive the ambitions of Suleyman the Magnificent, while Murad IV, who succeeded in 1623, although of great vigour and ability, was more concerned with his Persian campaigns, in which he reconquered Baghdad, than with the progress of events to the West of him, and he died in 1640. Thus the Hapsburgs were able to surmount the great crisis of the Thirty Years' War without interference from Constantinople.

The death of Murad IV was followed by a period of renewed weakness in the Ottoman Empire. So long as the Venetians held Crete, the Sultans felt that their control over the Eastern Mediterranean was incomplete, and so Murad's successor, Ibrahim, set about the task of reducing the island. It proved beyond his power, for although siege was laid to Candia in 1645, the town could not be taken, and it held out for just a quarter of a century. Ibrahim was deposed and murdered in 1648, but this did nothing to arrest a course of events which proved increasingly damaging to Ottoman interests. The Venetians won a considerable naval victory in the Ægean, and in 1656 their admiral, Mocenigo, occupied the Dardanelles, thus threatening Constantinople itself. Not for the last time it appeared as if the Ottoman Empire was on the verge of dissolution. From this fate it was preserved by the genius of the various members of the Kiuprili family, who for the next thirty years controlled its destiny as Grand Viziers under Mohammed IV.

This Indian Summer of the Ottoman Empire was marked by a revival of aggression in the West. The Venetians were soon driven away from the Dardanelles, and the civil disturbances were suppressed, while the Persians were still cowed by the victories of Murad IV, so that the way was clear for a return to the policy of Suleyman the Magnificent. Throughout the years 1661 and 1662 there were conflicts of minor importance in Hungary and Transylvania between the respective partizans of Austria and the Porte, but war on a first-class scale did not begin until 1663 when Ahmed Kiuprili took the field with the avowed intention of finally destroying the Habsburg power. At first he encountered little opposition, but before long various adverse factors began to operate. In the first place, he had alienated Louis XIV by an insult to the French ambassador, so that instead of enjoying the support of France, as in the previous century, the Turks had now to reckon with her enmity. Then, while the Ottoman troops in general, and the Janissaries in particular, had either been spending its time either in stagnation or mutiny, the art of war had progressed, and their tactics and weapons were obsolete. Above all, the Sultan's armies had no longer to meet the indifferent Christian commanders of an earlier age, for Leopold I had entrusted his forces to Montecuculi, one of the leading generals of the day. The consequence was seen in July, 1664, when at the battle of St. Gothard the Osmanli sustained an overwhelming defeat at the hands of Montecuculi, under whom was serving a strong French contingent, which materially contributed to the victory.

Indeed, the presence of the French not only affected the issue, but also the consequences, of the battle, for Leopold had no mind to be beholden any further to Louis XIV, and he determined to use his triumph for the purpose of making peace. Accordingly, in

August, 1664, he signed the Treaty of Vasvar, by which once more the suzerainty of the Sultan over Transylvania was recognized, and the Turks were allowed to retain the important Hungarian fortresses of Neuhausel and Grosswardein: the Emperor also agreed to pay an indemnity of two hundred thousand florins.

Reassured by this unexpected turn of fortune's wheel, Ahmed Kiuprili then turned to Crete, captured Candia in September, 1669, and made a treaty with the Republic of Saint Mark by which the entire island passed into Ottoman hands. This conquest of Crete was to have a double significance, for it was the last notable acquisition of the Turks in Europe, and it also marked the complete absorption of the last important remnant of the Byzantine Empire. It was not until 1913 that the island formally became Greek once more.

The next victim marked down by Ahmed Kiuprili was Poland, who was having serious difficulties with her Cossack subjects, who called upon the Sultan to protect them. War broke out in 1672, and the Turks laid siege to the fortress of Kaminiec, which was considered to be the key to Podolia. In less than a month it fell, and so dismayed was the reigning Polish monarch, Michael, that he negotiated the Treaty of Buczacz, by which he surrendered Podolia and the Ukraine to the Sultan, and also promised to pay tribute. The Polish Diet, however, refused to ratify these terms, and John Sobieski led the resistance to the Turks. Once again the Sultan's forces had to meet a master of the art of war, and in 1673 and 1675 they met with crushing defeats at Choczim and Lemberg respectively. Peace was made at Zurawno in October, 1676, and the difference between the settlement there and the Treaty of Buczacz is the measure of John Sobieski's success. The Sultan indeed retained Kaminiec and part of the Ukraine, and of Podolia, but the rest of his earlier gains, including the tribute, were abandoned. Seven days later Ahmed Kiuprili died, and was succeeded in office by his brother-in-law, Kara Mustapha.

The new Grand Vizier determined to take advantage of the unexpectedly favourable international situation to strike a blow at Vienna itself. All eyes were concentrated upon the struggle between Louis XIV and the United Provinces, in which Leopold had now been forced to participate, and even when the Treaty of Nimeguen had been concluded in 1678 it was clear that no substantial help would be forthcoming for the Emperor from the West. All the same, the Grand Vizier thought it advisable to renew the old understanding with France, and this was accomplished by the grant of fresh trade and other privileges. By such means Mustapha hoped to isolate the Emperor, and he was further assisted by a Hungarian rising against Leopold, for the Magyars not only resented what they considered to be the humiliating provisions of the Treaty of Vasvar, but they were alienated by his abolition of the office of Palatine and obvious determination to rule their country from Vienna.

The Osmanli, it must be remembered, could never fight more than one war at a time, and the attack on Austria was delayed by complications with Russia. There was severe fighting, in the course of which the Grand Vizier suffered one serious reverse, but a compromise was reached in 1681, when it was agreed that neither Power should erect any fortifications between the Bug and the Dniester.

The way was now clear for the attack on Vienna, and in the spring of 1683 the Grand Vizier crossed the Danube at the head of two hundred and seventy-five thousand men. He had not reckoned upon his allies in vain: Leopold was isolated, and it was only from Poland that help was forthcoming. John Sobieski, now King of that country, was officially at peace with the Porte, but he was under no illusions as to what would be his fate if Austria went down, and he concluded an alliance with the Emperor by which he promised to place forty thousand men in the field. Meanwhile the war went on: Leopold left his capital for the safety of Passau; and on July 9th the Ottoman standards appeared before Vienna.

What then ensued can be described in a few sentences. Mustapha could have stormed the city, but he delayed, for he preferred that it should capitulate, when his personal share in the booty would be more considerable. John Sobieski arrived in the nick of time, and on September 12th the Turks were decisively beaten. Thereafter the Crescent was pushed steadily back across the plains of Hungary. In 1684 the Holy League was formed between the Emperor, Poland, and the Republic of Saint Mark, and the Imperialist successes on the Danube were only matched by the Venetian victories at sea. At Constantinople the heads of Grand Viziers fell, and the Sultan was deposed, but nothing could arrest the march of events. By 1694 the Turks had been stripped of all their possessions in Greece and on the coast of the Adriatic, and the great Prince Eugene was entering the field against them. In 1697 he won at Zenta a resounding victory over Mustapha II in person, and there seemed to be nothing to prevent his early arrival at Constantinople. Nevertheless, the same factor, namely the approaching death of Charles II, which in the West was inducing Louis XIV to agree to the terms of the Treaty of Ryswick, was making for peace in the East: Leopold wished to have his hands free to deal with the Spanish succession, and accordingly in January, 1699, the Treaty of Carlowitz was concluded, largely, it may be added, owing to the good offices of British diplomacy.

This settlement reflected the result of the war. The Emperor was acknowledged suzerain of Transylvania, and he received all Hungary to the West of the Theiss, as well as most of Slavonia. Poland recovered Podolia and Kaminiec, while the Republic of Saint Mark retained its conquests in Dalmatia and the Morea, but restored those to the North of the Isthmus of Corinth. The Tsar, now Peter the Great, refused to be included in this treaty, but by an armistice he kept possession of Azov, and of the districts which he had conquered to the North of the sea of that name.

No such peace had ever before been made by an Ottoman Sultan, and the Treaty of Carlowitz was clear evidence that the Moslem tide was on the ebb at last. Never again was Europe to be threatened by the Power which for three centuries had constituted a perpetual menace to its security. For the future the Eastern Problem was to be changed, and the question was no longer how to protect Christendom from the Turk, but who was to take his place as the dominant Power in the Near East.

It was at this point that the Osmanli first came into contact with those who were to be their chief enemies for many years, namely the Russians. So long ago as 1492 there had been a protest from Ivan III against the treatment of some of his subjects by the Turks, and that same Ivan was interested in Constantinople, for he had married a niece of Constantine XIII, the last Byzantine Emperor; he had also assumed the two-headed eagle, which had been the symbol of the Eastern Empire. In the reign of Ivan IV the first clash between the two Powers had taken place over a Turkish project to unite the Don and the Volga by a canal. This would have necessitated an Ottoman occupation of Astrakhan, which the Russians successfully resisted, and during the course of the subsequent hostilities they inflicted a severe reverse on the Sultan's troops near Azov. The project was then abandoned.

A hundred years elapsed before the two Powers came into direct

conflict again, though the situation on their frontiers was very un-
settled, and a raid by the Tartars into Southern Russia would be
followed by a Cossack attack on Azov, which was then an Ottoman
town. As we have seen, there was another war in the eighth
decade of the seventeenth century, and the settlement reached in
1681 was a mere truce. Russia joined the Holy League in 1686,
and from that date until the conclusion of the Treaty of Carlowitz
the two countries were intermittently at war.

The reigning Tsar, Peter the Great, was determined to obtain
access to the Baltic and the Black Sea, and he saw in the embarrassments of the Porte an opportunity of achieving the second of these
ambitions. After several attempts to capture Azov he succeeded in
reducing the city in 1696, and he at once proceeded to improve the
fortifications and to enlarge the harbour with a view to the creation
of a naval base. Three years later he was able to retain his conquest
at Carlowitz.

Defeated though they had been, the Turks were far from reconciled to the terms of the peace which they had signed, and the first
opportunity to rectify them was, curiously enough, furnished by
the Tsar. After his defeat by the Russians at Pultava in 1709,
Charles XII of Sweden took refuge on Ottoman territory, together with Mazeppa, the Cossack chief. Peter the Great demanded
their extradition, which the Porte refused, and in November, 1710,
declared war on Russia. In the summer of the following year the
Tsar crossed the Pruth, but then proceeded to repeat the blunder
which had led to the overthrow of his Swedish rival at Pultava;
that is to say he pushed on too far and too fast, found himself surrounded by a greatly superior force of Osmanli, and was compelled to sue for peace.

The terms which he had to accept at the Treaty of the Pruth
in July, 1711, were sufficiently hard. Azov and the adjacent territory were restored to the Sultan; the Tsar promised to raze to the
ground the fortress of Taganrog, which he had recently built on
the Sea of Azov, and to destroy other fortifications and castles in
the neighbourhood, as well as to surrender guns and stores. He
undertook to leave the Cossacks alone, and not to interfere in the
affairs of Poland or the Ukraine. Finally, the Russians were no
longer to have an ambassador at Constantinople; they were to
hand over all Moslem prisoners in their custody; to afford the
King of Sweden free and safe passage to his own kingdom; and
not to keep a fleet in the Black Sea. No surrender could have been

more complete, and a quarter of a century was to elapse before Russia again tried conclusions with the Porte.

Encouraged by these successes, the Turks determined to upset the clauses of the Treaty of Carlowitz which affected the Republic of Saint Mark, and they were the more tempted to do this because the Venetians, as Roman Catholics, were far from popular among the Orthodox inhabitants of the Greek mainland. In 1715, therefore, the Ottoman forces attacked the Peloponnese by land and sea, and within a few months the Venetians had been expelled not only from Greece, but also from the Archipelago. The Porte then proposed to follow up these victories by operations in the Adriatic.

At this point the Emperor, now Charles VI, intervened. He had no desire to see another such revival of Ottoman power as had marked the days of the Kiuprili, and he had at his disposal a veteran army trained in the War of the Spanish Succession as well as one of the greatest generals of the age in Prince Eugene. Accordingly, in 1716 he accused the Porte of a gross violation of the Treaty of Carlowitz, and concluded an alliance with the Republic of Saint Mark. In August of that same year Eugene decisively defeated the Grand Vizier at Peterwardein; in November the city of Temesvar, the last fortress left to the Sultan in Hungary, was forced to surrender; and in August, 1717, the Austrians captured Belgrade. The road to Constantinople lay open, but Eugene was unable to take it. The ambitions of Alberoni in the Western Mediterranean and in Italy were distracting the attention of Charles from the Balkans. So when the Porte invoked the mediation of Great Britain and the United Provinces, the Emperor was found to be ready to treat.

The Peace of Passarowitz was signed in June, 1718, in the presence, as had been the case at Carlowitz, of British and Dutch observers. The Republic of Saint Mark gave up all claim to the Morea, and also surrendered several places in Dalmatia, which was necessary to keep open the Turkish communications with Ragusa. In future the Ionian Islands constituted the only Greek territory to remain her possession. On the other hand, the Habsburg gains were considerable, for the Emperor obtained not only Temesvar, which completed the recovery of Hungary from the Turks, but also Belgrade, Semendra, Rimnik, and Krasova. The river Aluta, in Wallachia, became the boundary of the two empires, thus assigning to Austria the whole of the country termed Little Wallachia. Six other rivers, namely the Danube, the Timok, the little Morava, the Dwina, the Save, and the Unna, then formed the frontier line, so that nearly all Serbia, and a part of Bosnia, exchanged the rule of Constantinople for that of Vienna.

The Treaty of Passarowitz possessed special importance on two counts: it marked the beginning of the end of Venetian power, while the populations transferred from the Sultan to the Emperor were not Turks but Rumanians and Southern Slavs. The significance of this distinction was not perceived at the time, but two hundred years later it was to matter a very great deal.

CHAPTER XX

NORTHERN EUROPE, 1632–1721

WHEN Gustavus Adolphus was killed at Lutzen, his country had gained the hegemony of Northern Europe, but he died before the position could be consolidated. His aim had been to turn the Baltic into a Swedish lake, and to wrest from Denmark control of its exit into the North Sea. Gustavus was succeeded by his daughter, Christina, a child of four-and-a-half, but his work was carried on by Axel Oxenstjerna. For ten years all went well, and Swedish foreign policy was almost wholly concerned with the Thirty Years' War and its repercussions; then broke out another of those fratricidal conflicts with Denmark which are so conspicuous a feature of Scandinavian history.

Christian IV and his people were beginning to recover from their unfortunate participation in the Thirty Years' War, and the Danish monarch thought the opportunity a good one to reassert control of the Sound and the Belts. Free navigation through these channels was also a matter of concern to Great Britain and the United Provinces, but at this particular moment neither was in a position to interfere. In the British Isles civil war was imminent, and the Dutch were involved in their apparently interminable struggle with Spain. Secure in his position astride the islands, with one foot on Halland and the other on Jutland, Christian felt himself master of the situation, and he proceeded to raise the tolls on the Sound. Never was man more wholly undeceived, for Oxenstjerna fell upon Denmark without any declaration of war, and, defeated on land and sea, the Danish King was compelled to sign the Treaty of Brömsebro in February, 1645. Sweden thereby acquired the islands of Ösel and Gothland, the provinces of Jemtland and Herjedal, and Halland for a period of thirty years: she was also entirely relieved from the payment of tolls on the Sound and the Belts. At the same time the Treaty of Kristianopel conceded very considerable reductions in the Sound and Norwegian tolls to the Dutch, who had assisted the Swedes in the recent fighting.

Three years later there occurred the Peace of Westphalia, which made Sweden a Germanic Power, but she was not destined to be free from war for long. In 1654 Christina abdicated, and was succeeded by her cousin, Charles X, whose reign was marked by a series of struggles against his neighbours. These conflicts had their origin in a revival of the old quarrel between Sweden and Poland, and in this Denmark, Brandenburg, and Russia kept on interfering. Charles X found that it was a great deal easier to defeat the Poles than to conquer Poland, and from his consequent embarrassments the other Northern Powers were by no means unwilling to profit. Sweden had some difficulty in making head against so many enemies, but in the later stages of the war Charles X struck what proved to be a decisive blow at Denmark by marching an army in the depth of winter across the ice of the Belts, and captured a number of islands without the use of ships.

Finally the conflict, or rather the series of conflicts, was brought to an end as the result of pressure from Great Britain and the United Provinces, neither of whom was prepared to tolerate the continued interference with their trade. Accordingly, in May, 1660, the Treaty of Oliva was concluded between Sweden, Poland, and Brandenburg; in the following month peace between Sweden and Denmark was reached by the Treaty of Copenhagen; and in 1661 the pacification of the North was completed by the Treaty of Kardis between Sweden and Russia. By these arrangements John Casimir V of Poland renounced all the old claims of his branch of the Vasa family to the throne of Sweden, and he acknowledged the independent sovereignty of the Great Elector in East Prussia, while the new King of Denmark surrendered almost all the remaining Danish possessions on the Scandinavian peninsula: the Tsar, Alexis, restored to the Swedes the Livonian fortresses which he had occupied. This settlement strengthened still further the hold of Sweden on the Baltic, and following on the Treaties of Xanten and Westphalia it marked out Brandenburg as the rising force in North Germany. It also stressed the steady decline in the fortunes of Denmark.

Charles X had died before peace was made, and his son and successor, Charles XI, being a minor, the country was for some years governed by a council of regency, whose venality was only equalled by its incompetence. Its vacillation during the War of Devolution has been noticed in an earlier chapter, and soon after the conclusion of the Treaty of Aix-la-Chapelle the Francophil party regained their ascendancy. When, therefore, Louis XIV declared war on the United Provinces in 1672 the Swedes espoused the cause of France, and this in its turn implied hostilities with the Great Elector, the ally of the Dutch, for which the council of regency had made no adequate preparation. In June, 1675, Frederick William won a resounding victory at Fehrbellin, and then pushed on into Swedish Pomerania, which without any serious opposition he occupied in its entirety. These misfortunes encouraged the other enemies of Sweden to try their luck, and the Danes made a strenuous effort to regain their lost provinces. By this time Charles XI had come of age, and he soon showed that he possessed his share of his family's energy and ability. In two pitched battles he defeated the Danes, and drove them out of Sweden, but the navy had been allowed to decay to such an extent as to render impossible any attempt to recover his overseas possession. Fortunately for the Swedes, however, Louis did not forget them when the time came to make peace: the French had occupied Cleves during the war, and this was only restored to the Elector of Brandenburg by the Treaty of Saint Germain-en-Laye in June, 1679, on condition of the return to Sweden of all his conquests in Pomerania, except for a small strip of land on the Oder.

For some years after this settlement the Northern Powers were at peace until 1697, when the death of Charles XI appeared to afford an opportunity to the enemies of Sweden to wreak their vengeance upon her. The excuse was provided by one Patkul, a Livonian nobleman who had offended Charles XI, and who had in consequence been compelled to leave his country. He appealed to Denmark, Poland, and Russia for assistance, nominally to restore to Livonia its lost independence. These Powers agreed to support Patkul, and in 1699 a coalition was formed against Sweden and her new monarch, Charles XII.

The Swedish King realized that his great hope lay in striking at his enemies before they could concentrate, so early in May, 1700, he sailed straight to Copenhagen, and ended the Danish war at a blow. Frederick IV was unable to defend his capital, and, largely owing to the good offices of Great Britain and the United Provinces, he concluded the Treaty of Travendal, by which he withdrew from his alliance with Poland and Russia. Charles XII then turned on Peter the Great, who was besieging Narva, and routed him in a battle in which the Swedes numbered a mere eight thousand against some sixty thousand Russians.

Only Poland now remained to be dealt with. John Sobieski had died in 1696, and in his place Augustus, Elector of Saxony, had been raised to the throne. Fresh from his victory over the Tsar, the Swedish King marched through Livonia and Courland into Poland, where he defeated Augustus at the battle of Clissow, and drove him into Saxony. In 1703 Charles captured Thorn and Danzig, procured the deposition of Augustus in an assembly held at Warsaw in the opening weeks of the following year, and imposed Stanislaus Leszczynski upon the Poles as their sovereign. He then resumed his career of conquest, drove the Russians out of Lithuania in 1705, and finally invaded Saxony itself in 1707. In September of that year Augustus was compelled to sign the Treaty of Altranstadt, by which he recognized Stanislaus as King of Poland and handed over Patkul to his conqueror. Charles had the unfortunate Livonian broken on the wheel, and so came to an end the coalition against Sweden.

By this time the War of the Spanish Succession was in full swing, and both sides endeavoured to enlist the support of the King of Sweden. Louis XIV reminded him of the old friendship between their two countries, and entreated him to acknowledge the benefits of the Treaty of Saint Germain-en-Laye by drawing his sword for France at the crisis of her fate. Marlborough, fresh from his victories at Blenheim and Ramillies, came to Altranstadt to ask Charles not to listen to the arguments of Versailles. The Swede hesitated, and then decided to let the War of the Spanish Succession take its couse. He preferred to deal a final blow to the Tsar by the capture of Moscow, so in the spring of 1708 he turned his back on Germany and the Rhine and marched away to the North.

Like Napoleon and Hitler in succeeding centuries, Charles determined to strike at Moscow, but he was not destined to reach the city. The promises of substantial Cossack support proved illusory, and the problem of supplies was insuperable. In June, 1709, the crisis was reached when, at Pultava, the Tsar defeated the Swedes in what has proved to be one of the really decisive battles of history. Charles was himself wounded, though he managed to reach Turkish territory, but the Russian victory marked the end of Sweden as a Power of the first rank. As was the case with the United Provinces, for lack of the necessary resources she could not maintain her position for more than a couple of generations.

All the same, Sweden did not go down without a fight. Charles XII remained in Turkey until the failure of the Tsar at Azov enabled him to return to his own country, which he found threatened on all sides by Russians, Danes, and Poles. For seven years he struggled in vain against superior forces abroad and the disaffection of the nobles at home. By 1716 he had lost every acre of German soil, and two years later he was killed while besieging the fortress of Fredrikssten in Norway.

The death of Charles XII paved the way for a general pacification of Northern Europe which completely transformed the Balance of Power in that quarter. By the Treaties of Stockholm, in February, 1719, and February, 1720, the Elector of Hanover, now also *de facto* King of England, obtained the bishoprics of Bremen and Verden, while Stettin and district went to the new kingdom of Prussia, as Brandenburg had become. There was some delay before a settlement was reached with the Tsar, and three Russian descents on the Swedish coast took place before, in August, 1721, the Treaty of Nystad was signed: by this Russia obtained Livonia, Esthonia, Ingria, the province of Kexholm, and the fortress of Viborg, while Finland to the West of Viborg and North of Kexholm was returned to Sweden, who was also granted an indemnity of two million thalers and freedom of trade in the Baltic.

This settlement marked the end of one era and the beginning of another. Just as Sweden had displaced Denmark as the dominant state in the Baltic so now Sweden yielded up that rôle to Russia, while across the sea Prussia was rapidly building up in the Reich the position to which Gustavus Adolphus and his successors had aspired.

CHAPTER XXI

THE PARTITION TREATIES AND THE WAR OF THE SPANISH SUCCESSION, 1698–1713

As the seventeenth century drew to its close it became clear that Charles II of Spain had not much longer to live, and that it behoved those who considered themselves his heirs to bestir themselves. Louis had, it is true, come to an agreement with Leopold in 1668 as to the division of the Spanish dominions, but circumstances had changed, and the monarch whom it was most important to conciliate was no longer Leopold but William. The Treaty of Ryswick gave Louis the opportunity of opening negotiations with his old enemy, and he lost no time in doing so. William, on his side, was quite ready to discuss the matter. When the war came to an end England had an army of eighty-seven thousand men, but hardly had peace been signed than a wave of pacifism and disarmament swept across the country, and Parliament refused to vote supplies for more than seven thousand soldiers. Louis, it may be added, fully realized that in these circumstances William had no option but to negotiate, and with one hand tied behind his back.

The method of communication was through the Comte de Tallard, the French ambassador in London, and all through the spring and summer of 1698 the negotiations continued. The problem was sufficiently complicated to tax the most astute intelligence. The claimants to the Spanish throne were three in number, namely the Dauphin, the Electress of Bavaria, and the Emperor. The Dauphin was the nearest heir by blood, for he was the son of the eldest daughter of Philip IV, but his mother had renounced all claim to the Spanish crown when she married Louis XIV, though it was a moot point whether this renunciation stood in view of the fact that her dowry had never been paid. The Electress of Bavaria, the daughter of the Spanish King's younger sister and of the Emperor Leopold I, was next in succession, but her mother had likewise renounced her rights when she married the Emperor. Lastly, there was Leopold himself, for his mother, the aunt of Charles II, had, unlike her nieces, made no renunciation. If, therefore, the renunciations held good, the Emperor's claim was the best, but if not, then the Dauphin was the lawful heir.

Nevertheless, it was clear from the beginning that in the regulation of the succession legal interpretations would have to give place to practical considerations, for in spite of the encroachments of France during the previous forty years, the Spanish monarchy was still by far the greatest of all Christian realms. If the Emperor succeeded to this inheritance, the empire of Charles V would be revived, whereas if the prize went to France the rest of Europe would not unnaturally feel its very independence threatened.

Of these alternatives the former would have suited England the better, for the Habsburg dominions were but loosely knit together, were inefficiently governed, and did not constitute a threat to vital English interests. At the same time William knew quite well that Louis would never consent to this, and in view of the state of his subjects' opinion he was by no means certain that he would be in a position to oppose French pretensions by force. Such being the case, a compromise was effected without any difficulty, and in October, 1698, the First Partition Treaty was signed. This stipulated that the Electoral Prince of Bavaria, the weakest of the three claimants, should have Spain, the Indies, and the Low Countries; Naples, Sicily, the Tuscan ports, and Guipuzcoa were to fall to the Dauphin; and the Milanese was to go to Leopold's son by his second wife, the Archduke Charles. The problem that had confronted Europe for a generation seemed to have been solved.

Fate willed otherwise, for hardly had this solution been reached than the Electoral Prince died. Louis heard the news on February 8th, 1699, and before a week had elapsed he had, with his accustomed energy, drawn up fresh schemes for the partition of the Spanish Empire. The principle on which they were based was the Balance of Power. "I know", he wrote to Tallard, "how alarmed Europe would be to see my power raised to a greater height than that of Austria. . . . But the Emperor's power is also so greatly increased by the submission of the princes of the Empire and by the advantageous peace which he has just concluded with the Porte, that it is in the general interest, if he becomes stronger, that my power also should be sufficient to counterbalance that of the Emperor." During the course of the negotiations no detail escaped his vigilant eye, and he displayed a shrewd appreciation of the interests of the other Powers. "I foresee," he said, "great difficulties in the way of obtaining the consent of the King of England to the addition of the Milanese to my son's portion. Should you see that it is impossible to overcome the objections raised, you can make a suggestion for bringing to a satisfactory conclusion this important matter". As for the Low Countries, "the King of England and the States-General would be equally irritated at seeing them in my hands, or in those of the Emperor", while "the Spaniards are jealous of any attempt to dismember their empire, which they wish to preserve entire. I shall be obliged to take up arms and conquer that portion of the Spanish dominions assigned to my son."

Months of hard bargaining took place before the Second Partition Treaty was concluded in May, 1700, between France, Great Britain, and the United Provinces. By this the Archduke Charles was given Spain, the Low Countries, and the Indies, while the Dauphin was to have the two Sicilies, the Milanese, and Guipuzcoa. It was not a very satisfactory arrangement from the point of view of France, but, even so, the Emperor protested against it. As for the Spaniards, their indignation knew no bounds: the Queen of Spain broke all the furniture in her room, and the Spanish ambassador in London used such strong language that he was requested to leave the country. That Louis was perfectly sincere in his statements that he intended to abide by this agreement cannot now be seriously doubted, and if proof of this be required it is surely supplied by the fact that in the following October he told Talland to insist that the English and Dutch should hasten their military preparations so that the treaty could be enforced when the necessity arose. "I cannot believe", he wrote, "that they will fail in executing agreements so formal and so precise, when the time shall arrive to carry them out."

Meanwhile, in Madrid all was confusion. The Queen Mother had died in 1696, and the Queen, who was a sister of the Empress, inclined to the party which favoured Austria, but the partizans of France, headed by Cardinal Portocarrero, steadily gained ground. The reason for this somewhat paradoxical development was that the one point on which all Spaniards were agreed was opposition to the dismemberment of their empire, and it was obvious that if anyone could prevent its partition it was Louis. So far as the King of Spain could appreciate any argument, this carried great weight with him, although his natural inclinations

were in favour of his relatives at Vienna. In these circumstances
he made a will leaving the whole of his dominions to Philip, Duke
of Anjou, the younger son of the Dauphin, and appointed a council
to carry on the government until the new King arrived in Spain.
If Philip refused to accept the inheritance the right to it was to
pass wholly to the Archduke Charles. Having sown this crop of
dragon's teeth Charles died on November 1st, 1700, in his fortieth
year.

Louis was now called upon to take the most important decision
of his reign, and it was not an easy choice that had to be made.
Only a few months had elapsed since the conclusion of the Second
Partition Treaty, and for the French King to go back on his word
would make him an object of contempt in every Court in Europe.
Moreover, France was in urgent need of a prolonged period of
peace, and to accept the will meant war, for it was impossible to
believe that the other Powers would make no effort to prevent such
an increase of French influence both in Europe and in the Americas.
It is true that the Second Partition Treaty would have placed a
Habsburg on the Spanish throne, but it also meant an enormous
increase of French territory when the Dauphin should succeed his
father. The Archduke Charles was, too, but the second son of the
Emperor, and there was always the possibility that with the passage of time relations between Madrid and Vienna would become
less friendly: in any event it would not be easy for the two branches
of the House of Habsburg to come to one another's assistance with
the French dominant in the Italian peninsula. On the other hand,
if the will were accepted Louis must abandon all hope of
advancing the frontiers of France in the direction of the Low
Countries.

There were equally weighty arguments on the other side. In
the first place, the attitude of the Emperor left no doubt that he
would fight sooner than agree to the terms of the Second Partition
Treaty, and if Louis had to go to war it was surely better to do so
for the whole than for a part. In the latter case, too, he would have
Spain against him, while it was more than likely that the English
and Dutch in their existing mood would prove unable or unwilling
to come to his assistance. Then, again, with a Frenchman on the
Spanish throne the influence, if not the frontiers, of France would
be immeasurably increased, and in future wars Spain, far from
being an enemy as for so long, would prove an invaluable ally.
Louis called a council meeting of the Dauphin, the Chancellor, the

Minister of Finance, and the Foreign Secretary, and after hearing their views he decided to accept the will.

For the moment the French King had won, and at first it seemed as if William would be compelled to acquiesce in what had happened: in that event the Emperor would have little chance of making head against the joint forces of France and Spain. The English Parliament was at that moment being particularly fractious, and the Dutch were in favour of peace at almost any price. In these circumstances the acceptance of the will was received in England and the United Provinces with resignation, for as one of its provisions was that Spain was to remain independent, it was not considered that the balance of power in Europe would be upset to anything like the extent that would have been the case had the Second Partition Treaty come into operation. William was but stating the facts when he wrote to Heinsius, the Grand Pensionary, "I am troubled to the very bottom of my soul to find now that the business has become public, that nearly everybody congratulates himself that France has preferred the will to the treaty, insisting that it is much better for England and for the whole of Europe". In these circumstances there was nothing to do but give way, and by April, 1701, both England and the United Provinces had recognized Philip as King of Spain.

At this point Louis made a number of mistakes which, though to some extent explicable, were destined to be fatal. In spite of the recognition of Philip by the English and Dutch the French King seems to have considered war unavoidable, and by endeavouring to put himself in the best possible position should it break out he did in fact render it inevitable. Early in 1701 he seized the fortresses of the Dutch Barrier in the Spanish Netherlands, which were occupied in accordance with the provisions of the Treaty of Ryswick. This thoroughly alarmed the United Provinces, and enabled William to form a league with the Emperor to secure a settlement which was not unlike that which was ultimately effected at Utrecht. Even so, the disinclination for war in England was so strong that she might have refused to fight had Louis not taken one final step which provoked her beyond endurance.

In September, 1701, James II died, and, in defiance of the Treaty of Ryswick, his son was recognized by Louis as King of England, Scotland, and Ireland. The reason for this step is not far to seek: French diplomacy had blundered badly in 1660, and Louis did not want to be caught napping by a second Stuart restoration. This time the returned monarch should have cause to be grateful to France. On the other hand, Jacobitism in 1701 was at a discount, and more than one of those who were to draw the sword for James III fourteen years later was then forswearing the Stuart cause; nor was the ordinary Englishman, however much he might dislike the morose Dutchman who reigned over him, prepared to accept a monarch at the dictation of the King of France.

The immediate reaction, therefore, which Louis produced was the passing of a measure by the English Parliament attainting James of High Treason for having assumed the title of King of England, and compelling all who desired official employment to abjure his claim to the throne. This measure, it may be noted in passing, was to no small extent due to Henry St. John, later Viscount Bolingbroke, who was one day to be Secretary of State to the monarch whom he was now so anxious to proscribe. The ultimate effect of the French King's action was to bring England into the field against him. William had been working for this ever since the acceptance of the will, and the recognition of James played into his hands by making his policy popular with his English subjects. When Louis further proceeded to prohibit the importation of all British manufactured articles into France, the cup of his iniquities, so far as the English were concerned, was indeed full.

Leopold thus found allies in London and The Hague, and the War of the Spanish Succession began, with France, Spain, and Bavaria arrayed against the Grand Alliance of the Empire, Great Britain, and the United Provinces. It was not long before it became evident that Louis had undertaken a task beyond even his strength. The attempt to end the war at one blow by the capture of Vienna was foiled by Marlborough at Blenheim in 1704, and the following years were marked by further disasters on all fronts. In Spain alone were French arms ultimately successful, and that because the bulk of Spanish people made Philip's cause their own; against the Catalans and the Portuguese who were supporting the Archduke Charles.

In 1706 Louis offered to treat for peace, but the only terms which he was prepared to consider were those of the Second Partition Treaty, which were not acceptable to the Allies. Indeed, the object of the war was changing, and peace was becoming increasingly more difficult of attainment. By the terms of the Grand

Alliance it had been stipulated "that the kingdoms of France and Spain should never be united or governed by the same person, that the dominions and commerce of the Dutch should be secured, and that a reasonable satisfaction should be given to the Emperor and the English King." The passage of time extended not only the scope of the war, but also its objects, and at the end of 1707 the Whigs carried in both Houses of Parliament a resolution to the effect that no peace "can be safe or honourable for Her Majesty or her allies if Spain and the Spanish West Indies be suffered to continue in the power of the House of Bourbon". In this way the whole basis of the policy of Great Britain, the mainspring of the alliance against Louis, was altered, and the war, from being one to preserve the balance of power, became one to impose upon the Spanish people a monarch whom the majority of them were determined not to have.

In 1711 the situation was further complicated by the death of the Emperor Joseph I, for his successor was his brother, the Archduke Charles, so that the Allies found themselves fighting not merely to force an unwanted King on the Spaniards, but also to make the new Emperor the master of Europe by resurrecting the empire of his namesake Charles V. As these developments came to be realized in England, opposition began to grow to the continuance of a war in which English lives and English money were being sacrificed for what were no longer English ends.

Meanwhile the French arms continued to suffer reverse after reverse in Flanders. In 1708 Marlborough and Eugene defeated the Duke of Burgundy at Oudenarde, and after a long siege Lille surrendered to the Allies. It was not, however, so much military defeat that was bringing France to the verge of ruin as economic and financial chaos. As early as 1707 the task of supplying the armies in the field had become acute, and the more far-sighted realized that France was nearing the end of her resources. The extraordinarily severe winter of 1708-9 precipitated the crisis, for fruit-trees and vines were destroyed in province after province. The financial situation was as desperate as the economic, for taxation had reached a point beyond which it was impossible to go, and even births, marriages, and deaths were compelled to contribute to the revenue. There was discontent in Paris, and both Madame de Maintenon and the ministers were savagely attacked.

So menacing had the situation become that Louis was driven to ask for terms. The first negotiations took place at The Hague, and it soon became clear that the Allies were determined to have their pound of flesh: the terms of peace were not to be negotiated, but were to be dictated. Yet Louis was reduced to such straits that even this prospect did not shake his determination to treat. He was prepared to recognize the Protestant succession in Great Britain, which he had repudiated by the proclamation of James III; he promised to satisfy all the commercial demands of the Allies, to abandon on Philip's behalf the whole of the Spanish dominions, and to cede Dunkirk, Lille, Tournai, Maubeuge, and Strasbourg, together with various towns on the frontier of Savoy, while Newfoundland and Hudson's Bay were to be surrendered. If the Allies had still been pursuing the goal for which the war had been begun they could have achieved it now, but their appetite had grown with success, and they put forward demands which even in his extremity Louis found it impossible to accept. Philip was to abandon the whole Spanish monarchy in two months' time, failing which Louis was to turn his arms against his own grandson, and it was only in the event of this condition being fulfilled that the Allies would even grant an armistice. Desperate as his position had become, Louis had not sunk so low as to accept such humiliation. He recalled his envoy from The Hague, and broke off the negotiations. "If I must continue the war", he said, "I will fight against my enemies rather than against my own family", and he appealed to the people of France to come to his aid.

The appeal was not made in vain. Nobles melted down their plate, ladies contributed their jewellery, and the peasants sent their hoarded sous to organize resistance. Never, in all his splendid reign was Louis more truly the leader of his people than when he sent the last army of France to the front in the spring of 1709. This force was placed under the command of Marshal Villars, and although it was compelled to yield at Malplaquet to the greatly superior numbers of the Allies, the honours of the battle belonged to the vanquished, while the losses of the victors were out of all proportion to the results obtained.

Negotiations for peace were opened once more, this time at Gertruydenberg, as soon as the opposing armies were settled in their winter quarters, but the Allies soon discovered that the position of Louis had by no means weakened since they last met his representatives. The Pyrrhic victory of Malplaquet had shown that the French powers of resistance were certainly not negligible: the French armies were still in being; the Allies were quarrelling among themselves; and the loss of life was beginning to have its effect upon British public opinion, while the stories of Marlborough's personal interest in the continuance of hostilities were gaining increasing credence. In the middle of the winter of 1709–10 Louis came forward with proposals which it seems inconceivable should have been rejected. He consented to surrender Alsace, and offered not only to recognize Charles, who had not yet become Emperor, as King of Spain, but to forbid his subjects to serve in the Peninsula, and he declared his readiness to provide supplies for the Allied armies there: for the rest, the Elector of Bavaria was to be restored to his dominions, which he had lost after Blenheim, and James was to be allowed to retire wherever he pleased after his expulsion from France. The negotiations dragged on for several months, until the Allies demanded that, alone and unaided, Louis should dethrone his grandson, when the conference of course broke down. This was in June, 1710: three months later the situation had completely changed, the Whigs were out of office, and the Tories had come into power in England with the determination to put an end to the war.

In the new administration the control of foreign policy lay very largely in the hands of Henry St. John, and his conduct of affairs up to and including the Treaty of Utrecht has for consummate ability rarely been equalled, and never surpassed, in the course of English history. It was successful because it was based upon the realities of the European situation, and not upon theories of his own, or upon the facts of ten years before. St. John realized that there were two wars, one against France, which the Allies had won, and another against Spain, which they had lost, or were on the point of losing. He never forgot that the original object of the conflict had been to prevent a French hegemony of Europe. This was the basis of a policy which he had both the vigour and the knowledge to put into effect. He was in close contact with opinion in his own party, and he knew Europe in a way impossible save to those who have studied it on the spot.

On the French side was Torcy, a nephew of Colbert, and also a man of great ability. Each statesman knew that the other's need for peace was as great as his own, but St. John had the disadvantage that the Whigs had committed England to a policy which was incapable of realization, though to depart from it would be an act of treachery to the Allies. The aim of both negotiators was to arrive at a preliminary settlement, which should then be put to

the other interested parties at a conference. If St. John be criti-
cized on the score that he was negotiating with the enemy behind
the backs of his allies, as was indubitably the case, he had at least
the excuse that previous efforts to make peace had been wrecked
by the obstinacy of the Emperor and the Dutch.

In July, 1711, a few weeks after the new British Government's
case had been immeasurably strengthened by the death of
Joseph I, Matthew Prior was sent to Paris, where, incidentally, he
found that the Dutch were already trying to arrive at a separate
arrangement with the French. Prior was not authorized to conclude any agreement: all he had to do was to state the British
demands, and to return with the French reply. These demands in
brief were as follows: no peace without satisfaction for all the
Allies; barriers for the Dutch, the Emperor, and the Duke of
Savoy, while Victor Amadeus was to have restored to him such of
his possessions as were in Austrian or French occupation; the
crowns of France and Spain never to be united; all the Allies
who came into the treaty to be satisfied, and the trade of the
United Provinces to be secured. So far as Great Britain was concerned, Prior was instructed to put forward certain propositions;
a treaty of trade and commerce to be negotiated; the succession to
the British throne "as now settled to be recognized"; Gibraltar and
Minorca to remain British possessions; Dunkirk to be demolished;
the Asiento contract to be entirely in the hands of England; Newfoundland to be ceded to Britain, the trade in Hudson's Bay to
continue shared, and the *status quo* in America to be preserved;
equal commercial privileges both with France and Spain; the
existence of these articles not to be divulged save by mutual consent.

Torcy was taken aback by the extent of these demands, but
Prior refused to give way, and the conversations were transferred
to London. On two occasions they came within an ace of being
broken off: once over St. John's demand for "cautionary towns"
in the Spanish Indies to secure English trade there, which Philip
refused to grant; and once over French insistence on the return
of Lille and Tournai in return for the destruction of the fortifications of Dunkirk. In both cases there was a compromise. In
exchange for the abandonment of the claim for the American
towns, St. John obtained an extension to thirty years of the period
of the Asiento monopoly of the slave trade granted to the South
Sea Company, while the question of Lille and Tournai was postponed until the conference. It was hard bargaining between St.

John and Torcy, for, as Professor Trevelyan so rightly says, "It was Greek meet Greek and blade cut blade".

At last, however, all the matters in dispute were settled, and on September 27th according to the Old Style, and October 8th according to the New, the preliminaries were signed by St. John and the Earl of Dartmouth on behalf of Anne, and by Nicolas Mesnager, Comte de Saint-Jean, for Louis XIV.

CHAPTER XXII

THE TREATY OF UTRECHT

THE Peace Conference opened at Utrecht on January 29th, 1712, and the British representatives were the Bishop of Bristol and the Earl of Strafford. The first event was the presentation by the Marquis d'Huxelles, on behalf of France, of a series of proposals which maintained the terms of the agreement with Great Britain, but seriously threatened the position of her allies, for they included the suggestion that the Spanish Netherlands should be given to the Elector of Bavaria. This move was followed by counter-suggestions from the other Powers, and before long it was apparent that the Conference had reached a deadlock. When this happened St. John adopted the time-honoured device of leaving the Conference to mark time, while the real business was transacted elsewhere, in this case directly between London and Paris. "Her Majesty is fully determined to let all negotiations sleep in Holland", he wrote, and the bishop and the earl duly obeyed his instructions.

The position of the British Government was a delicate one in spite of the victory over the Opposition at home. In the previous year the bases of a settlement had been agreed between England and France, much to the discontent of the former's allies, and the French were taking advantage of this situation to impose terms upon the Emperor and the Dutch in the knowledge that their own agreement with England had rendered her suspect in Vienna and The Hague. Torcy on the other hand enjoyed the great asset that he had free hands, except for the Franco-British understanding, while St. John was hampered by the Barrier Treaty with the Dutch. This was one of those undertakings which are so lightly given during the course of a war, and which prove so inconvenient at the succeeding Peace Conference. It had been negotiated in 1709, and went far to establish the supremacy of the United Provinces in North-West Europe. It admitted the right of the Dutch to close the Scheldt, which they had obtained sixty years before, and it pledged England to obtain for them Spanish Guelderland: the Dutch were also allowed to garrison more towns on the French frontier than had previously been the case. Bad as this arrangement was from the British standpoint, it nevertheless existed, and it tied St. John's hands.

A further difficulty arose at this point, and it came very near to wrecking the negotiations altogether, in view of the fact that the Franco-British understanding of the previous year had provided for the retention by Philip of Spain and the Indies. At that time there had been four lives between Philip V and the throne of France in the event of the demise of Louis XIV, but the situation was suddenly changed by the death of the Dauphin, of his son the Duke of Burgundy, and of his grandson the Duke of Brittany. This left only a sickly child, later Louis XV, between Philip and the crown when the old King should die. St. John and the Government saw themselves placed in the same difficult position as the Whigs had been at the death of Joseph I, for it was no more to the interest of Great Britain to see Philip King of France and Spain than to assist Charles to become both Holy Roman Emperor and Catholic King.

The first of these complications was solved by recourse to the unilateral denunciation of the Barrier Treaty. Swift prepared the way with a pamphlet entitled *Some Remarks on the Barrier Treaty*, and the House of Commons then debated the matter. A vote was passed that the treaty contained "several articles destructive to the trade and interest of Great Britain", and the ministers who advised its ratification were declared "enemies to the Queen and kingdom". On March 1st the Commons addressed to Anne a long "representation on the state of the nation", and St. John contributed an article to the *Amsterdam Gazette* in its support. The States-General answered the allegations in a formal memorial, which the Lower House voted to be a "false, scandalous, and malicious libel". By the summer of 1712 the majority in the Commons (and probably in the nation) was so incensed against the Dutch that any attempt to carry out the terms of the Barrier Treaty was clearly impossible. St. John had skilfully surmounted his first difficulty.

The complication caused by the deaths of the French princes proved less easy of solution. St. John's first suggestion was that Philip should renounce the succession to the French throne, but Torcy advised him that this was impossible, since the Paris lawyers held that no renunciation by the rightful heir could be valid. However desirous the British statesman might be of reaching a settlement, he was not prepared to sacrifice a vital national interest out of respect for the French constitution, and he therefore made an alternative proposal. If Philip will not abandon his prospect of becoming King of France, let him hand Spain and the Indies over to the Duke of Savoy; in return he can have the Savoyard territories with the addition of Montferrat, Mantua, and Sicily; if and when Philip succeeds to the French crown, these North Italian provinces are to be incorporated in the French dominions, while Sicily is to go to Austria. This suggestion met with the entire approval of Louis XIV, who did not believe that his great-grandson would live, and who rejoiced in what appeared to him to be the practical certainty of a large extension of French territory to the south-east. Philip, however, preferred Madrid to Turin, even with the possible reversion of Paris, and the scheme came to nothing.

Meanwhile no effort was being spared by the Emperor to prevent the conclusion of peace, and early in 1712 he sent his great general, Prince Eugene, to see what could be effected by his prestige, but the Government rose to the occasion, and saw that he became nothing more than a social lion. Indeed, there appears to have been a Tory conspiracy to keep him drunk as the surest method of rendering him harmless. On the Continent hostilities had ceased so far as Great Britain was concerned. Marlborough had already been displaced as commander-in-chief by the Duke of Ormonde, and in May the latter received orders to "avoid engaging in any siege, or hazarding a battle": St. John, who had now become Viscount Bolingbroke, also communicated these instructions to the French.

Ormonde accordingly announced to the Allied troops that the British Government was arranging an armistice for two months, to which he invited them to accede. He then marched towards Dunkirk, which, by arrangement with the French, he was under orders to occupy, but the Dutch governors of Bouchain, Tournai, and Douai refused to open their gates. Ghent he easily secured, as it had an English garrison, and he occupied Bruges without resistance. The Dutch and Austrians soon proved unable by themselves to resist the French, and the campaigning season of 1712 closed with Marshal Villars not only as victor in the field, but as master of several fortresses, including Douai and Bouchain.

With an armistice concluded, and the renunciation of the French crown completed, it became desirable to settle the outstanding points as soon as possible, and with this end in view Bolingbroke himself went to Paris at the beginning of August.

His journey from Calais to the French capital was in the nature of a royal progress, so desirous were the French of peace after the long and exhausting war. When he arrived in Paris he took up his residence at the house of the Marquise de Croissy, Torcy's aunt, and the two statesmen soon became personal friends.

The business of Bolingbroke's mission was easily concluded. It was agreed that the Duke of Savoy was to have Sicily, and that his right to succeed to the Spanish throne after Philip and his heirs should be acknowledged in the acts by which the inheritance of the Bourbons was settled. Other points at issue were seemingly arranged with equal ease. On the Saturday after his arrival Bolingbroke was taken by Torcy to Fontainebleau, where he spent the night, and next day was received by the King. Louis expressed his desire for peace, and his respect for Anne; but he spoke so fast, and his articulation was so indistinct, that the Englishman, although an excellent French scholar, had some difficulty in understanding him. Everywhere Bolingbroke met with the most flattering reception, and when he went to the theatre to see Corneille's *Cid* the whole house rose to receive him, and the performance was suspended until he had taken his seat.

When Bolingbroke returned to London he found, like many another British statesman both before and since, that what had seemed so easy and pleasant in Paris took on a very different complexion once he had left France. His colleagues in the Cabinet by no means relished the ovation which he had received on the other side of the Channel, and they were only too ready to create difficulties. The French were not slow in making capital out of this situation, and the reverses which their armies were inflicting upon the Dutch gave them an added advantage. Then an unfortunate quarrel took place between the lackeys of the French and Dutch representatives at Utrecht; this was elevated to the dignity of a national conflict, and the work of the conference was for a time suspended. At this point the British government decided to send the Duke of Hamilton to Paris to expedite matters, but before he could set out this nobleman was killed in a duel. A further delay thereupon ensued until his successor was appointed.

Fortune was certainly smiling upon Louis once again as the position of the British government became increasingly more difficult. It was impossible to meet Parliament until peace had been made, and indefinite prorogation was out of the question. By February, 1713, it had been prorogued eleven times, and a decision was essential. In that month, therefore, Bolingbroke sent Torcy what amounted to an ultimatum. He laid down in precise terms the British demands relative to the questions still outstanding, namely, the fishing rights off Nova Scotia, the monopoly of the navigation of the Amazon by the Portuguese, and the addition of Tournai to the Dutch Barrier: failing compliance war would be resumed in the spring. The threat had the desired result, and on Good Friday, April 3rd, 1713, about two o'clock in the afternoon, a post-chaise rattled down Whitehall: as it stopped at the Cockpit there alighted, all covered with dust, Bolingbroke's half-brother, George St. John, with the Treaty of Utrecht in his hand. The statesman welcomed him on the doorstep with open arms, and his relief can be gauged by his words, "It is the Lord's work, and it is marvellous in our eyes". The lapse of a few months, and several defeats by Villars, were necessary before the Emperor gave way, and signed the Treaties of Rastadt and Baden.

By the Treaties of Utrecht, Rastadt, and Baden, generally grouped together under the name of the Peace of Utrecht, the following arrangements were effected:—

1. Philip V was recognized as King of Spain and the Indies, on the condition that the crowns of France and Spain were never to be united on the same head.

2. Naples, the Milanese, Sardinia, and the Netherlands were given to the Emperor, subject to the right of the Dutch to the military government of Furnes, Ypres, Ghent, Tournai, Mons, Charleroi, and Namur as their barrier against France. The Scheldt was to remain closed.

3. France was permitted to retain Alsace including Strasbourg, but she had to surrender the fortresses of Kehl, Breisach, and Freiburg, which she had seized on the right bank of the Rhine.

4. The Electors of Cologne and Bavaria were restored, the succession of the House of Hanover in England acknowledged, and James banished from France.

5. England received Gibraltar, Minorca, Newfoundland (subject to certain rights of fishing on the banks), Hudson's Bay, Acadia, and St. Kitts, and acquired by an Asiento, or agreement, with Spain the right to trade under strict limitations with certain towns in Spanish waters set apart for the purpose.

6. The Kingdom of Prussia was recognized, and received Upper Guelderland.

7. Sicily and part of the Milanese were given to the Duke of Savoy, and it was agreed that the fortifications of Dunkirk should be demolished.

Had Bolingbroke been able to have his way, the treaty would have been followed by a commercial agreement with France and a large step in the direction of freedom of trade between the two countries. In this respect he was too far in advance of his age. The manufacturers rose in revolt, the Whigs did everything in their power to foment the opposition, and a number of Tories voted against the Government. Bolingbroke was no longer in the Commons to sway members with his eloquence, and his colleagues were only too ready to give him a fall. The vital clauses in the proposed treaty were rejected by nine votes, and a commercial understanding with France had to wait until the time of the younger Pitt.

Such was the settlement which was principally the work of two relatively young men, for Bolingbroke was only thirty-four, while Torcy was forty-seven. The methods employed to effect this pacification certainly left a good deal to be desired where the British Government was concerned, but some, at least, of the blame must surely be shared with the Whig administration whose bellicosity had placed the country in so impossible a position. For the rest, the great merit of the treaty was that it recognized existing facts. France was the first Power in Europe, Philip was the monarch desired by Spain, Great Britain was building a colonial empire, and Prussia and Savoy were rising states: all these incontrovertible realities were admitted at Utrecht. As for Louis XIV, he had completed the work of Richelieu and Mazarin, and had given his country security. It is true that the more unjustifiable ambitions of the middle years of his reign had not been realized, but he had effected a very great deal. Spain was a friendly, almost a client, state; Italy and Germany were as disunited as ever: and to the north it was invasion of, not from, the Low Countries that had become the order of the day. If proof be wanted of the security which Louis XIV won for France, it lies in the fact that while the monarchy stood no invader established himself on French soil.

APPENDIX

CONTEMPORARY RULERS

THE EMPIRE

Frederick III	. . .	1440
Maximilian I	. . .	1493
Charles V	. . .	1520
Ferdinand I	. . .	1556
Maximilian II	. . .	1564
Rudolf II	. . .	1576
Matthias	. . .	1612
Ferdinand II	. . .	1619
Ferdinand III	. . .	1637
Leopold I	. . .	1658
Joseph I	. . .	1705
Charles VI	. . .	1711

FRANCE

Charles VIII	. . .	1483
Louis XII	. . .	1498
Francis I	. . .	1515
Henry II	. . .	1547
Francis II	. . .	1559
Charles IX	. . .	1560
Henry III	. . .	1574
Henry IV	. . .	1589
Louis XIII	. . .	1610
Louis XIV	. . .	1643

THE PAPACY

Alexander VI	. . .	1492
Pius III	. . .	1503
Julius II	. . .	1503
Leo X	. . .	1513
Adrian VI	. . .	1522
Clement VII	. . .	1523
Paul III	. . .	1534
Julius III	. . .	1550
Marcellus II	. . .	1555
Paul IV	. . .	1555
Pius IV	. . .	1559

Pius V	. . .	1566
Gregory XIII	. . .	1572
Sixtus V	. . .	1585
Urban VII	. . .	1590
Gregory XIV	. . .	1590
Innocent IX	. . .	1591
Clement VIII	. . .	1592
Leo XI	. . .	1605
Paul V	. . .	1605
Gregory XV	. . .	1621
Urban VIII	. . .	1623
Innocent X	. . .	1644
Alexander VII	. . .	1655
Clement IX	. . .	1667
Clement X	. . .	1670
Innocent XI	. . .	1676
Alexander VIII	. . .	1689
Innocent XII	. . .	1691
Clement XI	. . .	1700

ENGLAND

Henry VII	. . .	1485
Henry VIII	. . .	1509
Edward VI	. . .	1547
Mary I	. . .	1553
Elizabeth	. . .	1558
James I	. . .	1603
Charles I	. . .	1625
Republic	. . .	1649
Charles II	. . .	1660
James II	. . .	1685
William III } Mary II }	. . .	1689
William III alone	. .	1694
Anne	. . :	1702

SPAIN

Ferdinand V } Isabella II }	. . .	1479

SPAIN—*continued*

Ferdinand V } Philip I }	. . .	1504
Ferdinand V alone	. .	1506
Charles I	. . . .	1516
Philip II	. . . .	1556
Philip III	. . . .	1598
Philip IV	. . . .	1621
Charles II	. . . .	1665
Philip V	. . . .	1700

SAVOY

Emmanuel Philibert II	.	1482
Charles III	. . .	1504
Emmanuel Philibert III	.	1553
Charles Emmanuel I	.	1580
Victor Amadeus I	.	1630
Francis	. . .	1637
Charles Emmanuel II	.	1638
Victor Amadeus II	. .	1675

SCOTLAND

James IV	. . . .	1488
James V	. . . .	1513
Mary	. . . .	1542
James VI	. . . .	1567

PORTUGAL

John II	. . . .	1481
Emmanuel	. . .	1495
John III	. . . .	1521
Sebastian	. . .	1557
Henry	. . . .	1578
(United to Spain	. .	1580)
John IV	. . . .	1640
Alfonso VI	. . .	1656
Pedro II	. . .	1683
John V	. . . .	1706

TUSCANY

Cosimo I	. . . .	1537
Francis	. . . .	1574
Ferdinand I	. . .	1587
Cosimo II	. . .	1609
Ferdinand II	. . .	1621
Cosimo III	. . . .	1670

DENMARK

John	. . . . .	1481
Christian II	. .	1513
Frederick I	. . .	1523
Christian III	. .	1533
Frederick II	. .	1559
Christian IV	. .	1588
Frederick III	. .	1648
Christian V	. .	1670
Frederick IV	. .	1699

SWEDEN

John II	. . . .	1483
Christian II	. . .	1520
Gustavus I	. . .	1523
Eric XIV	. . .	1560
John III	. . . .	1569
Sigismund III	. .	1592
Charles IX	. . .	1604
Gustavus (II) Adolphus	.	1611
Christina	. . .	1632
Charles X	. . . .	1654
Charles XI	. . .	1660
Charles XII	. . .	1697

RUSSIA

Ivan III	. . . .	1462
Basil	. . . .	1505
Ivan IV	. . . .	1533
Feodor I	. . . .	1584
Boris Godounoff	. .	1598
(The Troublous Times	.	1605)
Michael	. . .	1613
Alexis	. . . .	1645
Feodor II	. . .	1676
Peter I	. . . .	1682

OTTOMAN EMPIRE

Bayezid II	. . .	1481
Selim I	. . . .	1512
Suleyman I	. .	1520
Selim II	. . .	1566
Murad III	. . .	1574
Mohammed III	. .	1595
Achmet I	. . .	1603
Mustapha I	. .	1617
Othman II	. . .	1618

OTTOMAN EMPIRE—*continued*

Murad IV	. . .	1623
Ibrahim	. . .	1640
Mohammed IV	. .	1649
Suleyman II	. .	1687
Achmet II	. . .	1691
Mustapha II	. .	1695
Achmet III	. .	1703

John Casimir	. . .	1648
Michael	. . .	1669
John Sobieski	. .	1674
Frederick Augustus I	.	1697
Stanislaus	. . .	1704
Frederick Augustus I again	.	1709

POLAND

John Albert	. .	1492
Alexander	. .	1501
Sigismund I	. .	1506
Sigismund II	. .	1548
Henry (of Valois)	. .	1573
Stephen Bathory	. .	1575
Sigismund III	. .	1587
Wladislaus VII	. .	1632

BRANDENBURG

John Cicero	. .	1486
Joachim I	. .	1499
Joachim II	. .	1535
John George	. .	1571
Joachim Frederick	.	1598
John Sigismund	. .	1608
George William	. .	1619
Frederick William	.	1640
Frederick	. . .	1689

SELECT BIBLIOGRAPHY

CHAPTER I

Gairdner, J.: *Henry the Seventh*. London. 1913.
Grant, A. J.: *The French Monarchy, 1483–1789*. Cambridge.
Jonquière, Vicomte de la: *Histoire de l'Empire Ottoman*. Paris. 1914.
Walsh, W. T.: *Isabella of Spain*. London. 1931.

CHAPTER II

Maulde de la Clavière, R. de: *Histoire de Louis XII*. Paris. 1889–1893.
Ranke, L. von: *History of the Latin and Teutonic Nations, 1494–1514*. London. 1909.
Seton-Watson, R. W.: *Maximilian I*. London. 1902.
Vernon, H. M.: *Italy, 1494–1790*. Cambridge. 1909.

CHAPTER III

Armstrong, E.: *The Emperor Charles V*. London. 1902.
Poris, G.: *François I*. Paris. 1888.
Ranke, L. von: *The History of the Popes*. London. 1913.
Wyndham Lewis, D. B.: *Emperor of the West*. London. 1932.

CHAPTER IV

Bain, R. N.: *Scandinavia*. Cambridge. 1905.
Bryce, Viscount: *The Holy Roman Empire*. London. 1910.
Dunkley, E. H.: *The Reformation in Denmark*. London. 1949.
Hallendorff, C., and Schück, A.: *History of Sweden*. Stockholm. 1929.

CHAPTER V

Brown, P. M.: *Foreigners in Turkey*. Princeton. 1914.
Eversley, Lord: *The Turkish Empire*. London. 1917.
Lybyer, A. H.: *The Government of the Ottoman Empire in the Time of Suleiman the Magnificent*. Cambridge. 1913.
Marriott, Sir J. A. R.: *The Eastern Question*. Oxford. 1918.

CHAPTER VI

Bertrand, L., and Petrie, Sir Charles: *History of Spain*. London. 1934.
Davies, R. T.: *The Golden Century of Spain, 1501–1621*. London. 1937.
Hume, M. A. S.: *Philip II of Spain*. London. 1911.
Walsh, W. T.: *Philip II*. London. 1938.

CHAPTER VII

Armstrong, E.: *The French Wars of Religion*. Oxford. 1904.
Meaux, M. de: *Les luttes religieuses en France au XVIᵉ. siècle*. Paris. 1879.
Poirson, A.: *Histoire du règne de Henri IV*. Paris. 1862–1867.
Romier, L.: *Les origines politiques des Guerres de religion*. Paris. 1913–1914.

Chapter VIII

Bindoff, S. T.: *The Scheldt Question.* London. 1945.
Blok, P. J.: *History of the People of the Netherlands.* New York. 1898–1912.
Kervyn de Lettenhove, J. M. B. C.: *Relations politiques de Pays-Bas et de l'Angleterre sans le règne de Philippe II.* Brussels. 1882–1900.
Wedgwood, C. V.: *William the Silent.* London. 1944.

Chapter IX

Belloc, H.: *Wolsey.* London. 1930.
Lang, A.: *History of Scotland.* London. 1929.
Neale, J. E.: *Queen Elizabeth.* London. 1948.
Pollard, A. F.: *Henry VIII.* London. 1913.

Chapter X

Black, J. B.: *Elizabeth and Henry IV.* Oxford. 1914.
Cecil, A.: *Life of Robert Cecil, First Earl of Salisbury.* London. 1915.
Rott, E.: *Henri IV, les Suisses, et la haute Italie.* Paris. 1882.
Willert, P. F.: *Henry of Navarre.* London. 1893.

Chapter XI

Fletcher, C. R. L.: *Gustavus Adolphus.* London. 1892.
Reddaway, W. F.: *A History of Europe, 1610–1715.* London. 1948.
Stefansson, Jan: *Denmark and Sweden.* London. 1916.
Stevens, J. L.: *History of Gustavus Adolphus.* London. 1885.

Chapter XII

Coxe, W.: *History of the House of Austria.* London. 1807.
Gardiner, S. R.: *The Thirty Years' War.* London. 1912.
Wedgwood, C. V.: *The Thirty Years' War.* London. 1938.
Wingfield-Stratford, E.: *Charles, King of England, 1600–1637.* London. 1949.

Chapter XIII

Acton, Lord: *Lectures on Modern History.* London. 1912.
Fagniez, G.: *Richelieu et l'Allemagne.* Paris. 1891.
Fagniez, G.: *Le Père Joseph et Richelieu.* Paris. 1894.
Lodge, Sir Richard: *Richelieu.* London. 1908.

Chapter XIV

Scherill, F.: *The Great Elector.* Chicago. 1947.
Tuttle, —: *History of Prussia.* Boston. 1884–1896.

Chapter XV

Gaxotte, P.: *La France de Louis XIV.* Paris. 1946.
Hassall, A.: *Louis XIV.* London. 1931.
Hume, M.: *The Court of Philip IV and the Decadence of Spain.* New York. 1907.
Petrie, Sir Charles: *Louis XIV.* London. 1938.

Chapter XVI

Clément, P.: *Lettres, instructions et mémoires de Colbert.* Paris. 1861.
Lefèvre-Pontalis, A.: *John de Witt.* London. 1885.
Roujon, J.: *Louvois et Son Maître.* Paris. 1934.
Traill, H. D.: *William the Third.* London. 1911.

Chapter XVII

Bryant, A.: *King Charles II.* London. 1931.
Feiling, K.: *British Foreign Policy, 1660–1672.* London. 1930.
Hartmann, C. H.: *Charles II and Madame.* London. 1934.
Hartmann, C. H.: *Clifford of the Cabal.* London. 1937.

Chapter XVIII

Clark, R.: *Sir William Trumbull in Paris, 1685–6.* London. 1938.
Grimblot, P.: *Letters of William III and Louis XIV, and of their Ministers.* London. 1848.
Rousset, C. F. M.: *Histoire de Louvois.* Paris. 1862–1863.
Turner, F. C.: *James II.* London. 1948.

Chapter XIX

Creasy, Sir Edward: *History of the Ottoman Turks.* London. 1878.
Eversley, Lord: *The Turkish Empire.* London. 1917.
Kluchevsky, V. O.: *History of Russia.* London. 1911–1931.
Morton, J. B.: *Sobieski, King of Poland.* London. 1932.

Chapter XX

Bain, F. W.: *Christina, Queen of Sweden.* London. 1890.
Bain, R. N.: *Charles XII.* London. 1895.
Bain, R. N.: *The First Romanovs, 1613–1725.* London. 1905.
Strindberg, A.: *Les relations de la France avec le Suède.* Paris. 1891.

Chapter XXI

Connell, N. *Anne.* London. 1937.
Curtis Brown, B.: *Letters and Diplomatic Instructions of Queen Anne.* London. 1935.
Macaulay, Lord: *History of England.*
Torcy, Marquis de: *Mémoires.* Paris. 1757.

Chapter XXII

Carte, T.: *History of the Life of James, Duke of Ormonde.* London. 1851.
Churchill, W. S.: *Marlborough: His Life and Times.* London. 1933–1938.
Petrie, Sir Charles: *Bolingbroke.* London. 1938.
Trevelyan, G. M.: *England under Queen Anne.* London. 1930–1934.

INDEX

242

PRINTED IN GREAT BRITAIN BY RICHARD CLAY AND COMPANY, LTD., BUNGAY, SUFFOLK.